I0810150

IMAGES
of America

ROCKWALL

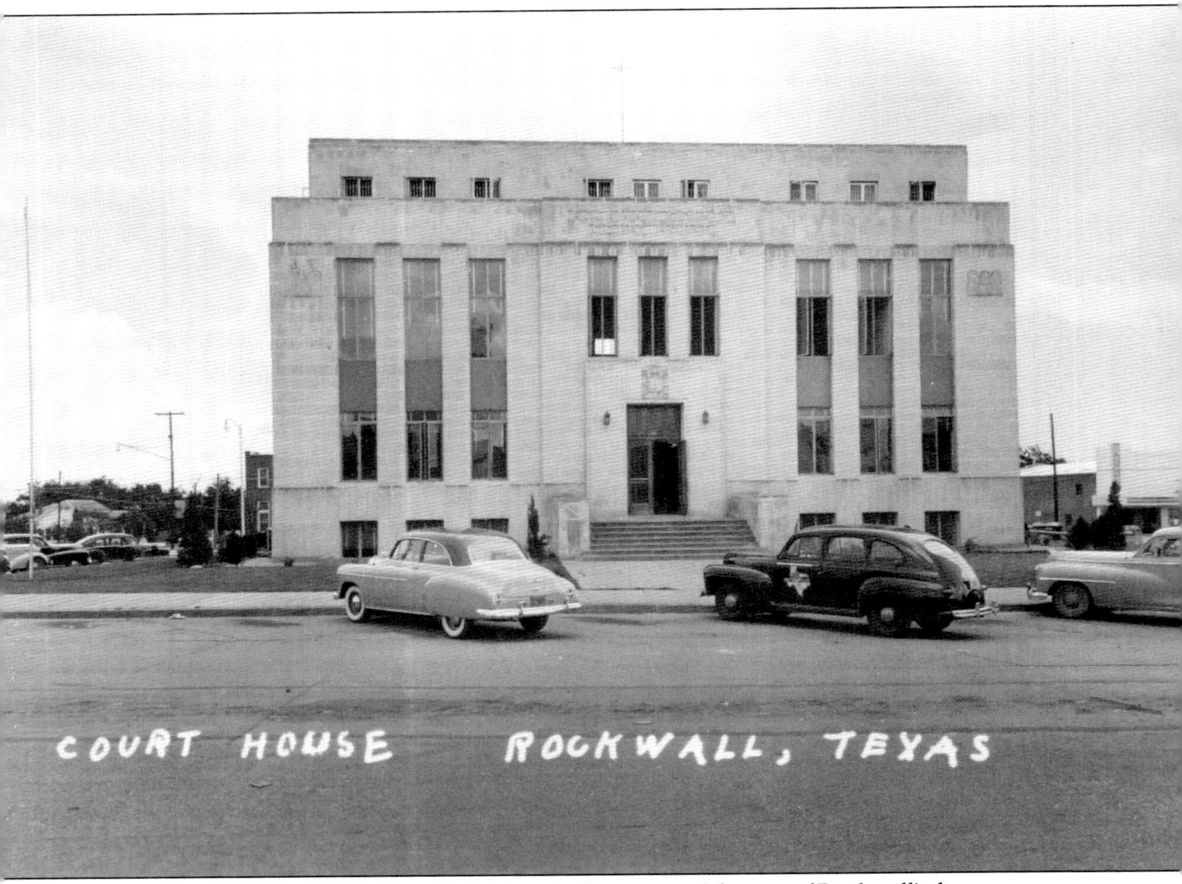

Rockwall County's historical courthouse sits in the center of the city of Rockwall's downtown square and is unquestionably the most recognizable historical building in the county. Although some current residents are not fond of the angular art deco architecture, at the time of its construction in 1941, the modern design was entirely appropriate for a city that sat in the shadow of Dallas. Art moderne architecture (the term art deco was actually not coined until the late 1960s) had gained prominence in Dallas in 1936 when Fair Park hosted Texas's Centennial Exposition and architect George Dahl had transformed the area into what he termed a Texanic style of modernism. The style represented progress—a vision for the future—and when Rockwall County leaders were settling on a new look for their government offices, they merely glanced west for their inspiration. Today Fair Park stands as one of the nation's preeminent examples of art deco architecture, and the Rockwall County Courthouse stands as one of the few remaining art deco–inspired courthouses in all of Texas. (Courtesy of Sheri Stodghill Fowler.)

On the Cover: The Paul Snow Ford Motor Company was located on the corner of Fannin and Rusk Streets in downtown Rockwall. (Courtesy of Martha Myers.)

IMAGES
of America

ROCKWALL

Sheri Stodghill Fowler

ARCADIA
PUBLISHING

Copyright © 2009 by Sheri Stodghill Fowler
ISBN 978-0-7385-5858-5

Published by Arcadia Publishing
Charleston, South Carolina

Printed in the United States of America

Library of Congress Control Number: 2008932139

For all general information contact Arcadia Publishing at:
Telephone 843-853-2070
Fax 843-853-0044
E-mail sales@arcadiapublishing.com
For customer service and orders:
Toll-Free 1-888-313-2665

Visit us on the Internet at www.arcadiapublishing.com

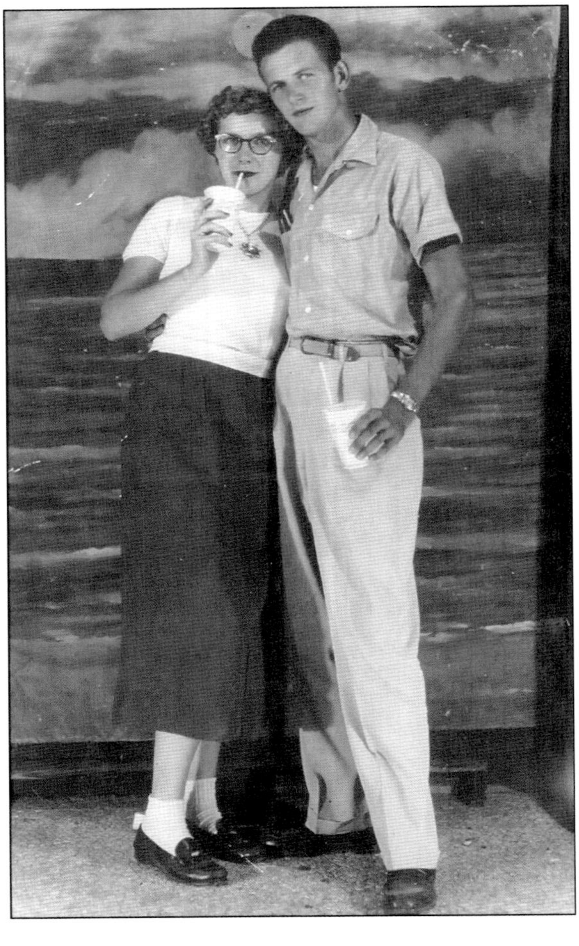

This book is dedicated to my mother and father, Don and Patsy Stodghill (pictured around 1955), who taught me to embrace my heritage and to love history . . . not just my own but all history. It is also for my children, Jake and Grace, who are the seventh generation on both my mother's and father's sides of my family to call Rockwall County home.

Contents

Acknowledgments 6

Introduction 7

1. Early Settlement and the Arrival of the Railroad: 1840–1900 9

2. Cotton is King in Rockwall's Agrarian-Based Economy: 1900–1945 27

3. The Fabulous 1950s and the Decline of King Cotton: 1945–1965 79

4. Construction of Lake Ray Hubbard and the Economic Shift to Suburbia: 1965 to Present 107

About the Rockwall County Historical Foundation 127

ACKNOWLEDGMENTS

History shared is history spared; otherwise it is lost forever. When a family allows a photograph to be published and shared with others, history has been saved. I am so thankful to all the individuals and families who reached into their own personal archives and have agreed to share photographs. Some have shared photographs specifically for this project, and their names are noted on the pages where the photographs appear. Others shared their family photographs with the Rockwall County Historical Foundation for general use in any history-related project, and that is how their photographs ended up in this publication. So, first of all, thanks to the dozens of families and individuals who have selflessly shared photographs and stories, and have graciously given the historical foundation permission to share those photographs and stories with others. By sharing a part of their personal history, each has significantly contributed to the collective history of our county.

A special thank-you goes to our Rockwall County and City of Rockwall elected officials who continue to support the projects and the efforts of the Rockwall County Historical Foundation (RCHF). Thanks to our past and current RCHF officers and directors, who always seek every opportunity to showcase and promote Rockwall history. The vast majority of the photographs in this book are part of a photograph archiving collection belonging to the RCHF.

A personal thanks to Billy Quinton, who has scanned countless photographs and done everything I ever asked. History never looked as good as when it is in his hands. I can never give enough praise to Kristie Kelly with Arcadia Publishing, who has the patience of a saint. She is, without a doubt, the easiest person in the universe to work with.

Finally, I have to thank my sweet cowboy Stacy Parks, who brought me coffee, cooked me dinner, and graciously (without even being asked) took care of every other crisis and mundane daily chore while I was busy at the computer sorting through photographs and writing captions. He made this project possible.

Introduction

In 1848, when Benjamin Boydstun decided to leave Illinois and transport his family to the great new state of Texas, he started out with a heart full of determination. He traveled the Mississippi River to New Orleans, then up the Red River to Shreveport. In Shreveport, he purchased a covered wagon with his ultimate destination Peter's Colony, the predecessor of Dallas. He left Louisiana with just $20 in his pocket.

As the Boydstun family crossed the prairie lands of Texas, they were greeted by buffalo, wild turkey, fox, and deer. Nearing the East Fork of the Trinity River, they traversed the same soil that Cherokee, Caddo, and Wichita Indians had once called home. This time of year, the rains were heavy, and the waters of the east fork were not safe for crossing. Delayed in their journey, the Boydstuns liked the look of the "blackland" soil and decided to settle on a 572-acre tract of land in Mercer's Colony, the exact land that would one day become the city of Rockwall.

On June 24, 1852, Boydstun sold 132.5 acres of that tract to pioneer settler W. B. Bowles. On February 25, 1854, Bowles sold 40 acres of that tract to Elijah Elgin. On April 17, 1854, Elijah Elgin platted the original site for a new town, and it was agreed that the city would be called Rockwall.

The unusual name was the result of an unusual discovery—an underground formation that resembled a rock wall. It had been unearthed in 1852 by Terry Utley Wade, Benjamin Boydstun, and William Clay Stevenson. The three pioneer settlers were digging a water well and discovered an underground rock structure. Local residents speculated that prehistoric man had constructed the wall to protect an ancient city, but future scientific studies would not necessarily agree.

Rockwall and the surrounding communities developed agrarian-based economies, and the first cotton gin was built in the area in 1866. However, the shipping of crops was still problematic because roads were poor and travel between major shipping points was difficult.

Rockwall County was created in 1873 with the city of Rockwall as the county seat. The railroad's arrival in 1886 was a major milestone for Rockwall's economic and social development. The city became a central shipping point for local crops, and Rockwall's business district, public school system, and population all grew. By 1900, there were 1,090 farms in Rockwall County.

Throughout the next few decades, cotton flourished as the county's main cash crop. In 1920, the Rockwall High School annual described the county with these words:

> Rockwall County, often termed the "Black Diamond of Texas," was created out of a division of Kaufman County and was organized in 1873. Its name comes from a pre-historic wall, surrounding the county seat, Rockwall, in a circular shape. Rockwall County contains one hundred and thirty-two square miles of choice black land. An oil well is being sunk near the town of Rockwall, and there are good prospects for the development of an oil field. The Bankhead Highway is in the course of construction and the bottom of the east fork of the Trinity River is being leveed so that about two thousand acres of the best black, waxy land will be added to the farm lands of the county. Cotton is the chief crop. Rockwall,

the county seat, is on the main line of the MK&T Railroad of Texas. There are up-to-date public school buildings all over the county, and rapid development of educational interest is felt everywhere. Rockwall County has a citizenship of the highest type, maintaining, in every community, churches on a high plane. There are two banks and six churches in the city of Rockwall. Prosperity and progress are imprinted upon the faces of everyone.

The oil field never developed, but nevertheless, Rockwall prospered for most of the 1920s. The Great Depression took its toll on the area, and both the number of businesses and the population declined during the 1930s. The arrival of World War II also marked the beginning of a shift in Rockwall's economic base. Workers began to abandon traditional agricultural jobs, instead opting to travel to Dallas or other nearby areas for industrial work. Throughout the 1940s and 1950s, agricultural production continued to decrease. By 1959, there were only 350 farms operating in Rockwall County.

Although the economy was changing in the 1950s, Rockwall was still quintessential small-town Texas. Friday nights revolved around Yellowjacket football. Kids could spend Saturdays watching serial Westerns or other first-run fare at the Ritz movie theater on the square. And if residents wanted to catch a quick bite to eat, they could stop in at one of the local cafés or soda shops. The 1950s were a time of segregation, and Rockwall was no different. At the Ritz, African American patrons sat in the balcony; white patrons sat on the main floor. The courthouse on the square had separate drinking fountains marked "white" and "colored." But that, in itself, made Rockwall typical for a small town in the South in the 1950s.

In the 1960s, Dallas began plans for construction of what would one day become Lake Ray Hubbard. As those plans became reality, Rockwall completely transitioned from a rural farming community into part of a growing Dallas metroplex. A few visionaries saw the possibilities. Art Wier developed Ridge Road Village, the first luxury residential development on the lake. Others followed with master-planned communities that appealed to city dwellers wanting to exchange the big-city lifestyle for a more small-town atmosphere but still remain within driving distance of metropolitan shopping and nightlife.

In 2009, the population of the city of Rockwall hovers at 30,000, with Rockwall County having approximately 60,000 residents. City and county officials struggle with balancing fast growth while maintaining small-town appeal. Rockwall County is consistently listed as one of the fastest-growing counties in the nation, so it is not likely that the growth will slow soon.

As Benjamin Boydstun looked across the prairie lands and surveyed his 572 acres of blackland soil, he never could have envisioned the future of this land now called Rockwall. In so many ways, it is so different. Yet it is still the same soil, the same land that the Boydstun family laid a plow to so many years ago.

One

EARLY SETTLEMENT AND THE ARRIVAL OF THE RAILROAD 1840–1900

In a movie version of Rockwall, this is the part where the piano music begins to play in the clapboard saloon and the county's first sheriff, Tom Shaw, throws the troublemaker out into the dusty street and tells him not to come back until he is ready to behave in a more civilized manner. Women and children do not frequent the square on Saturdays because the area's hired hands come to town for their weekly game of cards and their weekly baths. The baths are available at the barbershop, which stays open late for just such purposes.

The first Anglo settlers came to the area in the 1840s. Pioneers built their homes near the banks of the East Fork of the Trinity River, and during the next several decades, as the population grew, so did the towns of Rockwall, Heath, Barnes, Fate, Nadine, Munson, Locust Grove, Black Hills, Willow Springs, Blackland, Royse City, Rowlett, McLendon, Chisholm, and at least a dozen others. Some settlements grew and prospered and still exist today. Others succumbed to the realities of harsh weather, disease, and even war. Their populations dwindled, and the remaining residents combined with other nearby communities.

When two area businessmen, C. L. Jones and John Griffith, traveled by horseback to Austin in the spring of 1873 to obtain the charter for Rockwall County, the cities that were contained within its boundaries were still archetypal Old West towns. But in the mid-1880s, something happened that would change all that—the railroad was built directly through Rockwall County. This would change the accessibility, the economy, and even the aesthetics of the entire area in ways no one could imagine.

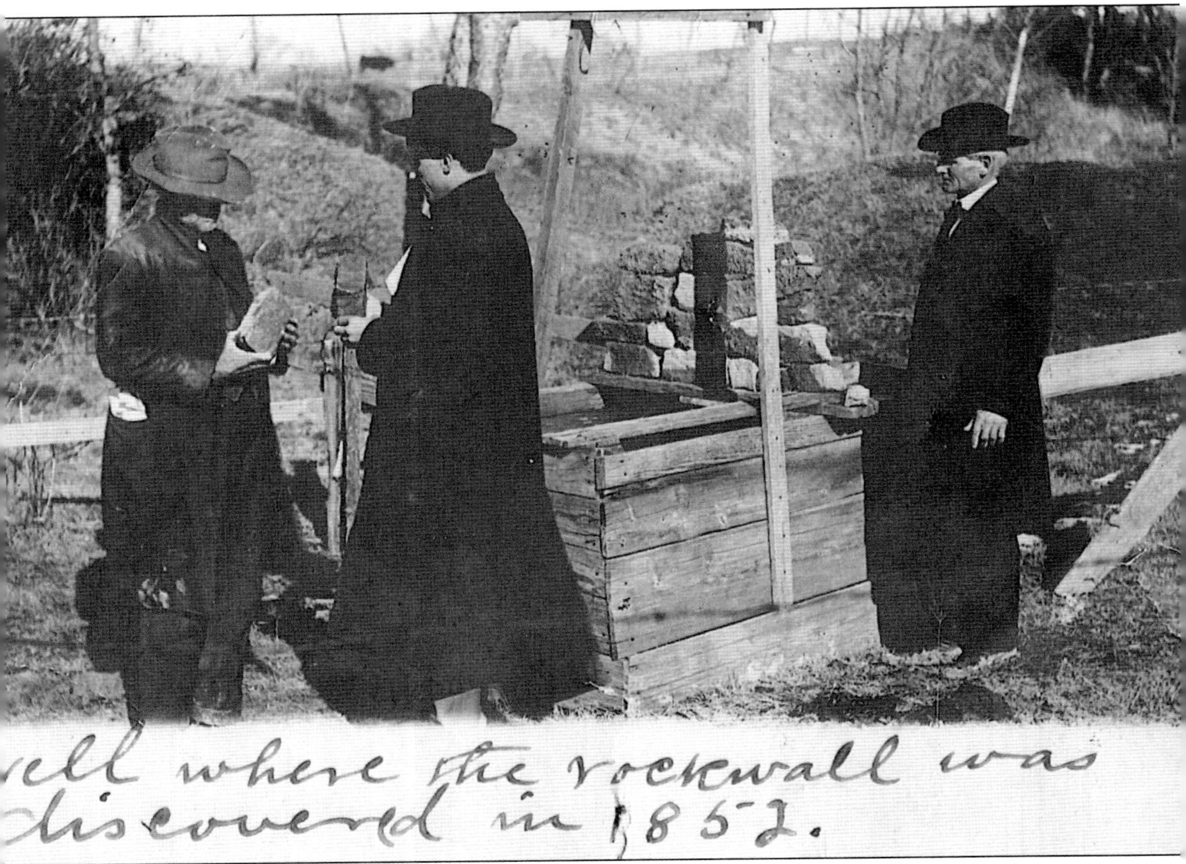

In 1852, three pioneer settlers, Terry Utley Wade, Benjamin Boydstun, and William Clay Stevenson, were digging a well and inadvertently discovered an underground formation they termed a "rock wall." The men dug alongside the strange wall to the full depth of the well and, still not finding the bottom, they used what they had already exposed as one side of that well. According to most accounts, this was the first documented discovery of the rock wall; almost immediately, a still-ongoing debate was ignited over whether the unusual formation was a natural, geological occurrence or a man-made structure. Two years later, in 1854, a new town was platted, and Terry Utley Wade's obituary states that he suggested the name city leaders adopted for the town—the name of "Rockwall." Taken many decades later, this photograph shows the original well site just west of downtown Rockwall and rocks from the underground formation.

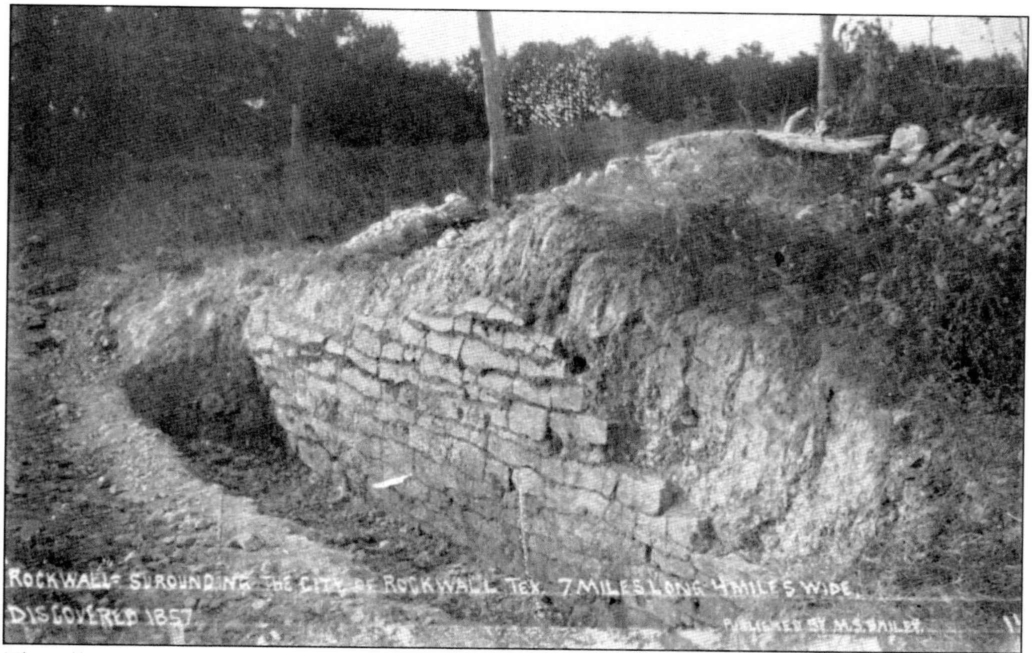

The official view by the Texas Historical Commission is that the rock wall is a natural geological formation, but to some locals who have seen unearthed portions of the symmetrical structure, it is hard to imagine the meticulous horizontal pattern of the rocks was made by anything other than the hands of prehistoric man. There are at least 11 known outcroppings of the wall.

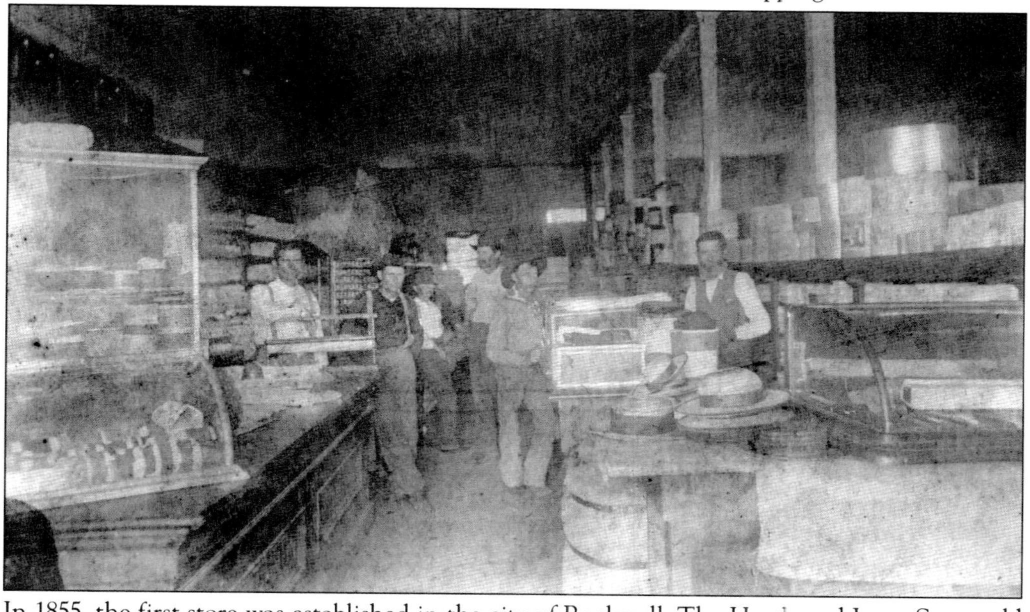

In 1855, the first store was established in the city of Rockwall. The Heath and Jones Store sold general merchandise and was located two blocks south of the current square. Soon after the store opened, one of the area's few remaining Native Americans tried to carry out a raid. Tom Shaw, a local resident who would eventually become the first sheriff, saw the attempted getaway, took aim, and shot the horse right out from under the robber.

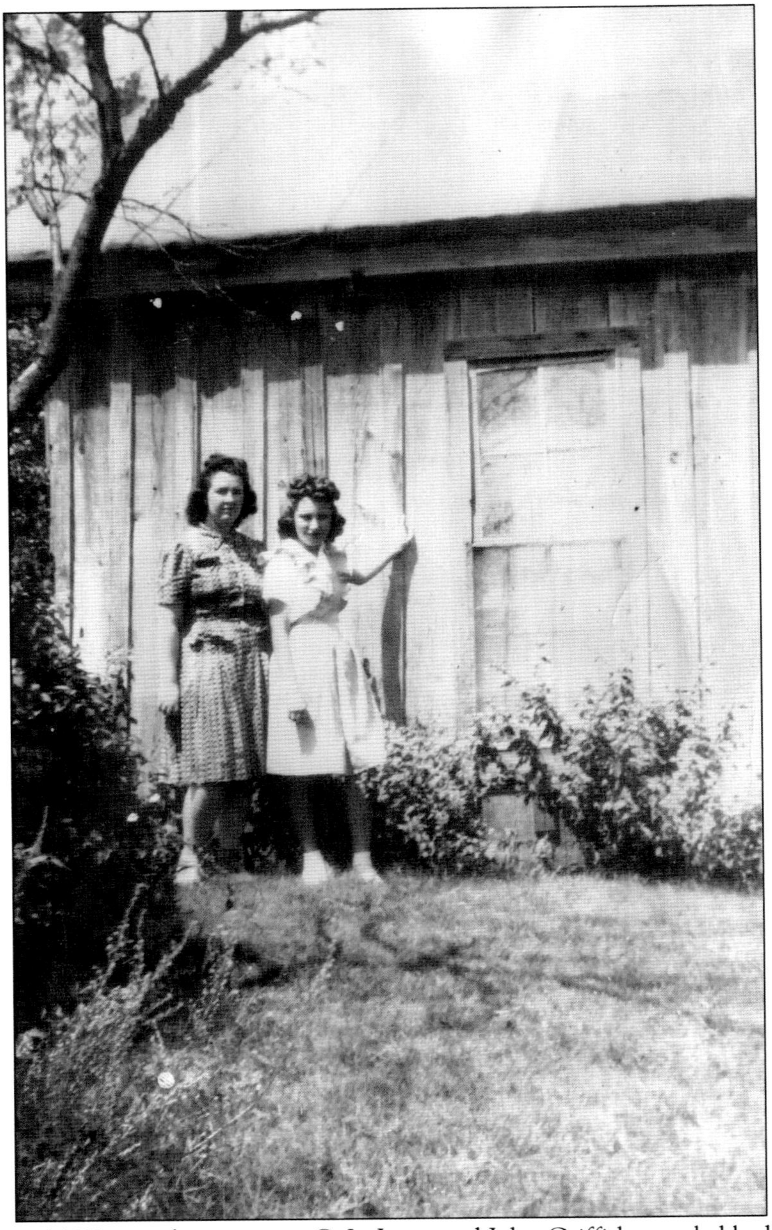

In the spring of 1873, area businessmen C. L. Jones and John Griffith traveled by horseback to Austin to obtain a charter for a new county to be called Rockwall. It was officially created on March 1, 1873, and organized on April 23, 1873, and it was—and still is—Texas's smallest county. It had previously been a part of Nacogdoches, Henderson, and Kaufman Counties, and the City of Rockwall was established as the county seat. Having no ready-made courthouse, the government offices were housed in a small store building just south of the public square. Constructed with solid oak timbers and wide doors, the building served the public well as the temporary seat of the Rockwall County government. In this photograph, Alice Townsend (left) and Katherine Anne Bischoff, both granddaughters of former Rockwall County judges, stand in front of the first building ever used as a Rockwall County courthouse.

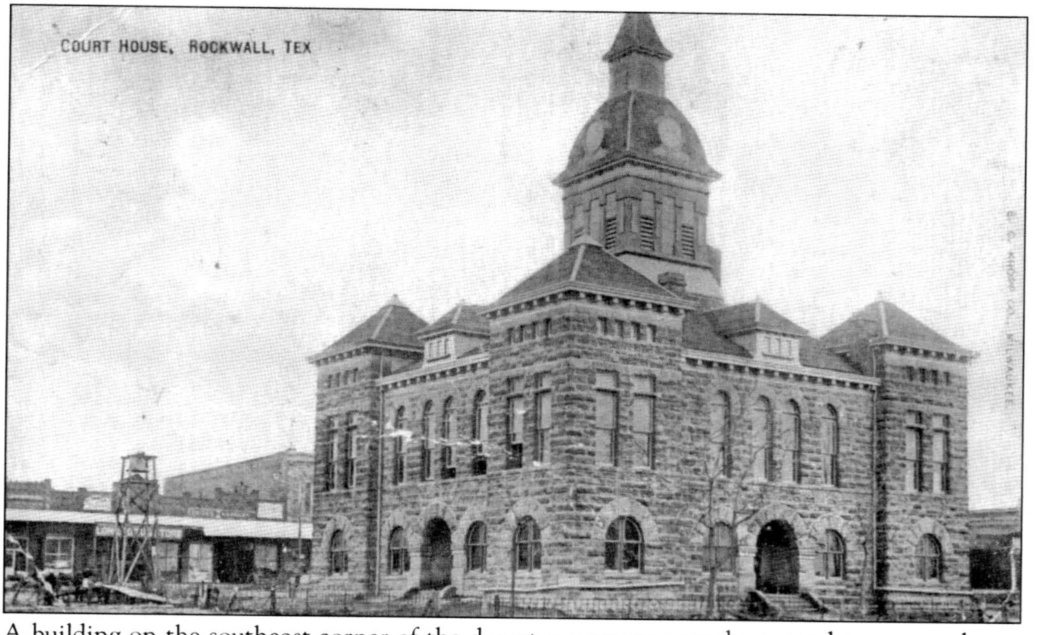

A building on the southeast corner of the downtown square was the second temporary home for Rockwall County's government offices. However, the accommodations were short-lived—on March 16, 1875, fire destroyed both the building and all the early county documents. In 1878, a wooden courthouse was built for a cost of $3,940. A separate stone structure was erected to house the county clerk's office and store the county's records. The wooden courthouse burned in the early 1890s, but the stone structure survived, along with its contents. In 1892, at a cost of $25,000, a native sandstone courthouse was built in the center of the downtown square. This courthouse would stand until 1941. Above is a picture postcard of the 1892 courthouse.

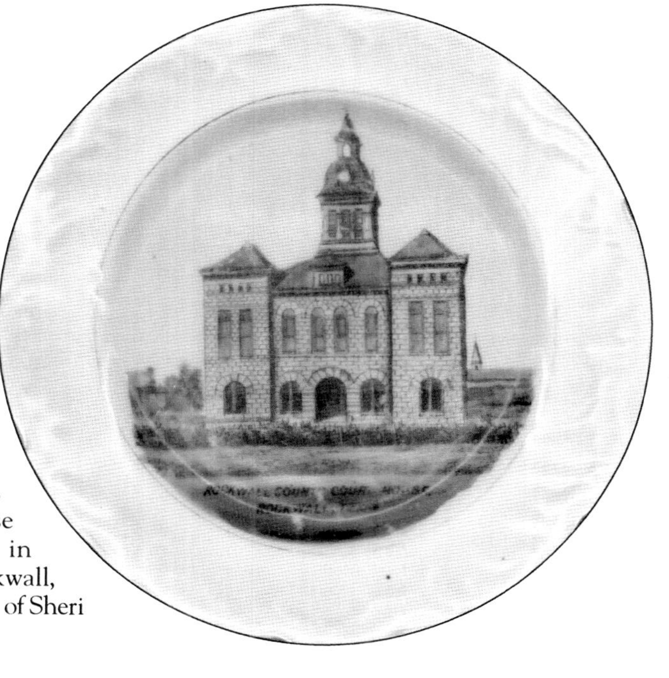

This commemorative plate bears the image of the 1892 courthouse with markings that read, "Made in Germany for James W. Vance, Rockwall, Texas, Wheelock China." (Courtesy of Sheri Stodghill Fowler.)

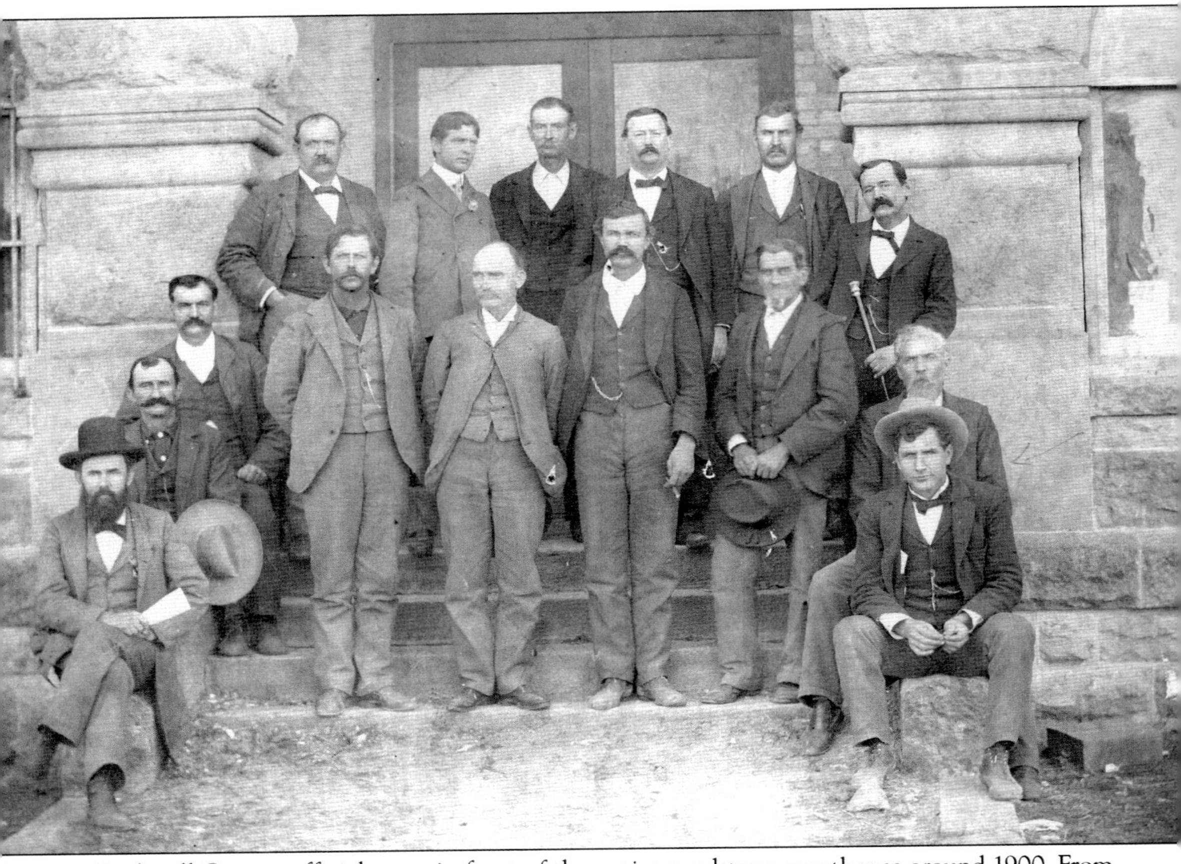

Rockwall County officials pose in front of the native sandstone courthouse around 1900. From left to right are (first row) Will H. Vernon and county commissioner (Precinct 4) James W. Reese; (second row) Jim Barringer and John T. Adams; (third row) tax assessor J. K. Browning, county commissioner (Precinct 3) W. A. Bunch, George Truitt, B. F. Spafford, district court clerk G. W. McCafferty, and county clerk Joe Chisholm; (fourth row) Jeff McCoulskey, county attorney Tom Ridgell, Sheriff Dan Anderson, county judge and ex-officio county school superintendent E. D. Foree, and Rascoe Payne. James Reese was just beginning his political career when this photograph was taken. He would go on to serve Rockwall as county attorney and county judge, and he would serve in the Texas Legislature as a representative of the Flotorial District, composed of Rockwall and Dallas Counties. His service to Rockwall in the political arena spanned 30 years. (Courtesy of the family of Evelyn Lofland.)

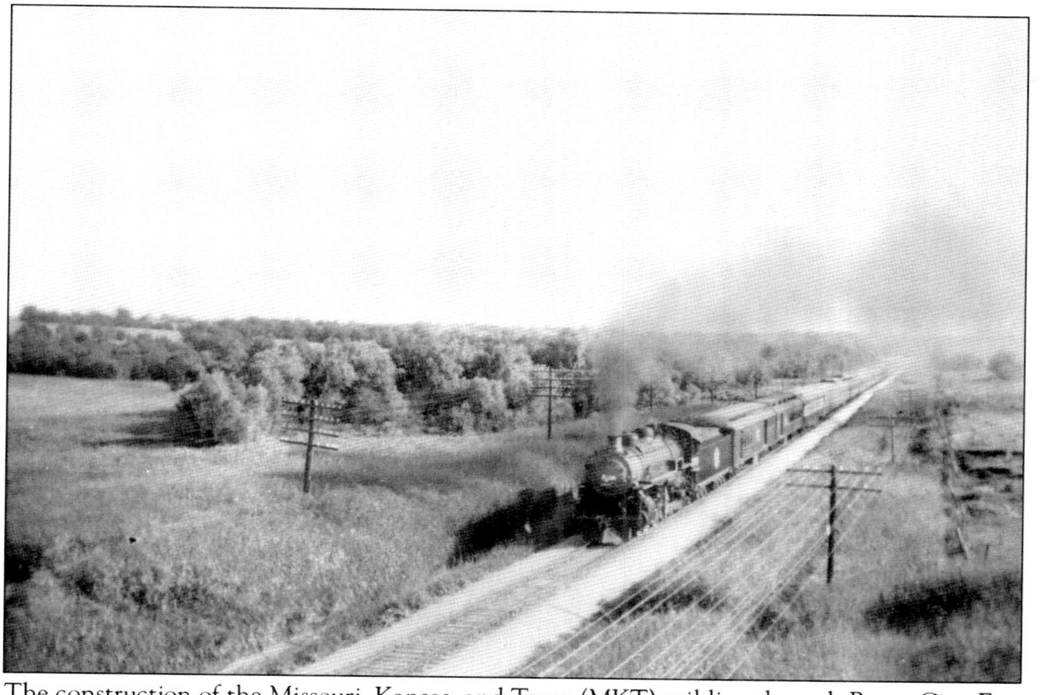

The construction of the Missouri, Kansas, and Texas (MKT) rail line through Royse City, Fate (then called Barnes), and Rockwall in the mid-1880s marked a major shift in Rockwall County's economy. Farmers could ship more cotton in less time. Business began to boom, and the entire area reaped the benefits. At the peak of its operation, the MKT scheduled eight passenger trains and five freight trains daily. Above is the MKT in the age of steam.

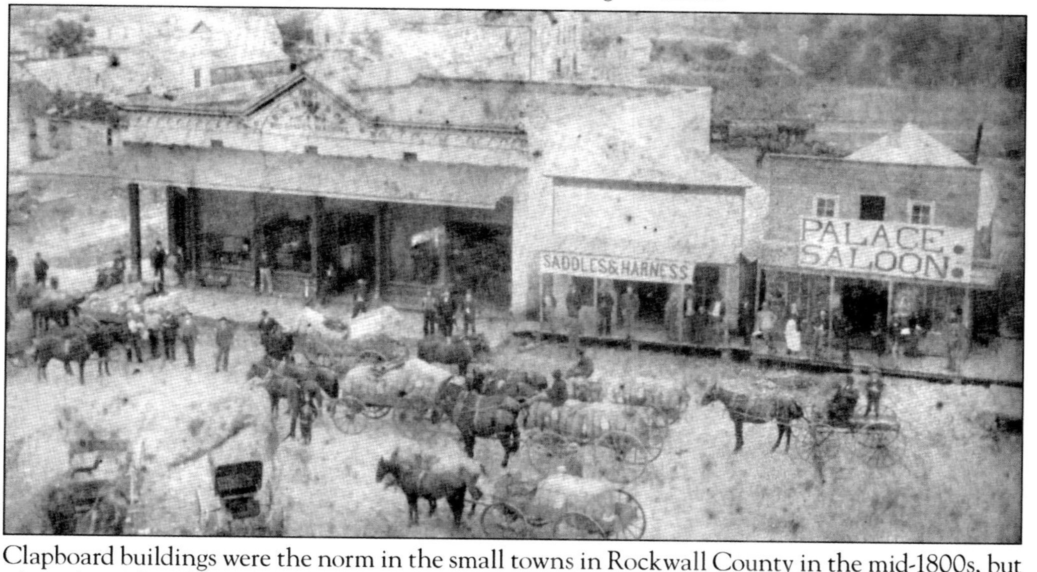

Clapboard buildings were the norm in the small towns in Rockwall County in the mid-1800s, but when the railroad came to town and shipping became easier—shipping cotton out and building materials in—the face of Rockwall began to change. In 1887, the first brick building was built on the south side of the Rockwall town square. Slowly but surely, the wooden storefronts were all replaced with sturdy brick construction.

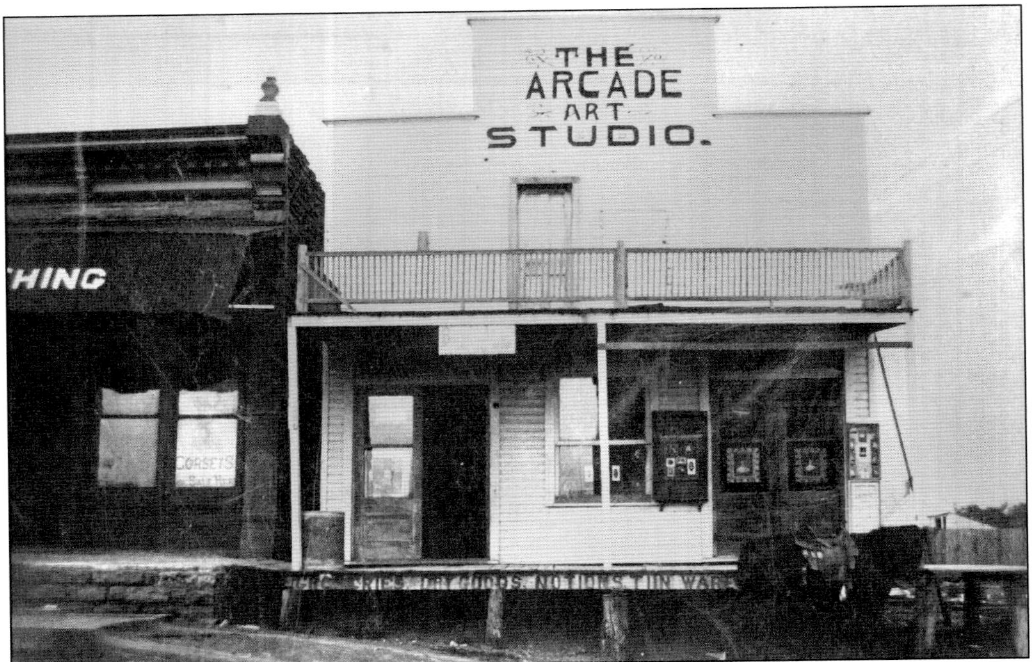

Henry W. Taylor offered "Up-to-Date High Grade Photographs" at his studio on the west side of the Rockwall square. In addition, he offered rooms to rent to earn extra money. Taylor's clapboard studio and hotel stands next to a newer brick building, a perfect example of Rockwall in transition in the late 1800s.

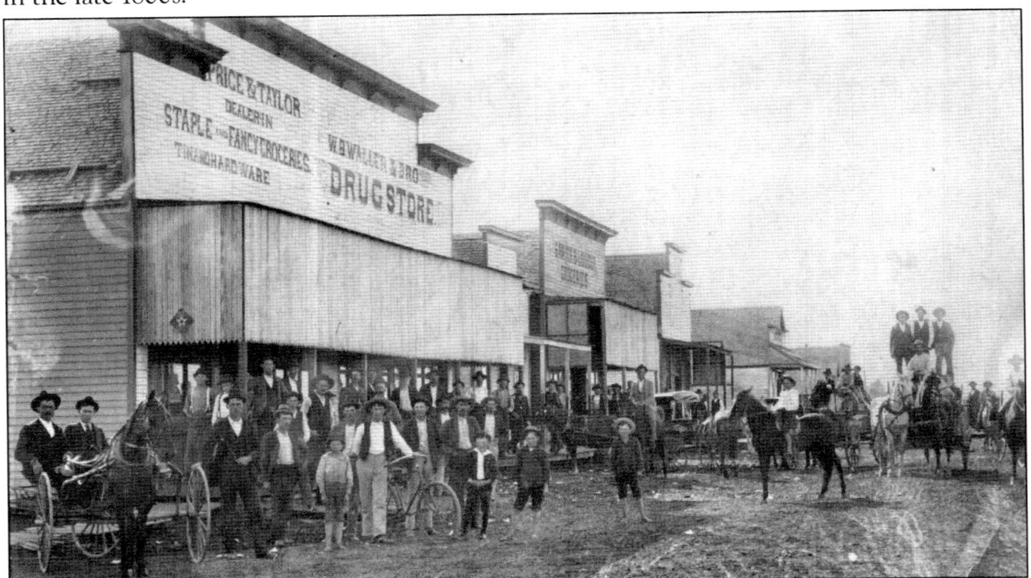

Just a few short years before this photograph was taken, the MKT railroad had been built through Fate, and this small Rockwall County community was now experiencing steady growth. This c. 1890 photograph was taken of the north side of Fate's main street. At this time, the city had 15 businesses, a two-room school, two churches, and a population of 100. These wood-framed buildings burned in 1910 and were later replaced with brick businesses.

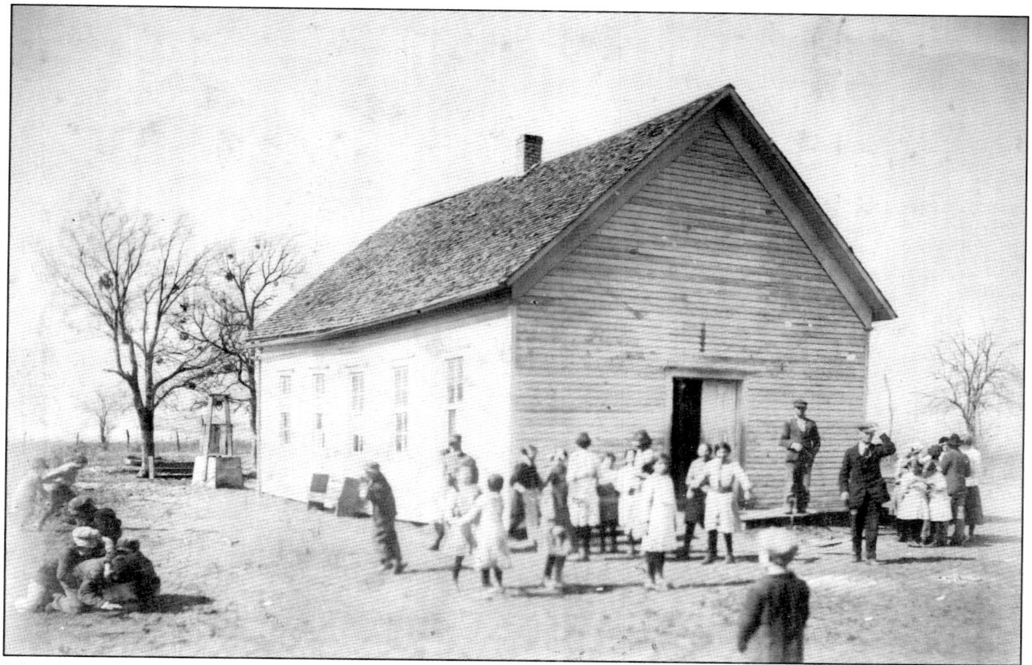

The first schools located in the area that would one day become Rockwall County were one-room country schoolhouses. Small communities gathered together to build a schoolhouse and pay a teacher to conduct classes for all grades. The Locust Grove School, pictured here around 1900, was located north of the city of Rockwall.

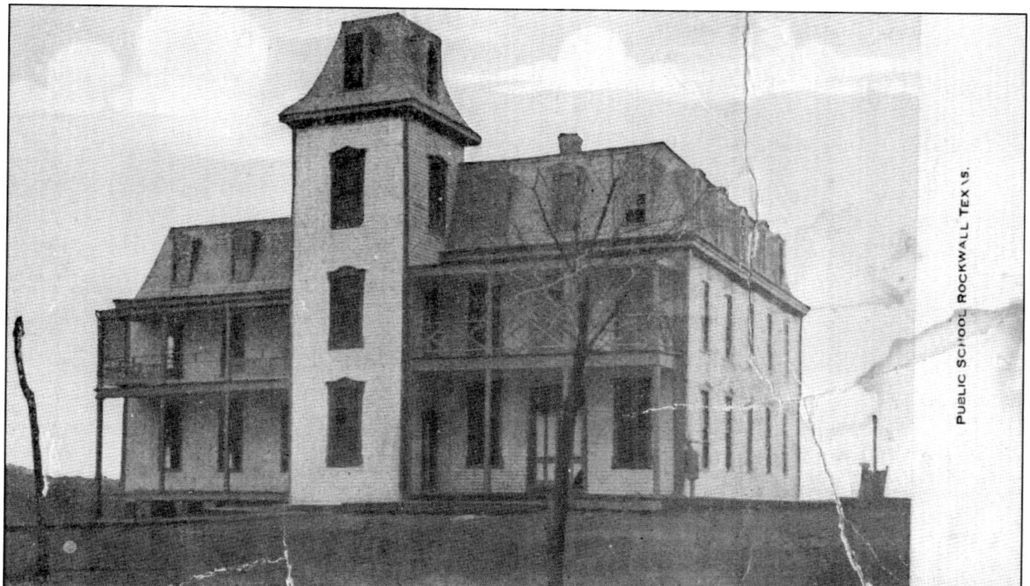

In 1878, the City of Rockwall constructed its first free public school. When city leaders received word that the railroad would be built through town and the population began to grow, it became obvious that a larger facility for public education would be necessary. In 1885, the city constructed the second free public school, shown in this picture postcard.

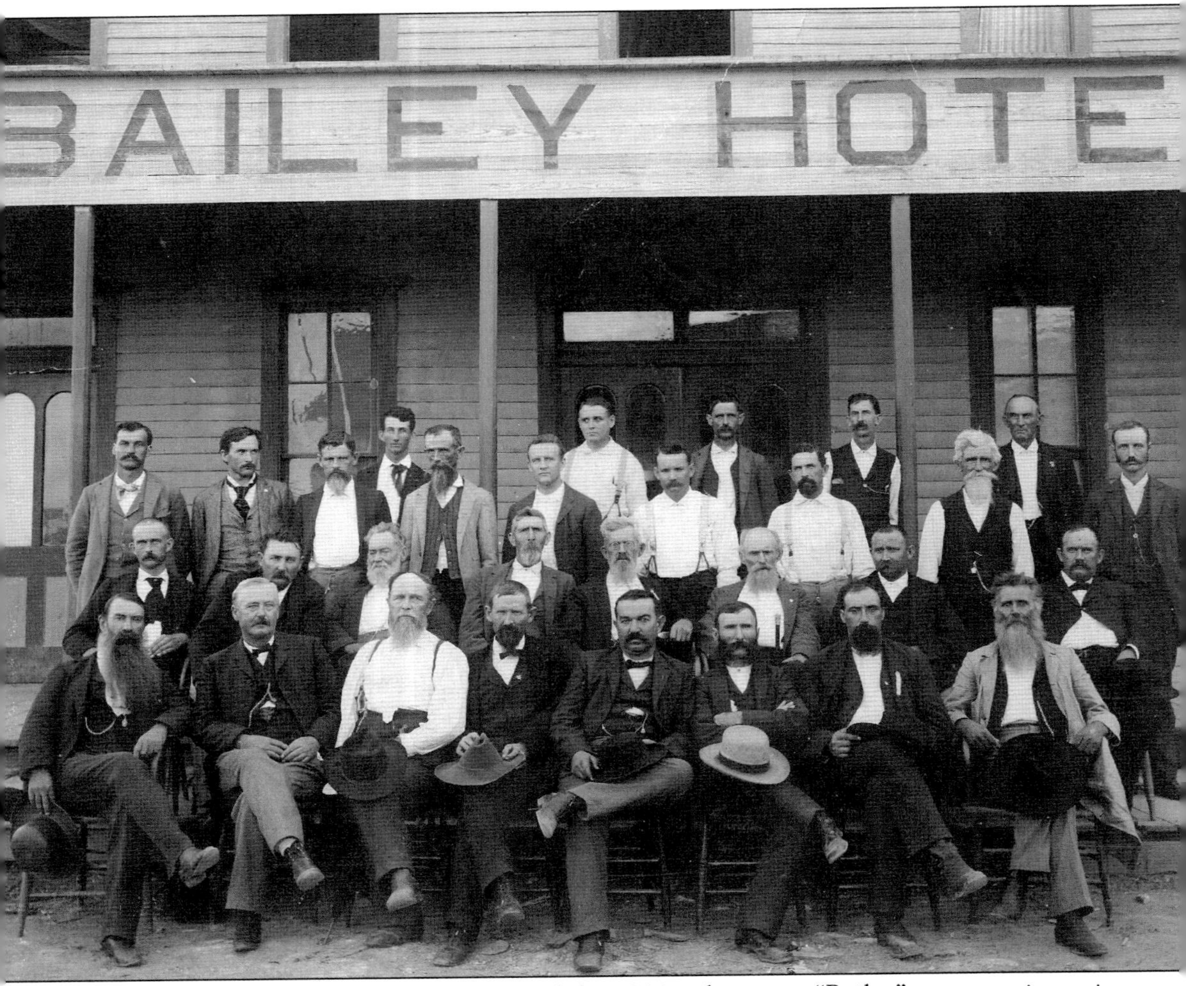

From the late 1800s to the early part of the 1900s, the name "Bailey" was prominent in Rockwall County. Having originally come from Kentucky and then settling near Fate for a short time, T. W. Bailey moved his family to the city of Rockwall in 1890. He and his wife, Hittie Squires, had six children and owned numerous businesses, including the Bailey Hotel (above) and a hardware store. He was also a prominent shareholder in the Rockwall Light, Ice, and Gin Company; his children carried on the tradition, owning or helping operate drugstores, banks, motor companies, and other businesses. In addition, the Baileys were active in civic organizations and politics. In this photograph, members of a fraternal organization gather for a meeting at the Bailey Hotel (note the matching pins and fobs).

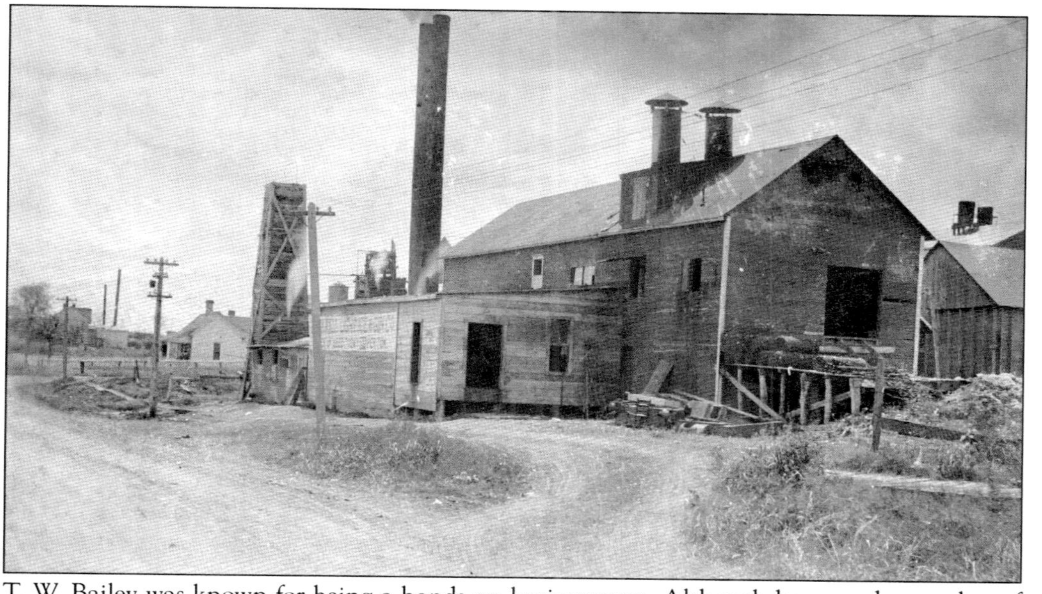

T. W. Bailey was known for being a hands-on businessman. Although he owned a number of businesses, he was still heavily involved in the day-to-day operations of each of them. He owned a large amount of stock in the Rockwall Light, Ice, and Gin Company, and he was actively involved in company management for many years.

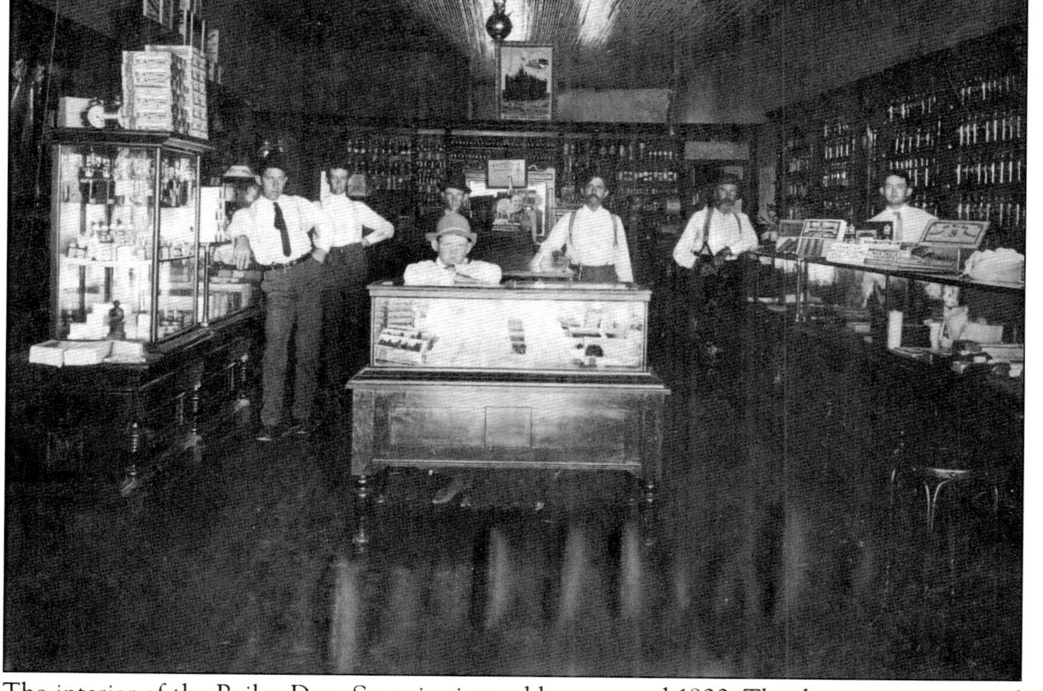

The interior of the Bailey Drug Store is pictured here around 1900. The drugstore was owned by Scott Bailey, one of the six children of T. W. Bailey and Hittie Squires Bailey. Scott was a pharmacist by trade. He was a prominent citizen and would go on to serve the city as mayor.

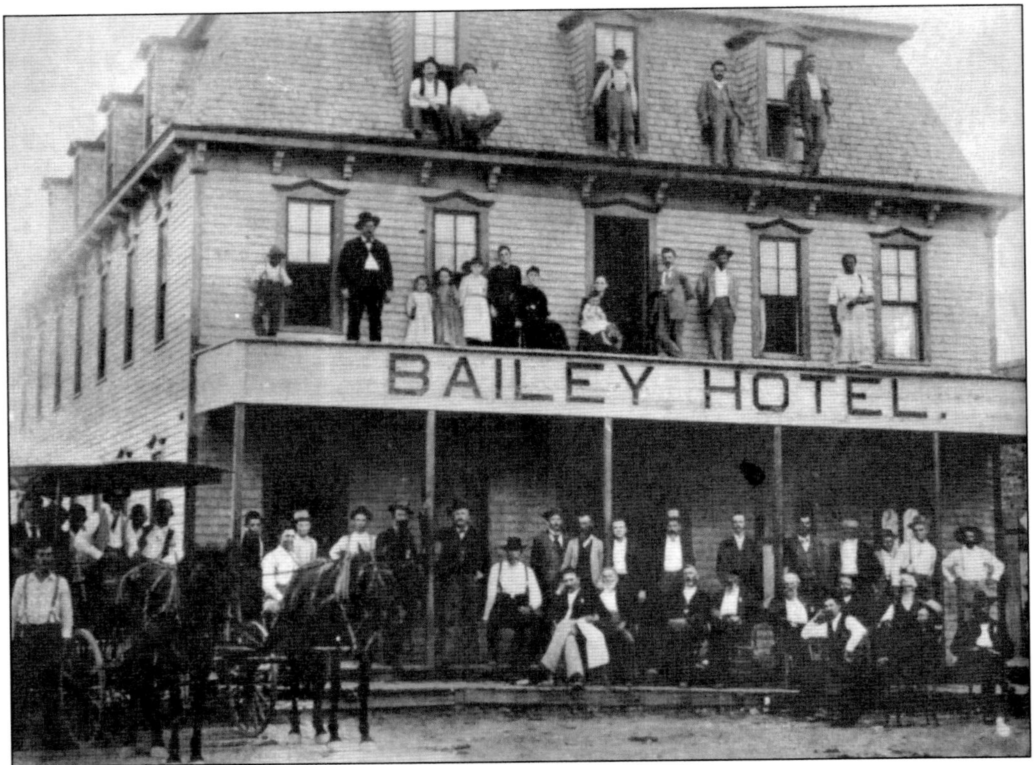

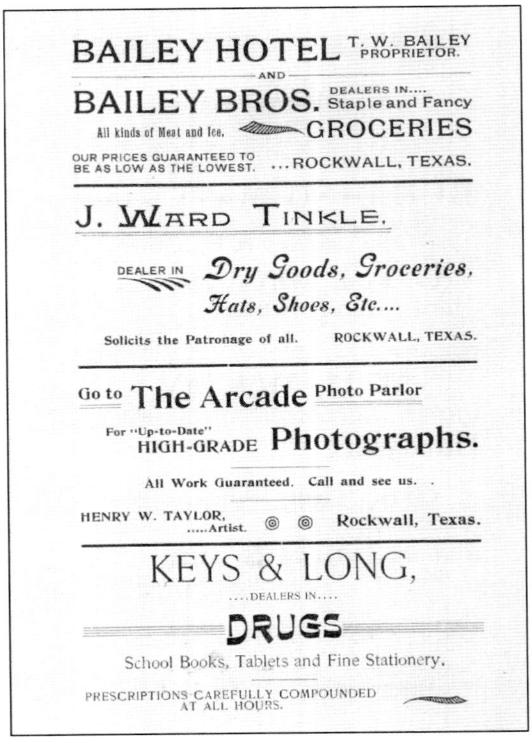

As a result of the railroad reaching Rockwall in 1886, several hotels were built around the city. The Bailey family built one of the most prominent. The Bailey Hotel was located on the corner of Washington and Goliad Streets one block off the downtown square. It was built in 1887 and burned in 1903.

T. W. Bailey advertises two of his business endeavors in the 1900 catalog of Rockwall College, a local tuition-based educational institution. The catalog was an extensive document, sent out both locally and regionally, containing course offerings, discipline rules, and a general section on the atmosphere and moral standing of the area. (Courtesy of the family of Evelyn Lofland.)

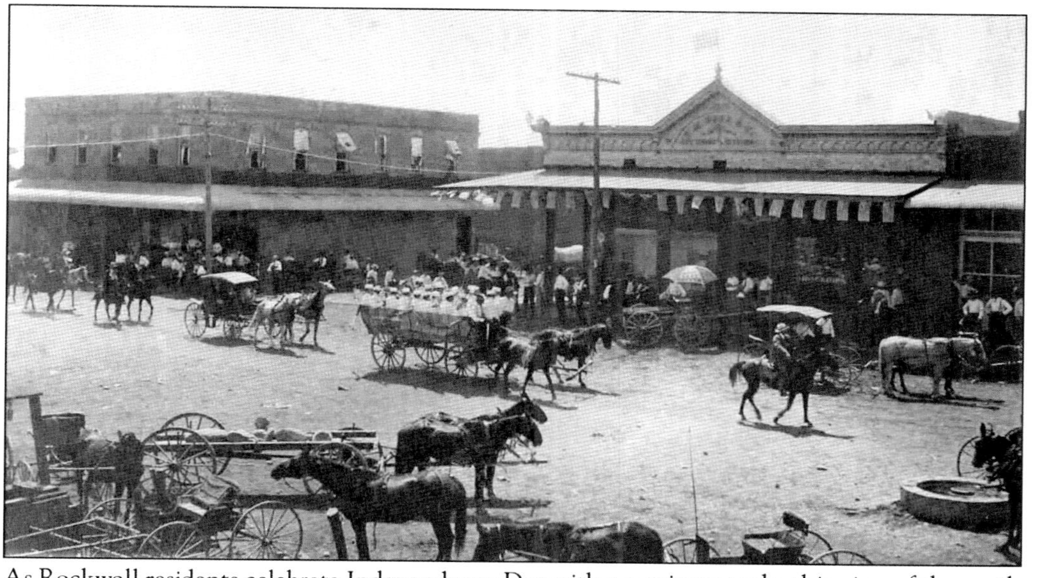

As Rockwall residents celebrate Independence Day with a passing parade, this view of the south side of the square shows that by the dawn of the 20th century, the city's transformation from frontier settlement to small-town respectability was complete. Brick buildings, many with unique architectural elements, now surrounded the public square, and each Saturday, the downtown area was filled with families shopping and socializing.

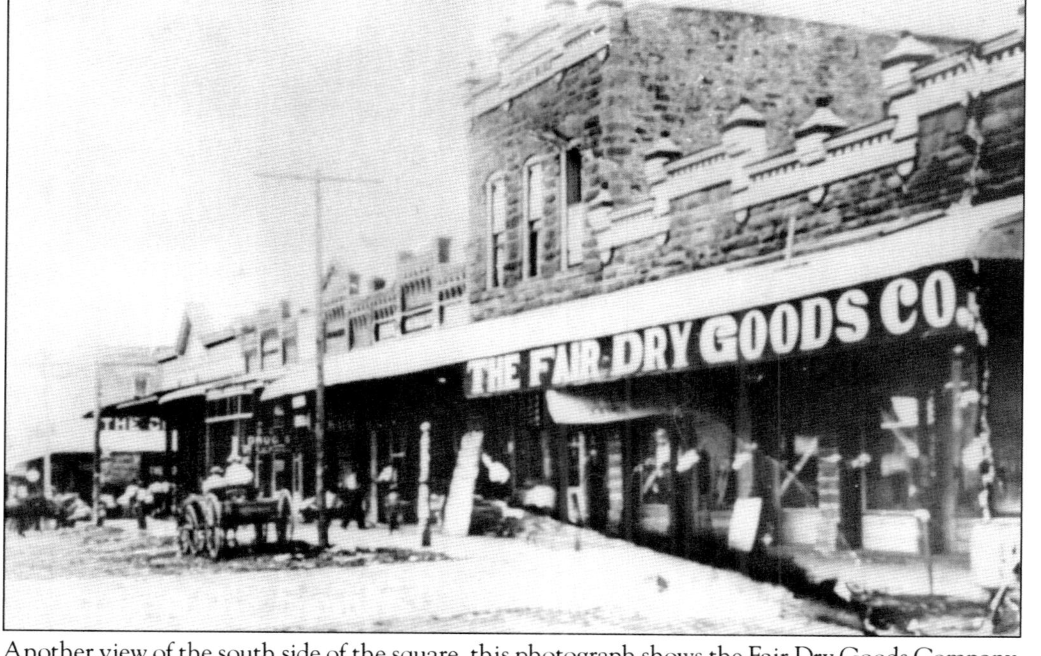

Another view of the south side of the square, this photograph shows the Fair Dry Goods Company, commonly called the Fair Store. It was operated by local businessman T. L. Townsend for 35 years. Townsend served as mayor, a member of the school board, and president of the chamber of commerce. The Depression wiped out his holdings, but he eventually was able to buy a grocery store on the square that he operated for 15 years.

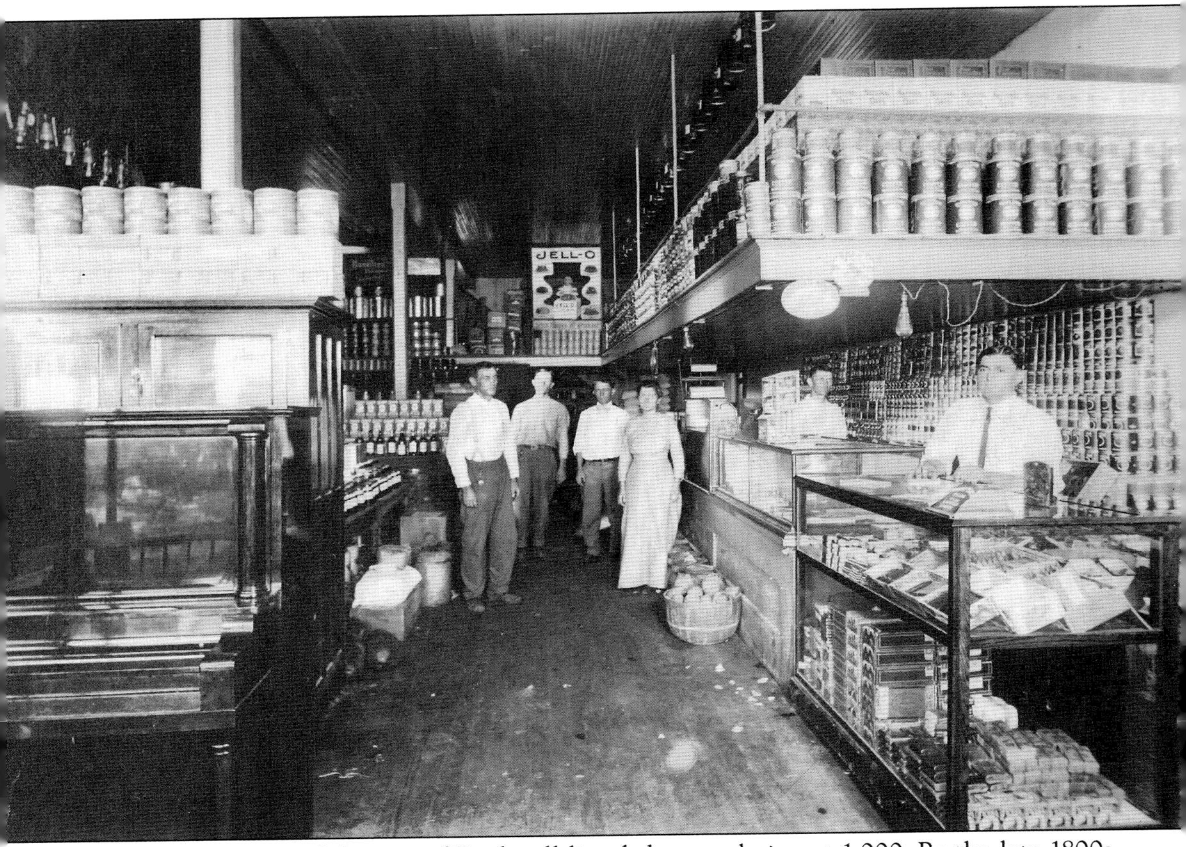

In 1893, a census of the city of Rockwall listed the population at 1,000. By the late 1800s, Rockwall's business district was flourishing. At that time, Rockwall boasted an ice cream factory, three blacksmiths, two wheelwrights, two banks, three drugstores, two hardware stores, two furniture stores (one that also sold caskets), several grocery and general merchandise stores, and two barbershops. This photograph shows one of Rockwall's general merchandise stores. While the railroad had made it easier for farmers to export their crops, it had also made it easier for goods to be imported into Rockwall. Stores began to display the latest discoveries in housewares and sundries, and things like Jell-O (sold as a prepackaged dessert item for the first time in 1895, with sales reaching $1 million by 1906) could be seen with fancy marketing displays even in small towns like Rockwall.

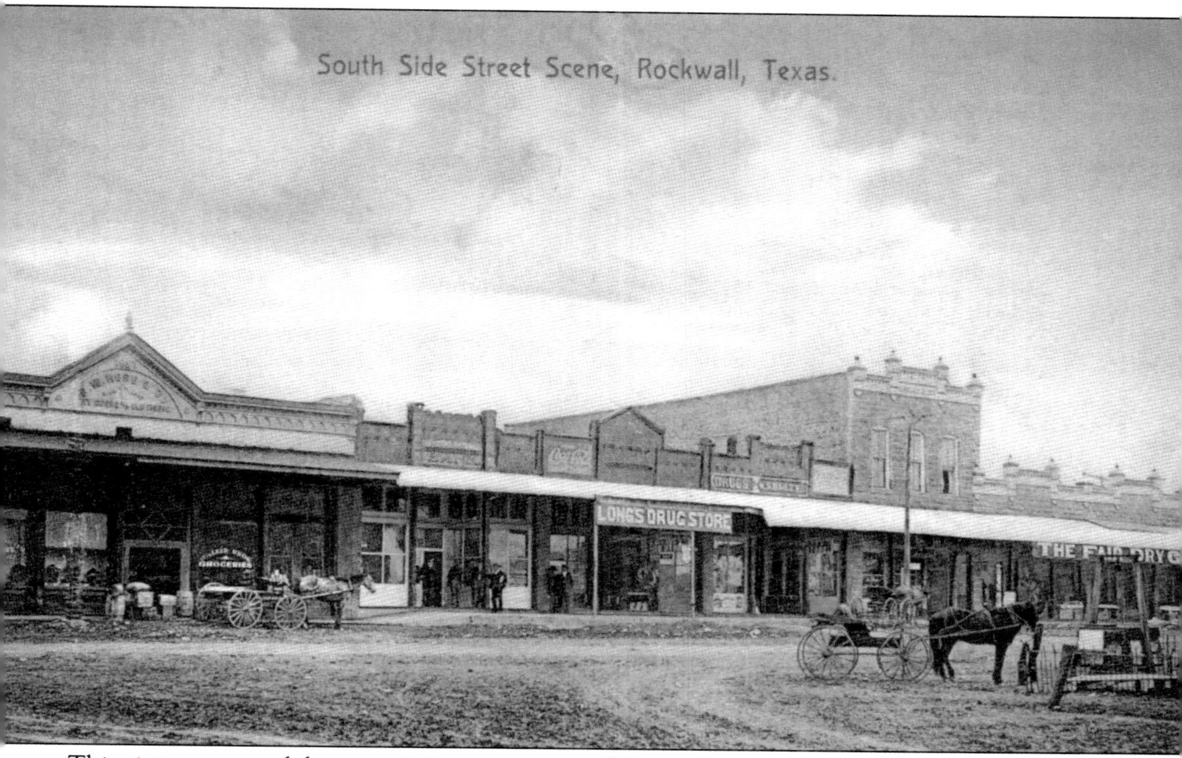

This picture postcard shows a pristine street scene of the south side of the Rockwall square around 1900. At this time, Scott Bailey's Drug Store was on this block, the Fair Dry Goods Store had already taken up residence, Citizens National Bank was operating, and one of the local stores was prominently advertising Coca-Cola for sale. In 1887, a man named Rose had built the first brick building on this block (far left). It housed Walker Brothers Dry Goods. The Walker brothers gave credit to farmers even when times were bad. As a result, the Walker brothers were well liked, and those who could pay on a regular basis were loyal customers, too. Current Rockwall residents can look at the south side of the downtown square today and still see several of the same architectural elements contained in this postcard.

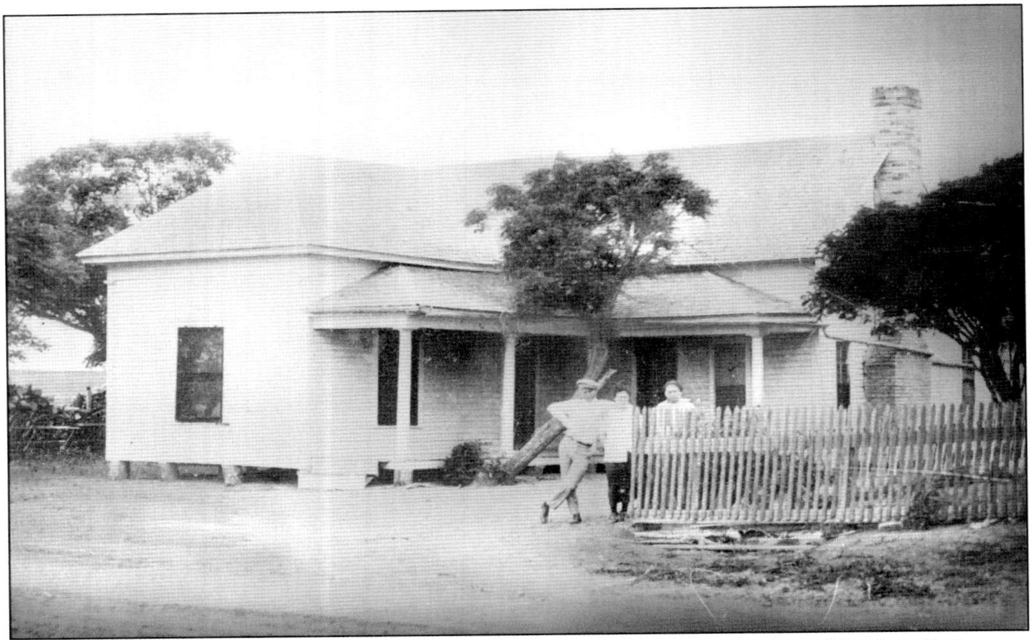

As the county seat of Rockwall was growing and developing, so was the rest of Rockwall County. Heath, Royse City, Fate, McLendon, and Chisholm, as well as areas such as Nadine, Blackland, Munson, and numerous other small settlements, were steadily increasing in population. By 1900, the economy was firmly agrarian based with the vast majority of farmers growing cotton. In 1880, records show Rockwall had 526 farms. By 1900, that number had increased to 1,090. Above, members of the Lofland family were local farmers and businesspeople in the Heath area. Pictured from left to right are James Thomas Lofland, Claudia Lofland Jones, and Martha Crawley Lofland-Raburn at their home on what is now Hubbard Road. Pictured below, the William Harris McLendon home was located northeast of Fate. Shown are Viola Truitt Willess McLendon (far left), daughters Eva and Chellie, and William Harris McLendon (far right).

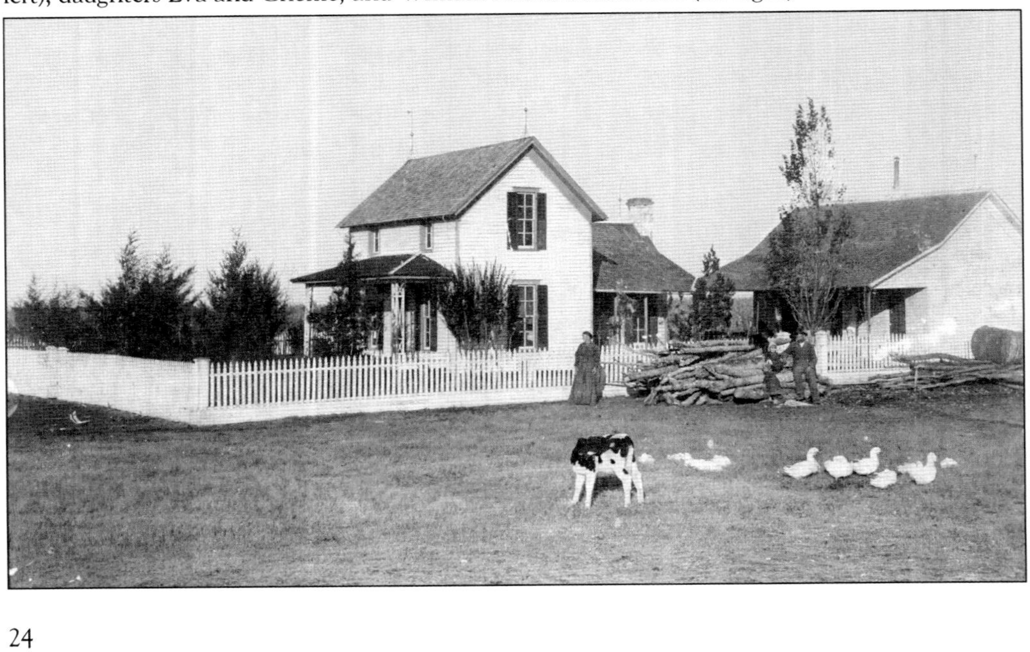

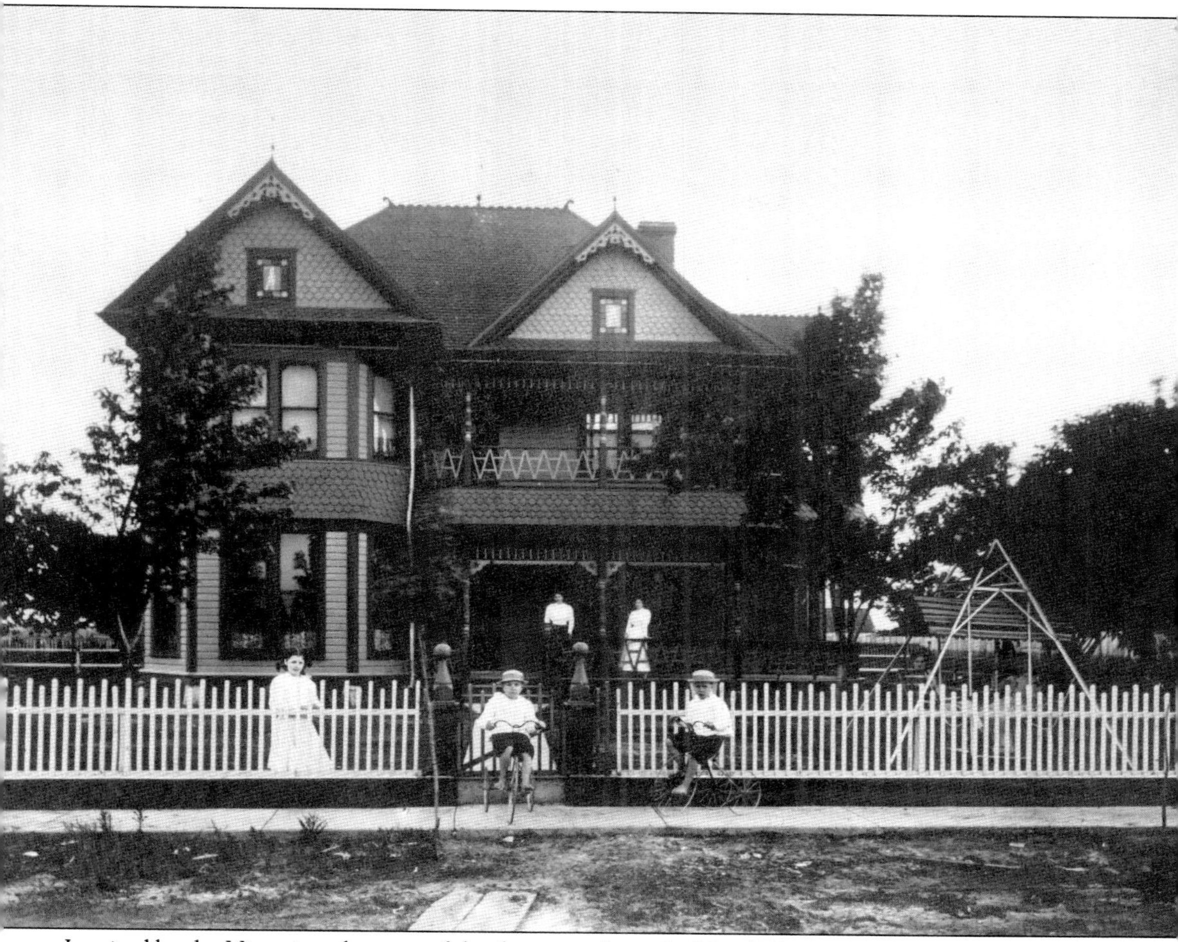

Inspired by the Victorian elegance of the day, near the end of the 19th century, Meredith Ephraim Reinhardt began to make plans to move his family into an impressive multistory home on what is now Old Greenville Road in Royse City. Reinhardt and his wife, Mary Sue Marvin Reinhardt, had three children—Mary Belle, Marvin, and Mike—and the sprawling home provided a perfect setting for a family that placed great emphasis on education, church, and civic awareness. There would be plenty of room for the constant coming and going of family, friends, and civic committees. M. E., known as Bose by his friends, farmed the land, and Mary Sue became accomplished at handiwork and gardening. Reinhardt passed away in 1932, followed by his widow in 1947. The beautiful Victorian home where they raised their children was later demolished. Descendants of the Reinhardt family still live in Rockwall County today.

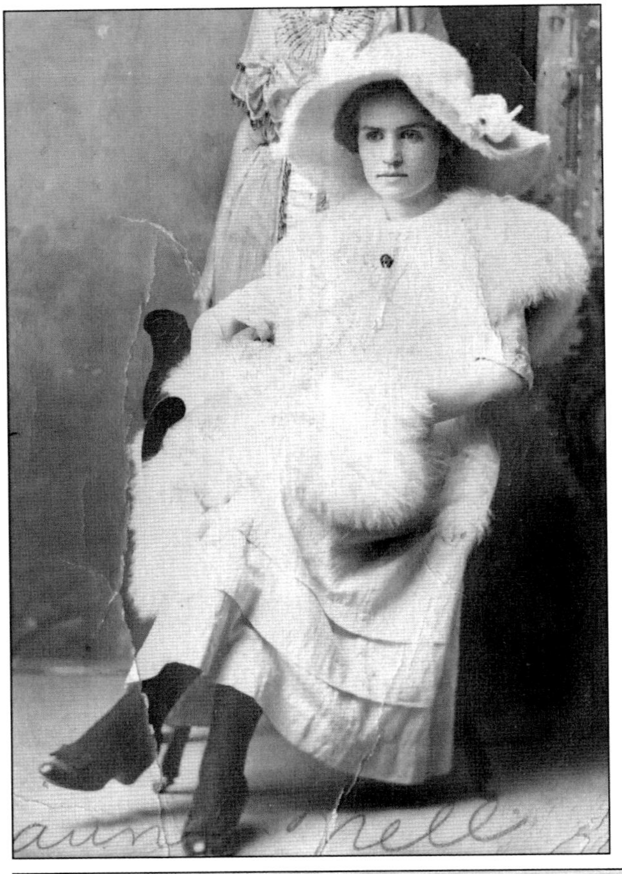

Although the vast majority of Rockwall County residents were rural farmers at the dawn of the 20th century, there were a number of merchants and businessmen—and a few prosperous landowners—whose families were obviously influenced by the Victorian protocols so popular in larger societal circles. At left, Nellie Manson Bost displays the newest fashions of the day. Below, a Rockwall calling card lets neighbors know the family will be accepting visitors. During the Victorian era, calling or visiting was considered the most important leisure activity in proper social circles, and calling card etiquette dictated the length of a stay and the time of a visit. Families had visiting days and "at home" days. Calling cards even had their own language—turning down a certain corner of the card conveyed a particular message to the recipient without having to write a word.

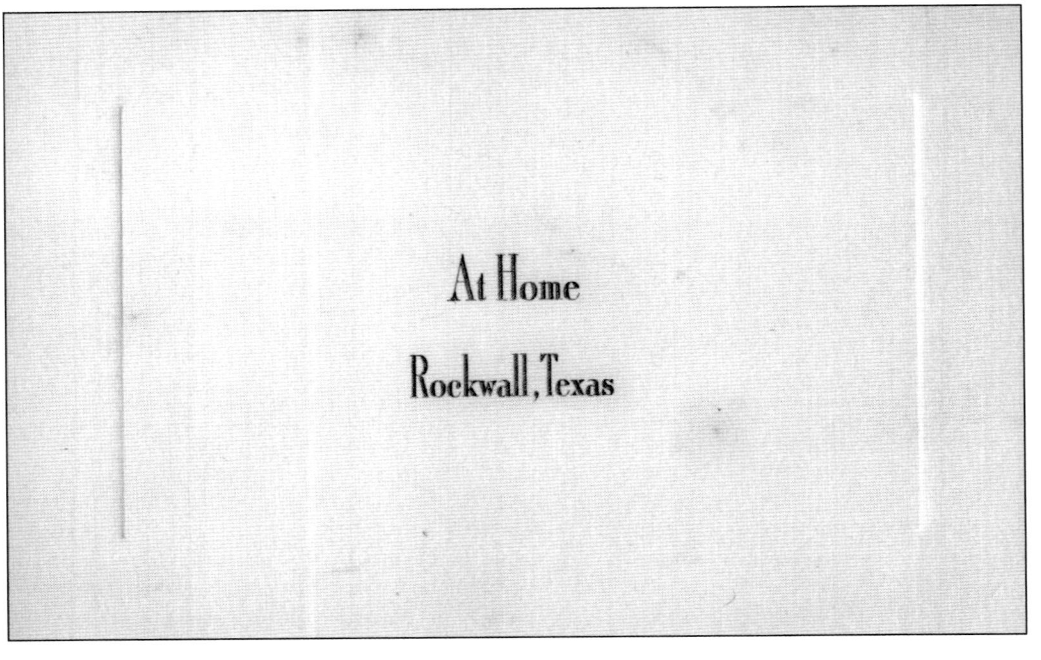
At Home

Rockwall, Texas

Two

Cotton is King in Rockwall's Agrarian-Based Economy 1900–1945

The first settlers described the blackland soil as so dense and strong that it took eight oxen to pull a plow through it. While the land was tough, it was also fertile. From the time the earliest settlers established their homes in what would one day be Rockwall County, they began farming in that blackland dirt.

When the railroad was built through Rockwall County in 1886, the increase in the ease of shipping guaranteed that, for at least the next 50 years, "Cotton was King."

Throughout the years, there were a total of 18 cotton gins built in the county. During the first 20 years of the 1900s, there was a steady count of approximately 1,000 farms in operation in Rockwall County, mostly producing cotton. By 1925, Rockwall County boasted more than 60,000 acres of cotton and produced approximately 20,000 bales of cotton each year.

Cotton farming was such an integral part of community life during this time that area schools often dismissed classes for several weeks in the fall and in the spring so children could help their families with the planting and harvesting of crops. Education was important, but cotton was their livelihood.

In addition to cotton becoming Rockwall's main cash crop during this period, the large number of small settlements in the area was slowly giving way to several main communities. Heath, Fate, Royse City, McLendon, Chisholm, and, of course, Rockwall thrived as the area's largest cities, each with their own schools, churches, and business districts.

During this time, life for the typical Rockwall County family revolved around the family, the farm, the school, the church, and taking a trip to town on Saturday for supplies and sundries.

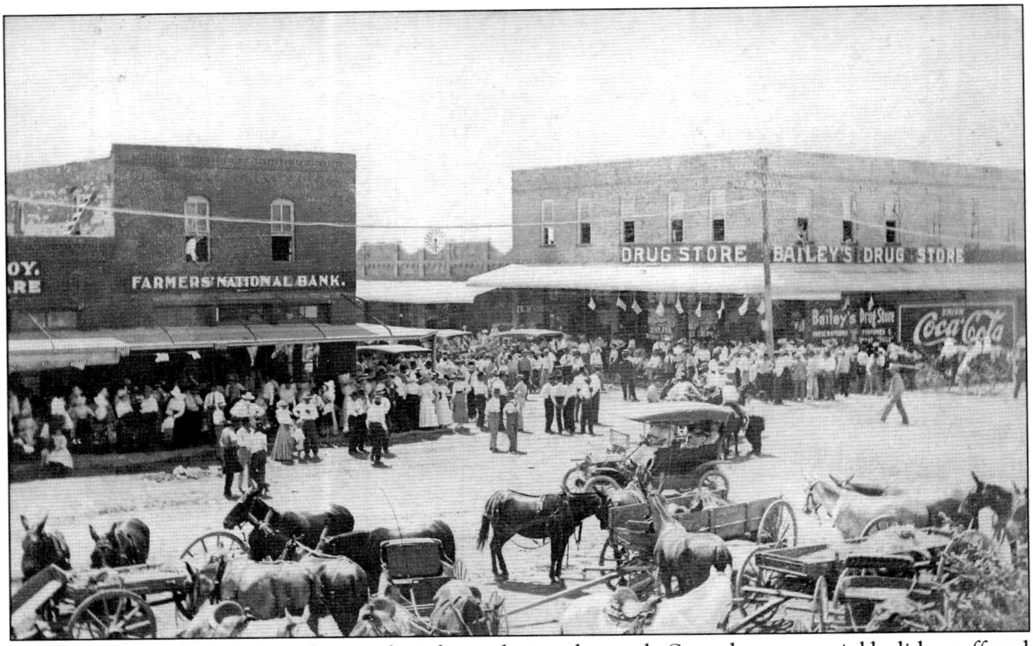

While most families were tending to their farms during the week, Saturdays or special holidays offered a reason to travel to town. During the late 1800s and the early 1900s, area merchants sponsored Trades Days, enticing residents to spend the day on the square with raffles of everything from a horse and buggy to cold hard cash. City and county leaders also planned special celebrations to invoke civic pride and build community spirit. Above, area residents stand on the southeast corner of the square during a special celebration in 1911. Below, citizens prepare for an Independence Day parade in one of the few known early images showing the north side of the square.

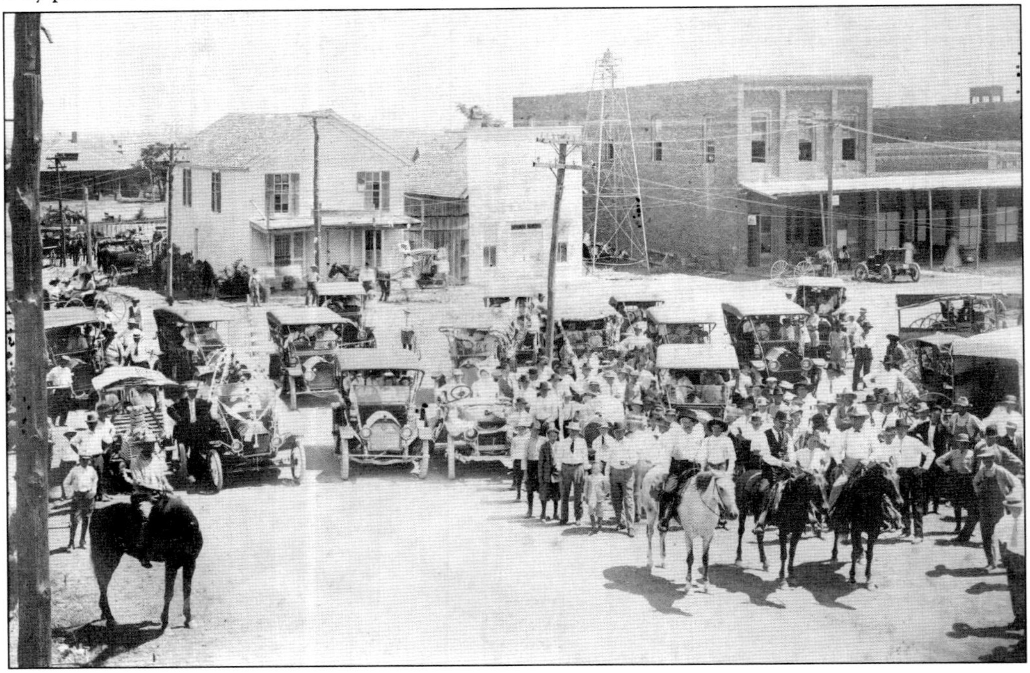

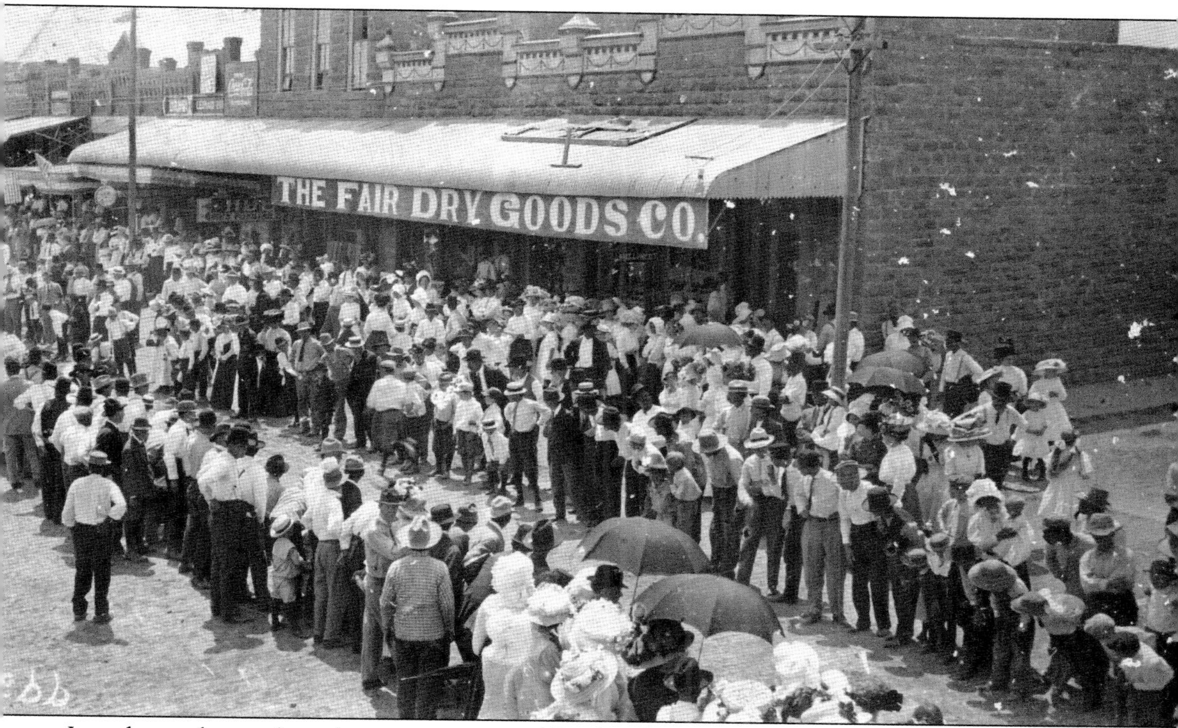

In a day and age when the vast majority of Rockwall residents were farmers, time for leisure activities was limited. When there was time off, the community provided a variety of offerings. Civic celebrations included parades and competitions. In the photograph above, Independence Day revelers await racers to pass by on Rusk Street. On less structured days off, families might enjoy a picnic at Katy Lake. In 1901, the railroad had constructed a tank 2 miles south of the square where the rail line intersected with what is now Farm-to-Market Road 740. The trains that passed through Rockwall would stop and get water for their steam engines, and families began to use this tank and the surrounding acreage as a recreational area. Rockwall's City Park was located off the town square near Squabble Creek and served as the location for countless family and school outings. For more fast-paced entertainment, a sports track north of town offered regular horse races.

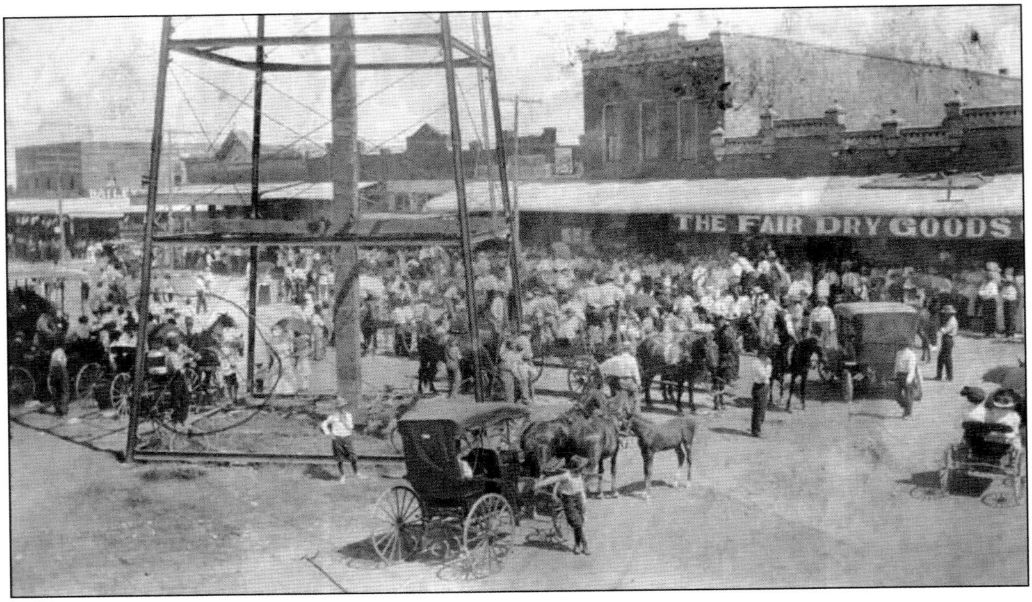

A number of photographs taken during community celebrations ended up on picture postcards. The scene above shows the south side of the square, and a local resident circled a family member then mailed the postcard to an out-of-state relative. The heavily damaged photograph below shows another view of the north side of the square and the two-story brick building that was home to Rockwall's first telephone exchange when it opened in 1902. The white frame building next door housed the volunteer fire department. Sitting between the two buildings was the city's fire alarm—a bell mounted on a wooden tower. If someone called in a fire, an operator yelled out the window and a passerby would sound the alarm.

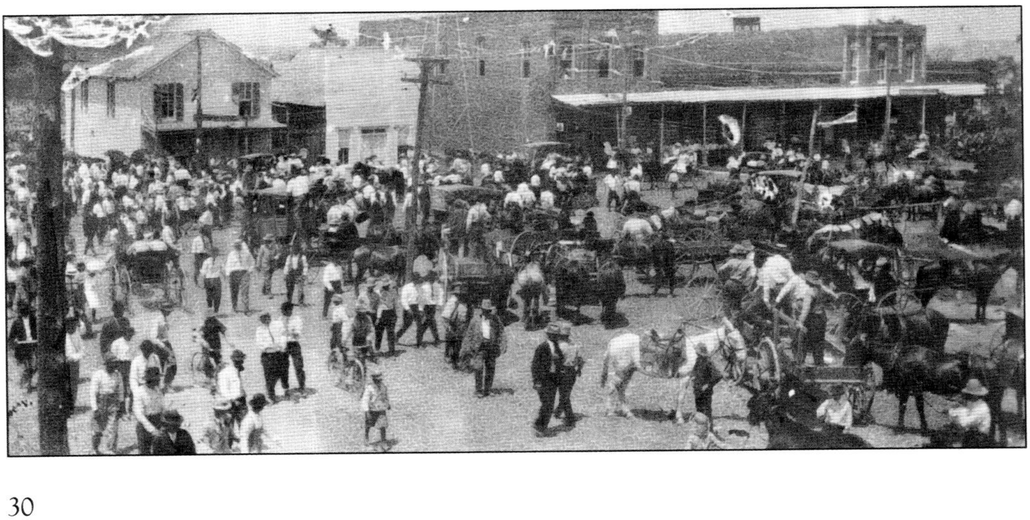

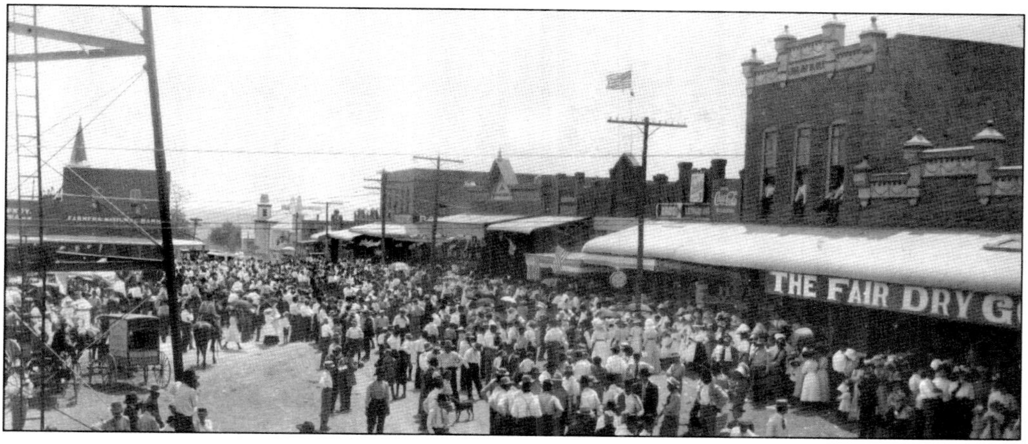

The photographs above and below show different angles of the square taken on the same day. In the left side of both photographs, Farmers National Bank is visible. Farmers National Bank sat on the northeast corner at Rusk and San Jacinto Streets, and was an integral part of Rockwall's early banking industry. The bank set up shop in this brick building in the early 1900s. In 1916, a new brick building was constructed to house the bank, and despite a series of name changes because of consolidation, a bank occupied this corner of the square for many decades.

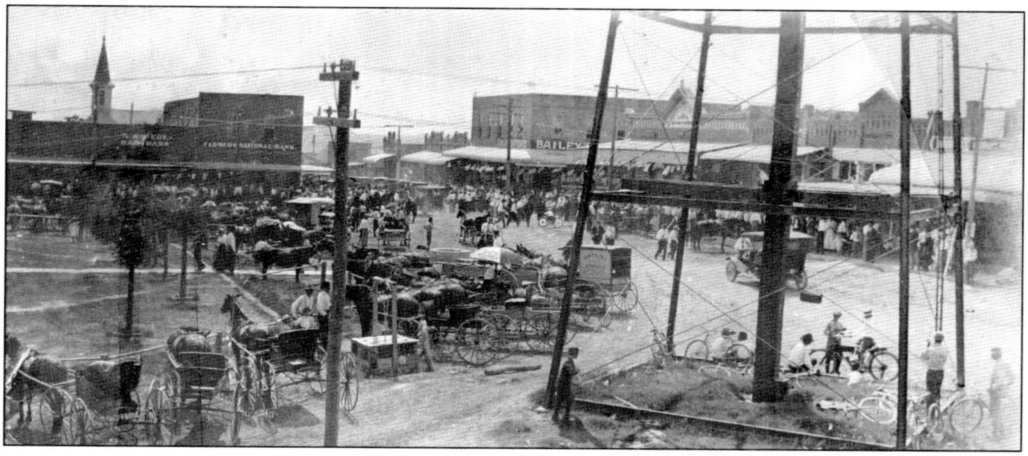

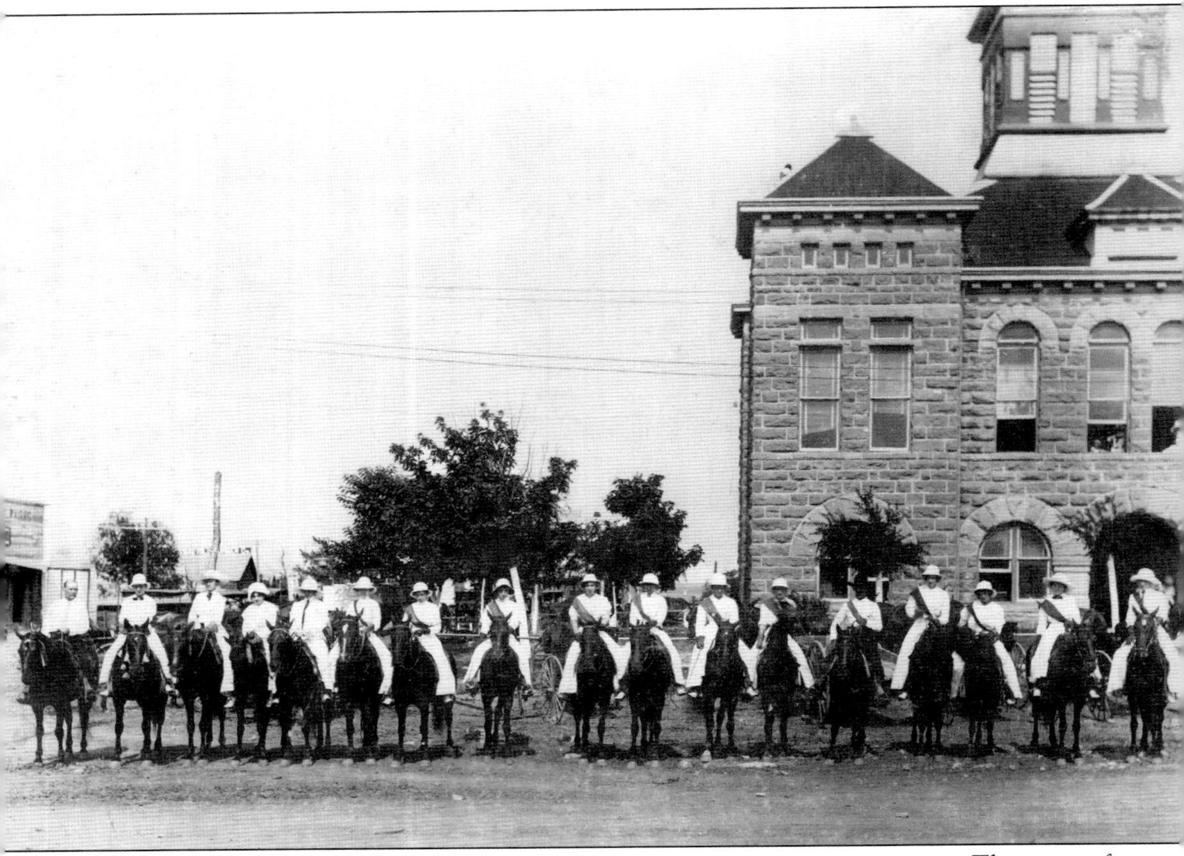

Many Rockwall residents participated in civic and community organizations. This turn-of-the-20th-century volunteer drill group lines up in front of the 1892 courthouse to pose for a photograph. Pictured from left to right are (as identified on the back of the photograph) Joe Chisholm, ? Wisdom, Annie Lofland, Mable McCoulskey Stephenson, Ben Guinn (Mrs. John Walker), Edith Ryan, Gay Ridgell, Winnie Anderson, Allie Snead, three unidentified, ? Meadows, Kate Austin, Emma Rochell, Blanche Corry, and Ethna Anderson. In the early part of the 1900s, the Woodmen of the World, the Masonic Lodge, the Eastern Star, and other social and service organizations enjoyed immense popularity. Throughout the next decades, a number of groups were organized in Rockwall County, many of which still remain today. In 1919, Rockwall's Friday Study Club was organized as a social, cultural, and civic club for women. It remains the oldest civic club in the city of Rockwall. (Courtesy of the family of Evelyn Lofland.)

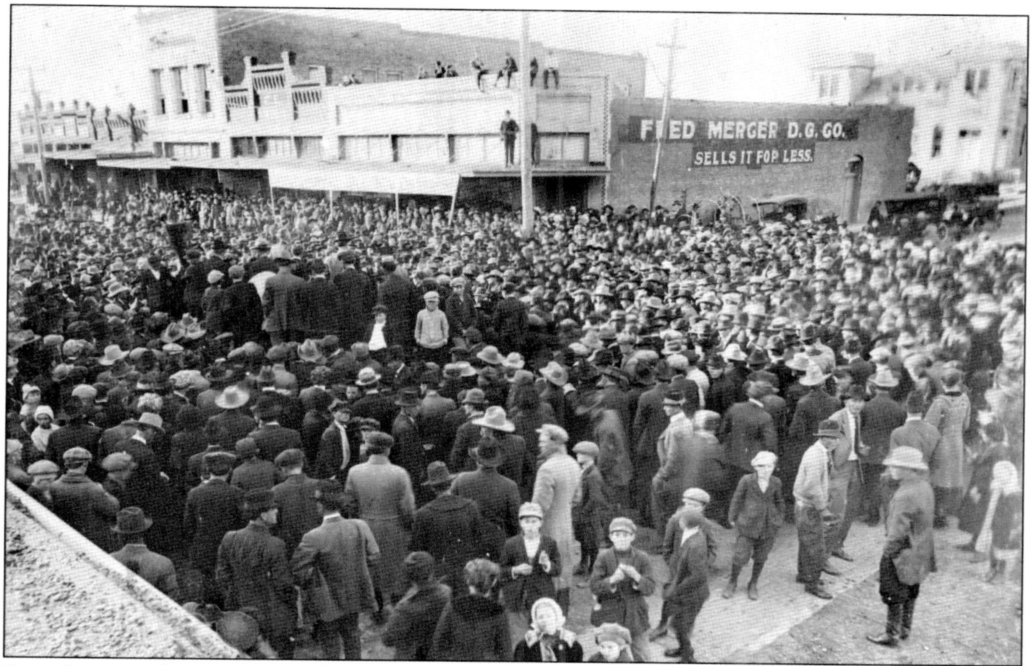

Saturdays were busy on most of Rockwall County's main streets, but holidays and special occasions always drew a particularly large crowd. On this Saturday in 1912 in downtown Royse City, a large group of residents awaits a drawing that would award a Ford car to a lucky ticket holder. Below, a picture postcard features Royse City's main street around 1910. The first documented family to come to the area that is now Royse City was Nancy McCasland and her three sons around 1849. Other families followed, and in 1886, G. B. Royse platted the town site. By 1890, the population of Royse City was approximately 1,000 residents.

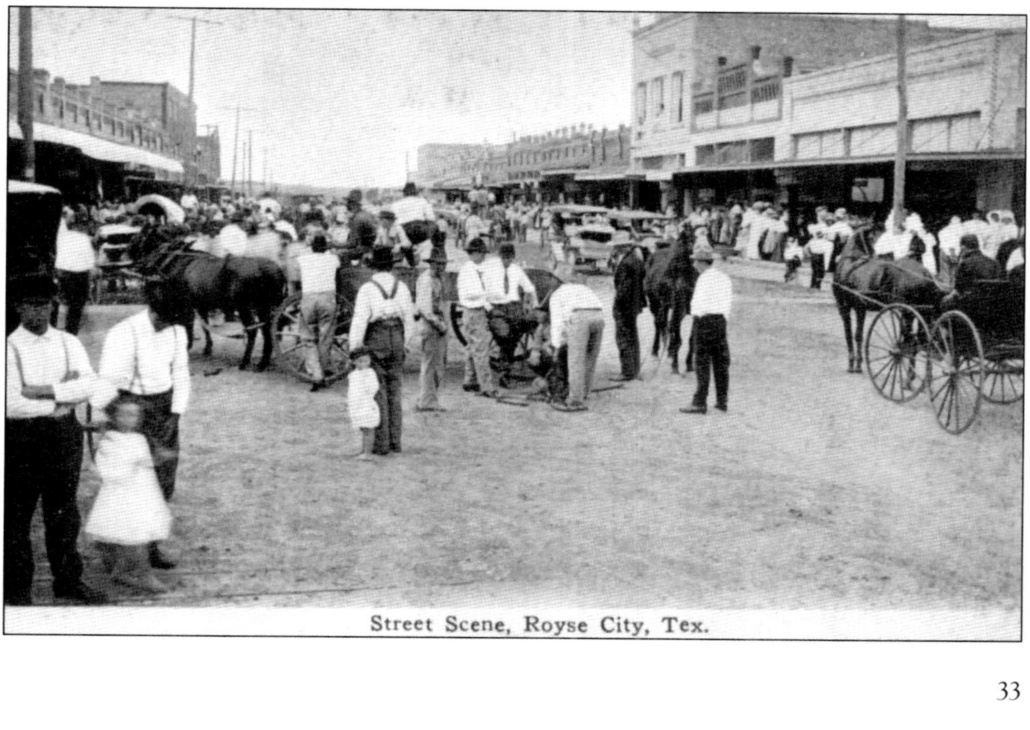

Street Scene, Royse City, Tex.

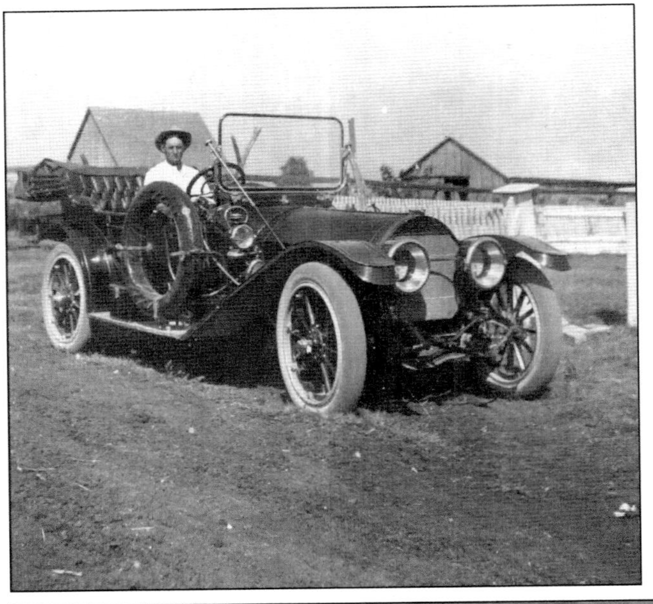

By 1910, a small number of automobiles could be seen around Rockwall, but it was not until a number of years later that they permanently replaced the horse and buggy as the primary method of transportation. In the early days of automobiles, gasoline was shipped to Rockwall in 50-gallon drums at a cost of 32¢ a gallon. In this photograph, N. L. Lofland poses in his car. (Courtesy of the family of Evelyn Lofland.)

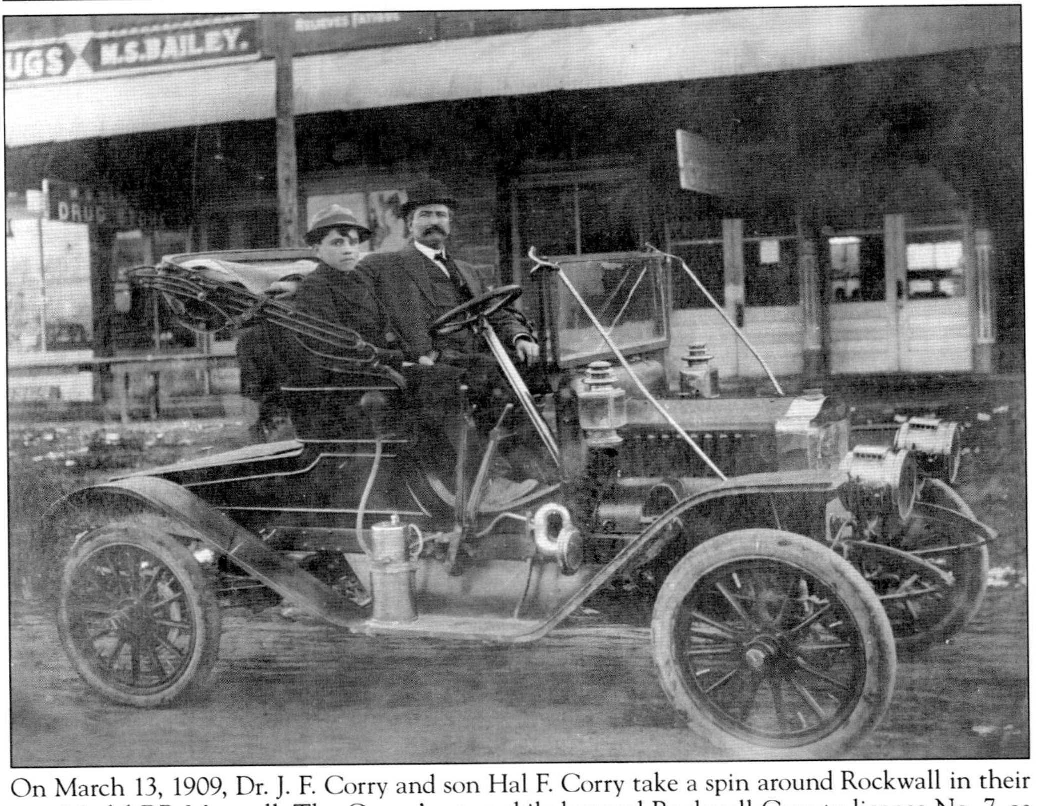

On March 13, 1909, Dr. J. F. Corry and son Hal F. Corry take a spin around Rockwall in their new Model DR Maxwell. The Corrys' automobile boasted Rockwall County license No. 7, as it was the seventh automobile in Rockwall County. According to family records, the car was purchased from the Sackstetter-Potter Company in Dallas and was personally delivered by one of the salesmen.

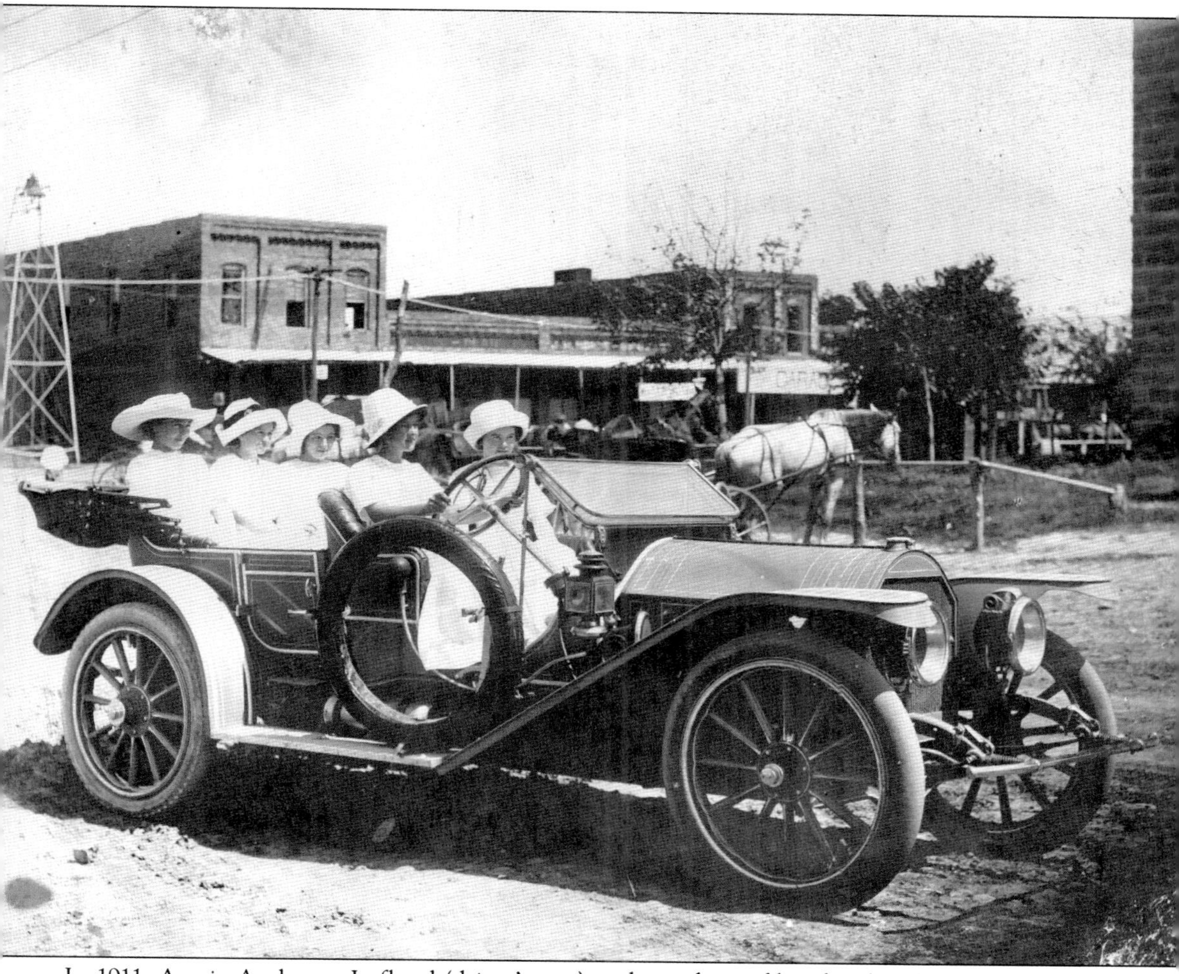

In 1911, Annie Anderson Lofland (driver's seat) and members of her family take in the sights around Rockwall's downtown square. Seated in the front seat with her is Blanche Anderson Corry. From left to right in the back seat are Ethna Anderson, Lucile Anderson, and Ruby Raines. The north side of the town square can be seen in the background. The Anderson sisters were members of a prominent and civic-minded Rockwall family. Their father, Dan Anderson, was a successful rancher. However, he and their mother, Julia Ann Raines Anderson, moved their family to town in the late 1890s so their children could have the best educational opportunities available at the time. Dan was well respected in the community, serving as sheriff and tax collector for the county as well as president of Guaranty State Bank, all the while expanding his ranching operations. (Courtesy of the family of Evelyn Lofland.)

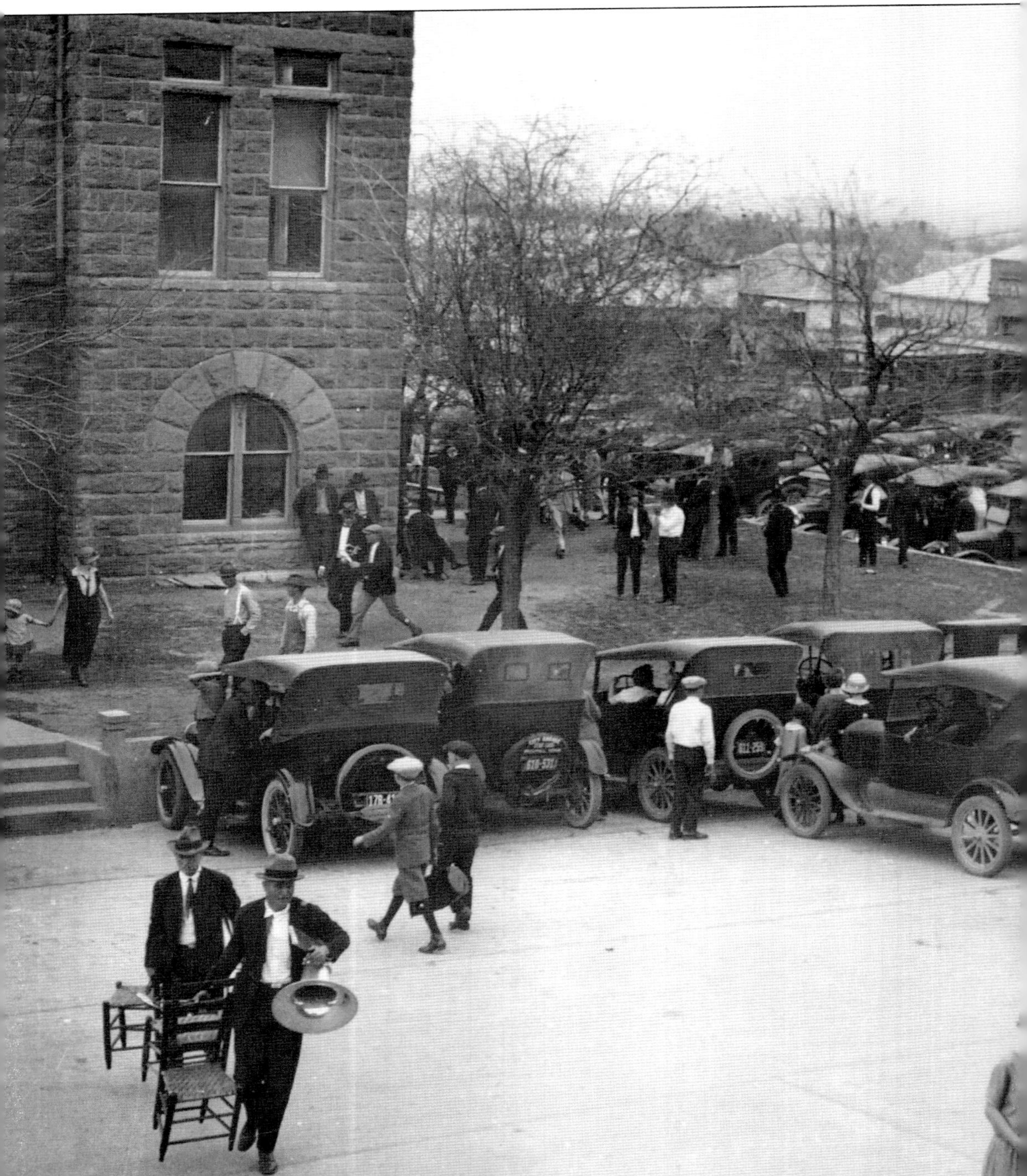

Many of Rockwall's roads were still dirt, but the town square had been paved, and that was worth a county-wide celebration. As long as horses had been the primary mode of transportation, paving had been unnecessary, but as automobiles took over the roads, the dust and dirt that surrounded the square became bothersome and sometimes even dangerous if the weather was particularly

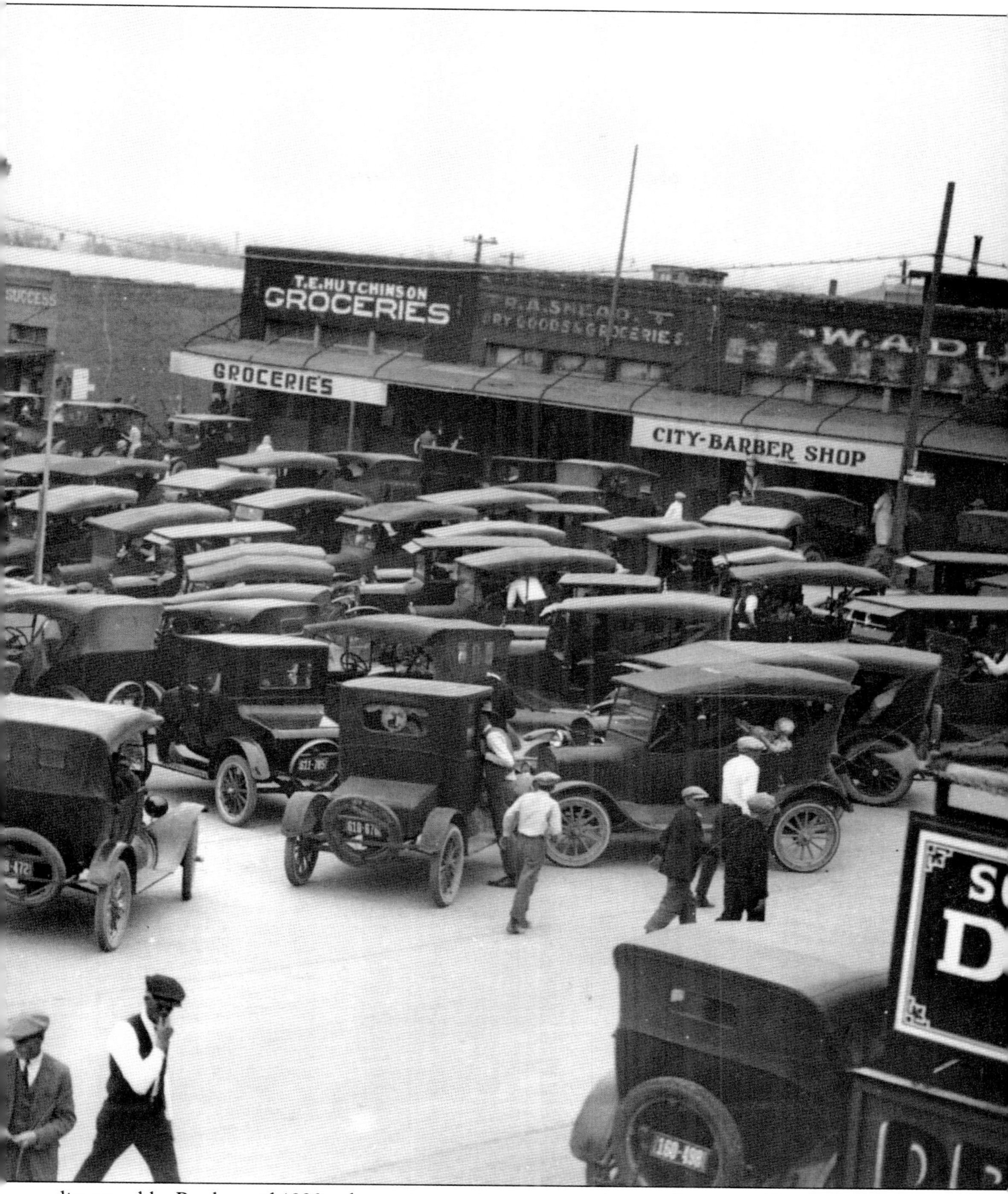

disagreeable. By the mid-1920s, the paving project was complete, and county officials decided to declare a Saturday for a dedication ceremony and celebration. Speeches were made, and a local band performed. In this photograph, the crowd disperses following the ceremony.

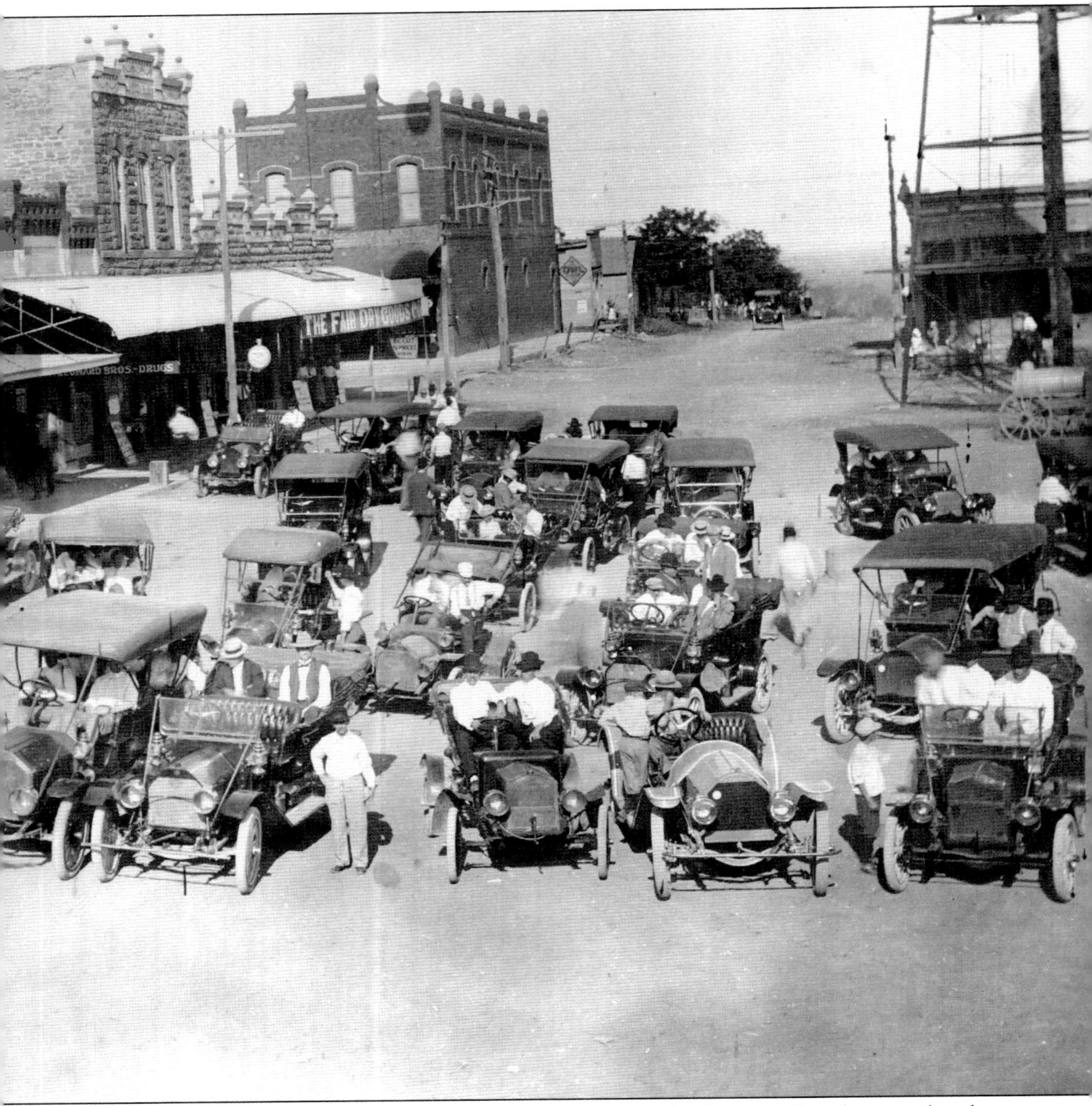

By 1915, automobiles were becoming more and more popular (as shown in this photograph, taken on the square around that time), but the dirt roads provided a difficult journey for the new machinery; if the weather was bad, the roads were basically impassable. The first concrete roads constructed in the county were slab roads—9-foot concrete slabs on the left-hand side of the old road beds. Approximately 40 miles of slab roads were constructed throughout the county. Concrete bridges were built to replace tenuous wooden ones, and smaller communities were suddenly connected in ways that made travel and commerce easier within the boundaries of the county. But the East Fork of the Trinity River was constantly overflowing, so travel to Dallas was still a problem. Around 1917, a Levee District was formed, and voters approved bonds to construct a levee along the East Fork river bed. The construction of this levee created some of the richest farmland in the state, wit much of the soil never having been touched by a plow.

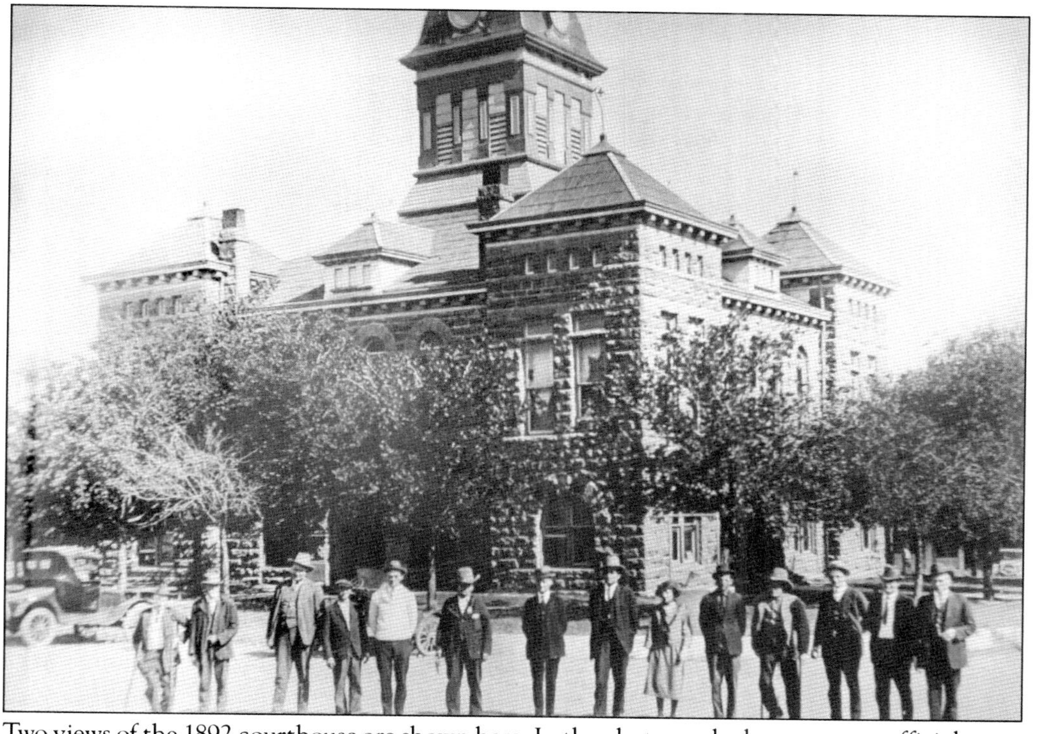

Two views of the 1892 courthouse are shown here. In the photograph above, county officials pose in front of their government offices. In the far left of the photograph is Miles Lannie Stimson, who held elective office in Rockwall County for 53 consecutive years despite facing the physical handicap of being crippled by polio in infancy. Lannie Stimson moved to Rockwall when he was six years old, and at the age of 19, he went to district court to have his minor's status removed so he could legally run for the office of Rockwall County treasurer in 1912. He was elected and served four years, then ran for tax assessor in 1916 and served four years in that capacity. In 1920, he again ran for county treasurer and served until November 16, 1965, when he resigned from office. He ran opposed only four times.

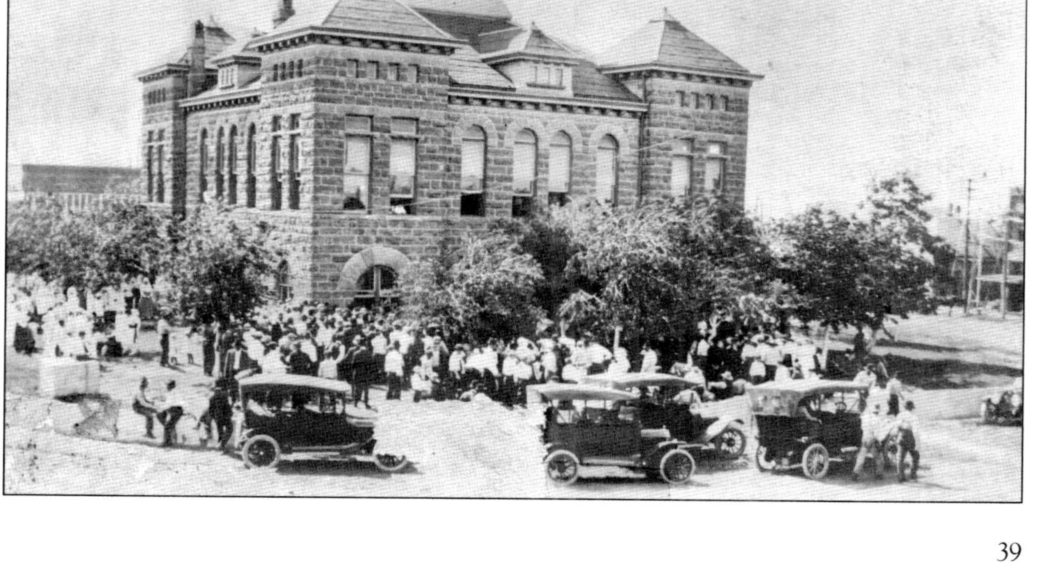

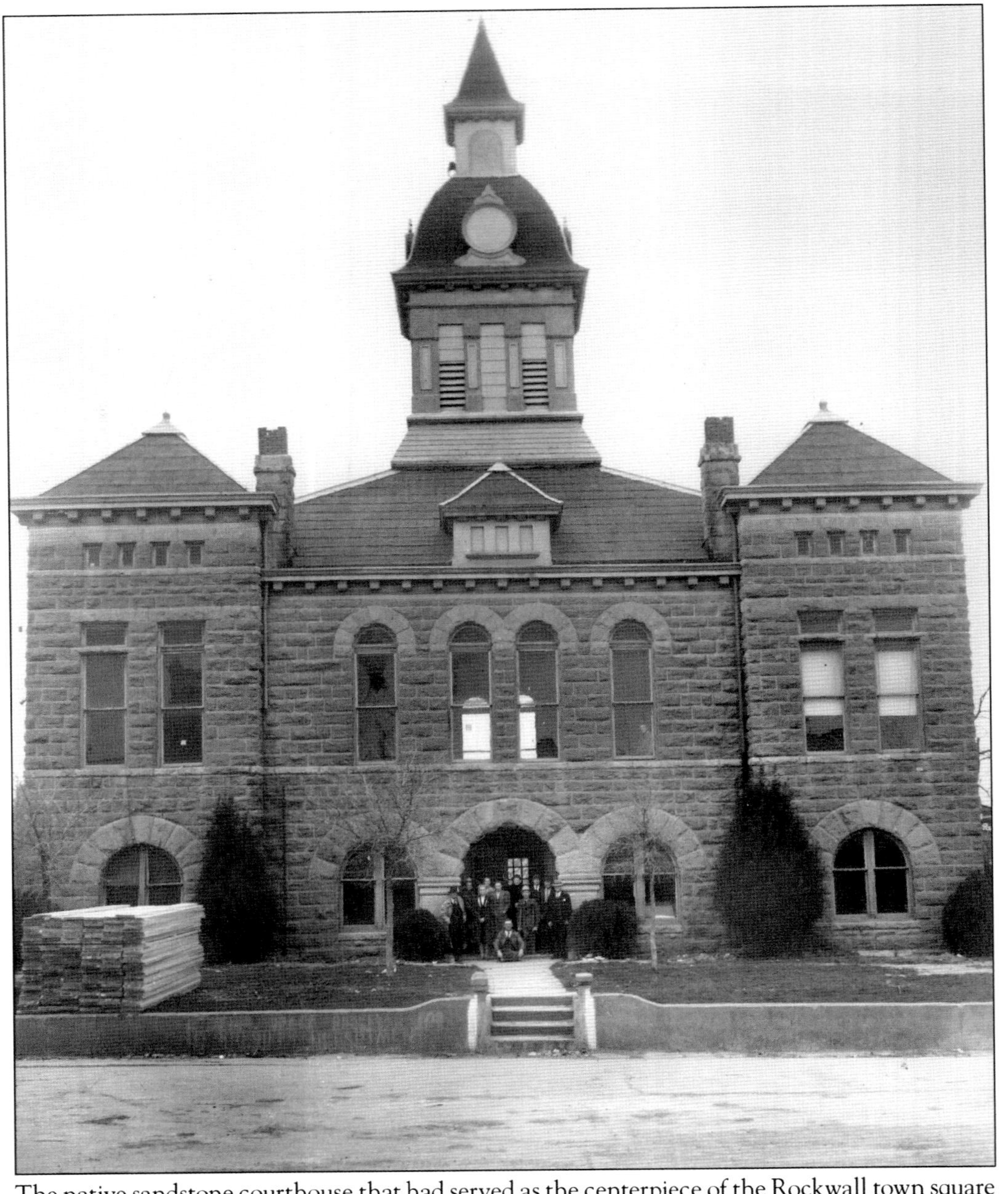

The native sandstone courthouse that had served as the centerpiece of the Rockwall town square since 1892 was showing wear and tear by the mid-1930s. The original stones had been quarried about 4 miles north of the city, but the mortar used to hold them together was crumbling, and the building was deemed unsafe. County officials were told to vacate their offices, and this photograph is the last official one taken of the impressive 1892 structure as community leaders pose in front of it for the final time. A lone occupant looks out a second-story window. Lumber is already stacked on the front lawn, awaiting use. The new courthouse would be constructed as a part of the government's Works Project Administration (WPA). The WPA was established in 1935 in the aftermath of the Depression to provide work for unemployed artisans and laborers. WPA grants funded the construction of public buildings such as schools, hospitals, and courthouses.

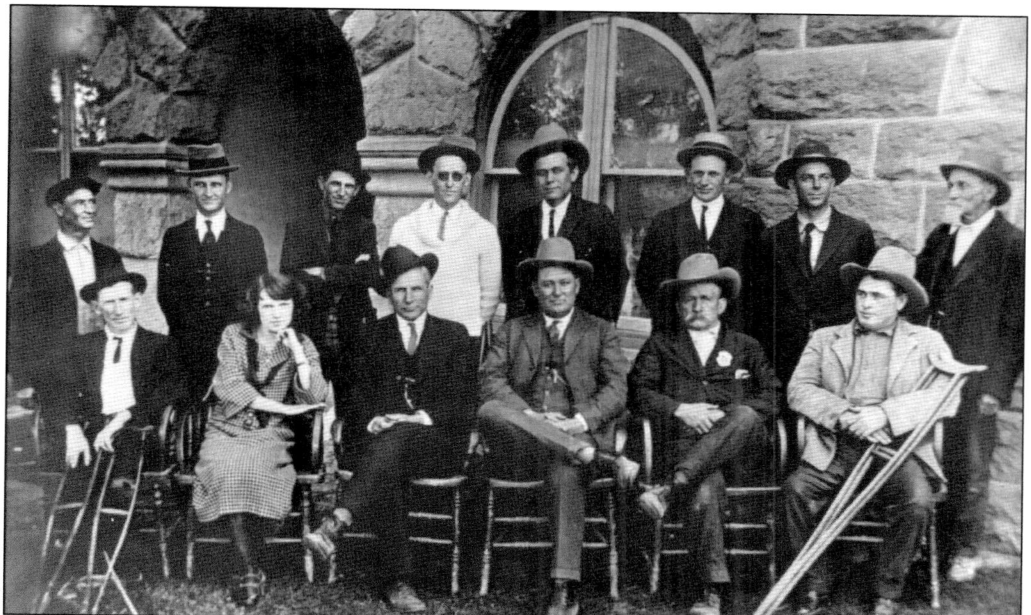

Above, county officials pose in front of the courthouse in 1923. From left to right are (first row) county treasurer Lannie Stimson, deputy county clerk Jessie Jones, county judge James Reese, sheriff/tax collector E. W. Hall, Constable John King, and deputy tax collector Oscar Horton; (second row) county abstracter Chester White, county attorney Carl Miller, county tax assessor O. L. Steger, county clerk Jack Stephenson, Deputy Sheriff Bob Maclin, Highway Patrolman Jim McCarter, county highway engineer Johnie Fout, and courthouse custodian ? Dunn. Below, Deputy Sheriff and tax assessor/collector Jim Lofland is pictured in his office in the courthouse in 1938. Lofland, a lifelong resident of Heath, served the county in that capacity for 26 years.

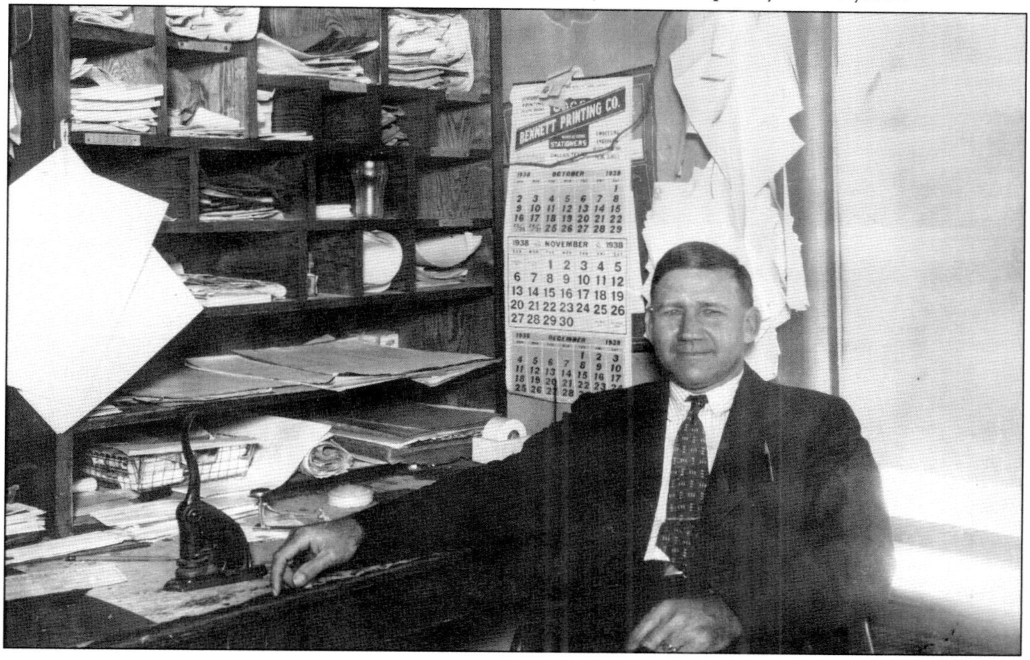

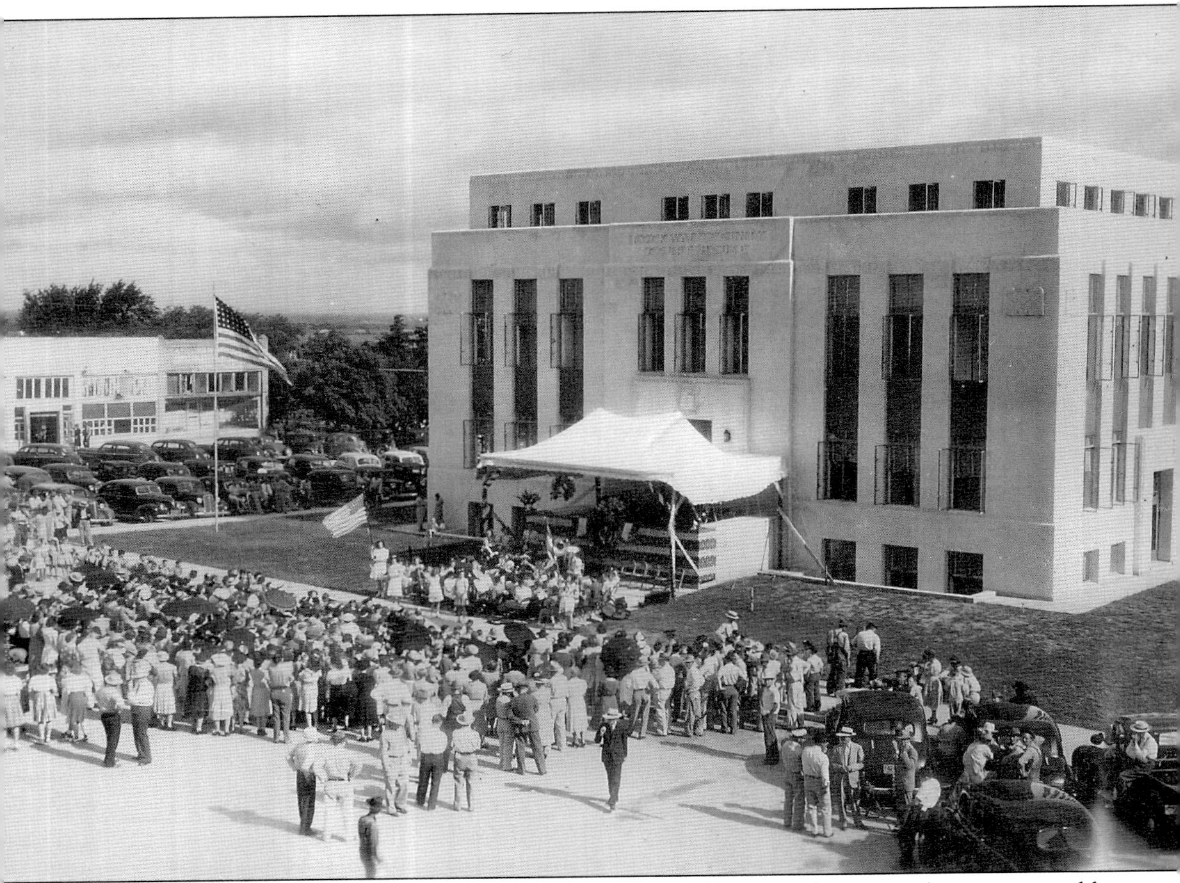

In the 1930s, Rockwall's 1892 courthouse was condemned because the mortar began to crumble, and it was considered unsafe for occupancy. Funds were scarce, so in January 1940, Rockwall County judge Mike Reinhardt went to Washington, D.C., and asked for a WPA grant for courthouse construction. Judge Reinhardt was awarded $52,000 on behalf of Rockwall County, which would go toward the complete construction cost of $92,000. During the night, Judge Reinhardt contracted acute pneumonia and died in a Washington hospital. Honoring his legacy, Rockwall County continued with the construction of a new art deco courthouse. According to records from the local newspaper, the 1892 sandstone courthouse was razed in March 1941, and by December of that same year, the new courthouse was complete. A description of the courthouse from 1941 calls it "a modern and efficient building." This photograph was taken on the day of the dedication ceremony.

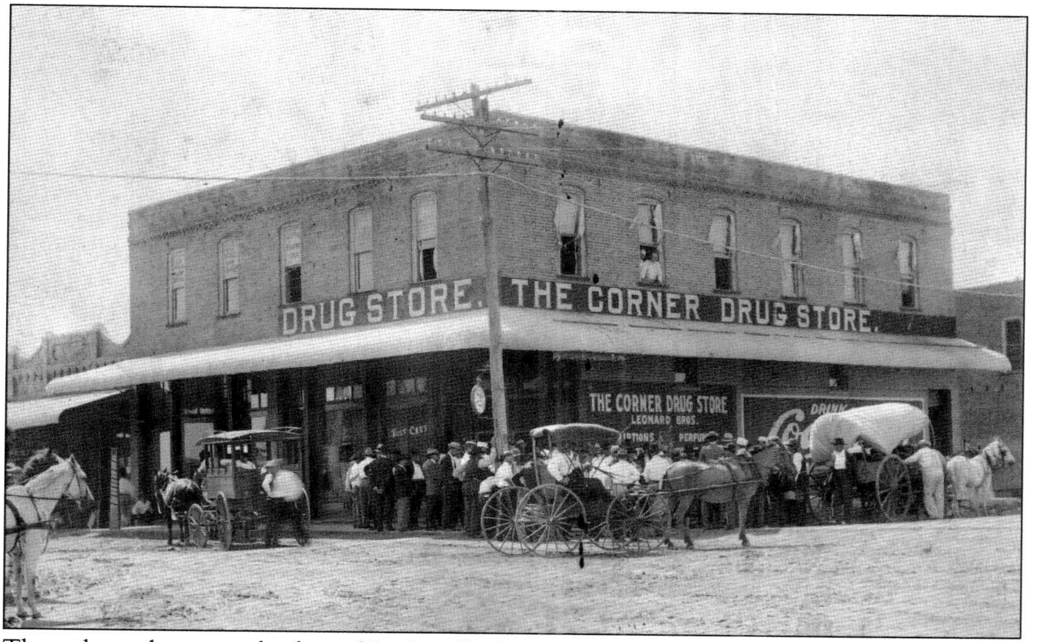

Throughout the years, the face of Rockwall's downtown square has changed dramatically. Prior to the dawn of the 20th century, the block that begins at the southeast corner of Rusk and San Jacinto Streets consisted of frame buildings with a plank sidewalk. Residents called it "rat row" because its main occupants were food establishments. In 1903, a brick building was erected on the corner. The building had several short-term occupants, including the Corner Drug Store (above) before Scott Bailey took over residency (below). His drugstore, which had previously been housed just a few storefronts toward the west on Rusk Street, occupied the building for more than 15 years.

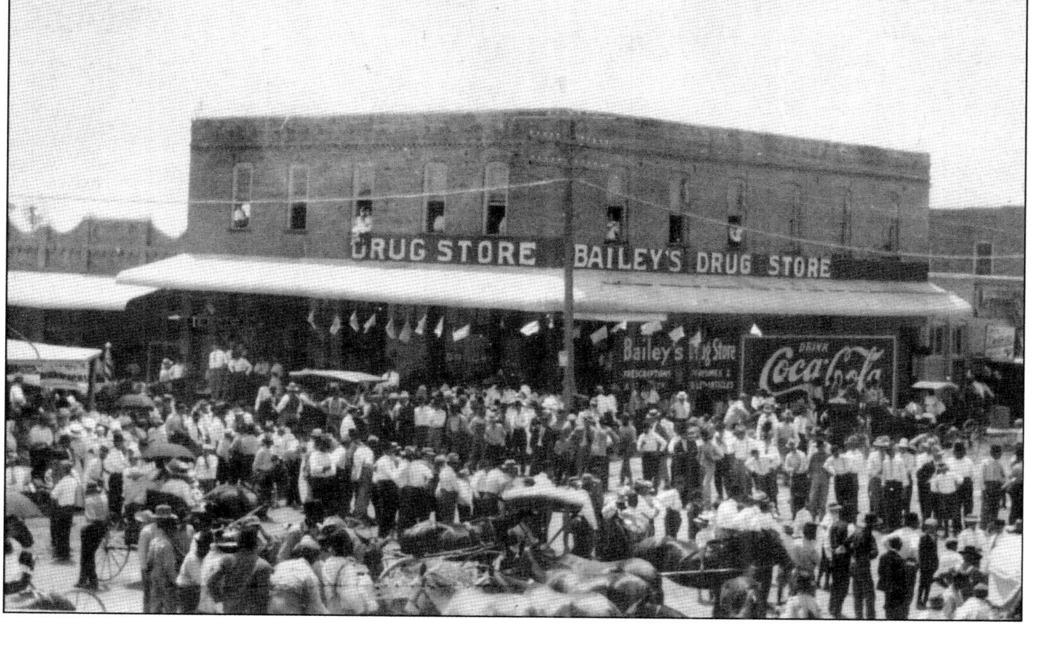

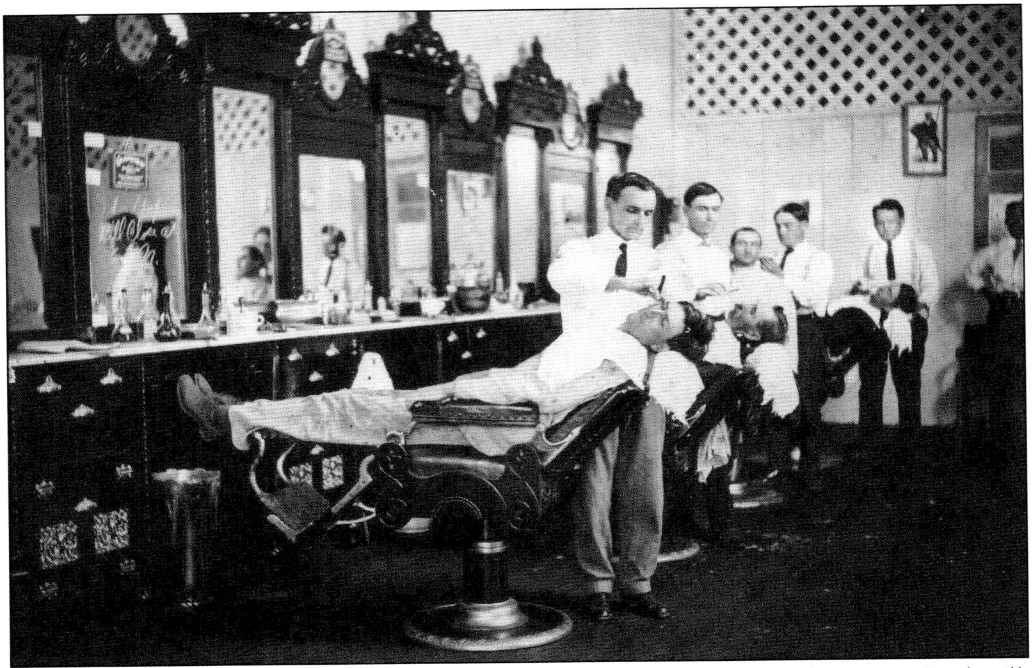

The Elite Barbershop, pictured around 1910, was located on Rusk Street in downtown Rockwall. Customers could get a haircut, a shave, a shoe shine, and a bath. The shop had four baths in the back with a potbellied wood-burning stove used to heat water. It stayed open late on Saturday evenings to accommodate hired hands or drifters who only made it into town once a week.

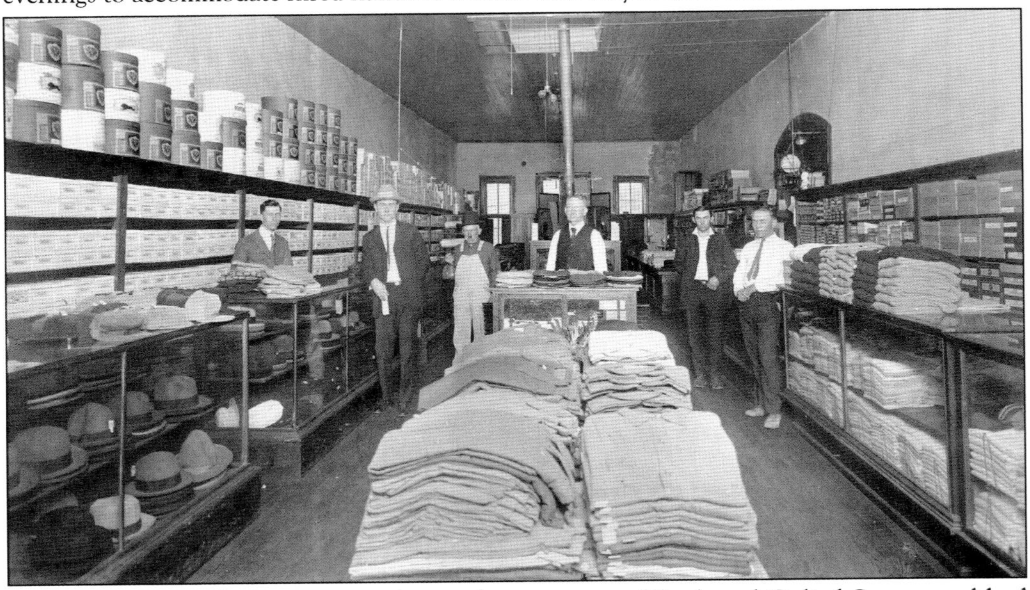

The Fair Dry Goods Store sat on the southeast corner of Rusk and Goliad Streets and had segregated sides for men's and women's clothing. For many years, it was the largest clothing store in Rockwall. Pictured in the men's area are, from left to right, A. D. Hartman, unidentified, Billy McCarter, proprietor T. L. Townsend, unidentified, and Homer Belew. The women's side was to the right and opened onto South Goliad Street.

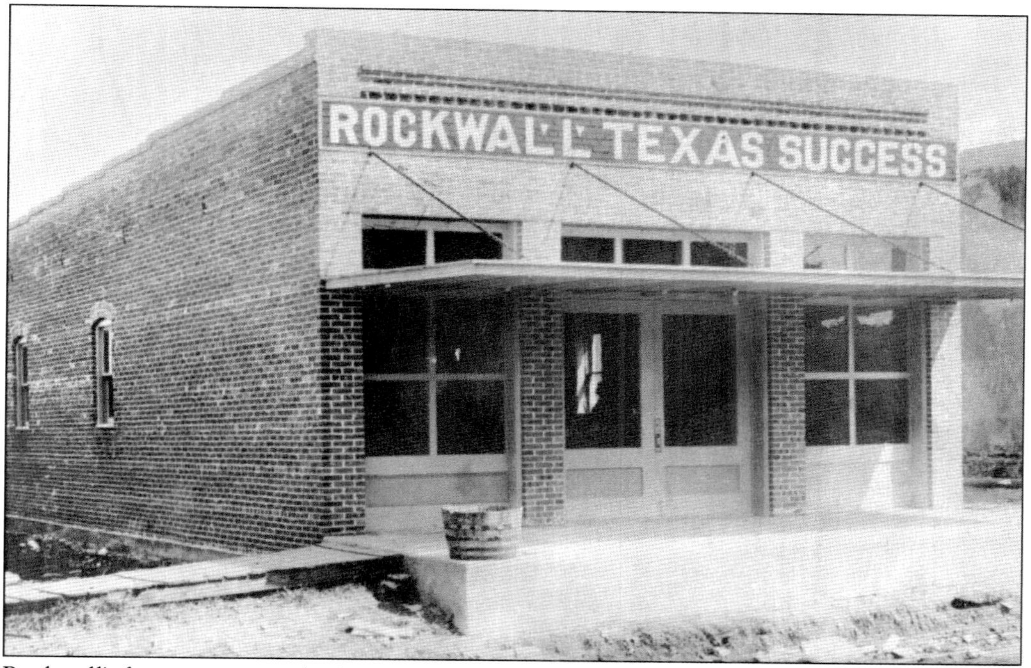

Rockwall's first newspaper, the *Success*, was founded by Sid Crosbyton in partnership with Lynn Charleston. Originally it ran out of a building on Rusk Street. In 1885, Dr. Hal Manson and Jeff Cox bought the paper. In 1910, Dick Gaines bought the business, and in the mid-1910s, he had a brick building erected on North San Jacinto Street to house the paper. In 1949, P. J. Bounds Sr. and P. J. Bounds Jr. purchased the business. The *Rockwall Success* remained within the Bounds family until 1988, when it was sold to an outside entity. Pictured above is the building on San Jacinto Street as it looked when built by owner Dick Gaines. Pictured below is Dick Gaines leaning on a showcase holding part of his pencil collection. Gaines had a collection of more than 3,400 pencils, with no two alike.

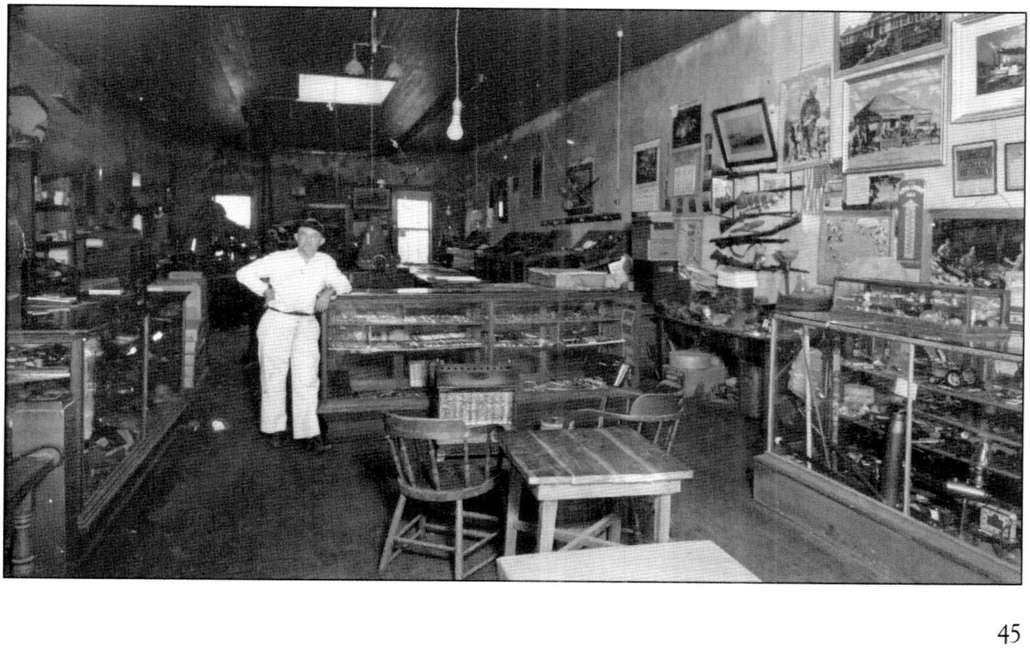

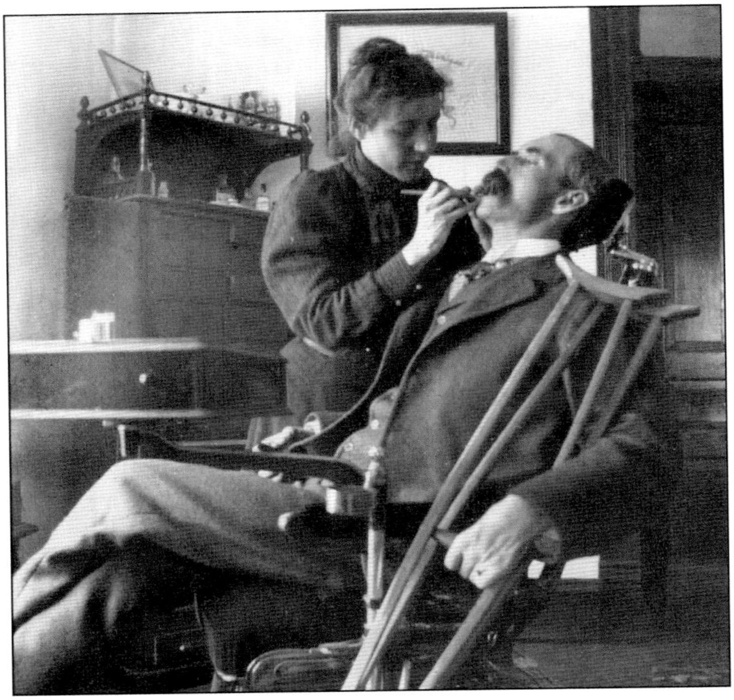

Dr. Jessie Castle LaMoreaux received her dental degree from the University of Michigan in 1896, then set up a practice in Dallas in 1898, thus becoming Texas's first formally trained female dentist. In 1901, she moved herself and her practice to Rockwall to be closer to her sister. She was active in the Rockwall community for many years. Dr. LaMoreaux passed away in 1954.

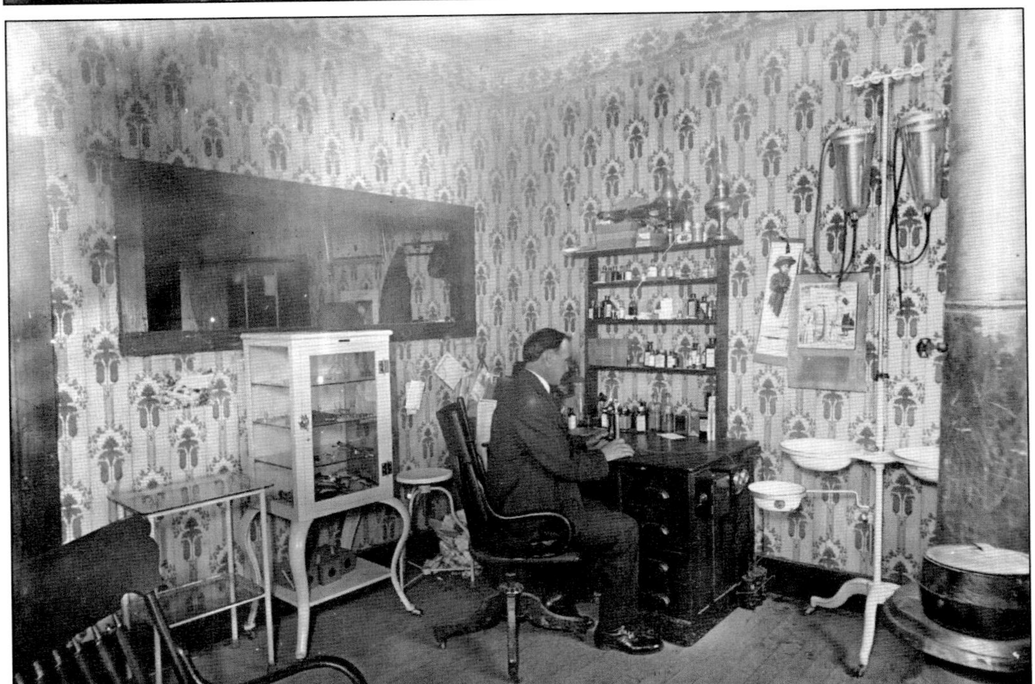

In 1905, Dr. Curtis Monroe Jackson moved with his wife, Lena, to Rockwall, where he had lived during part of his youth. They resided on Kernodle Street, and Dr. Jackson began making house calls in his Ford Model T. Dr. Jackson was active in the civic affairs of Rockwall, serving on the school board for several terms. He continued to practice medicine until his death in 1962.

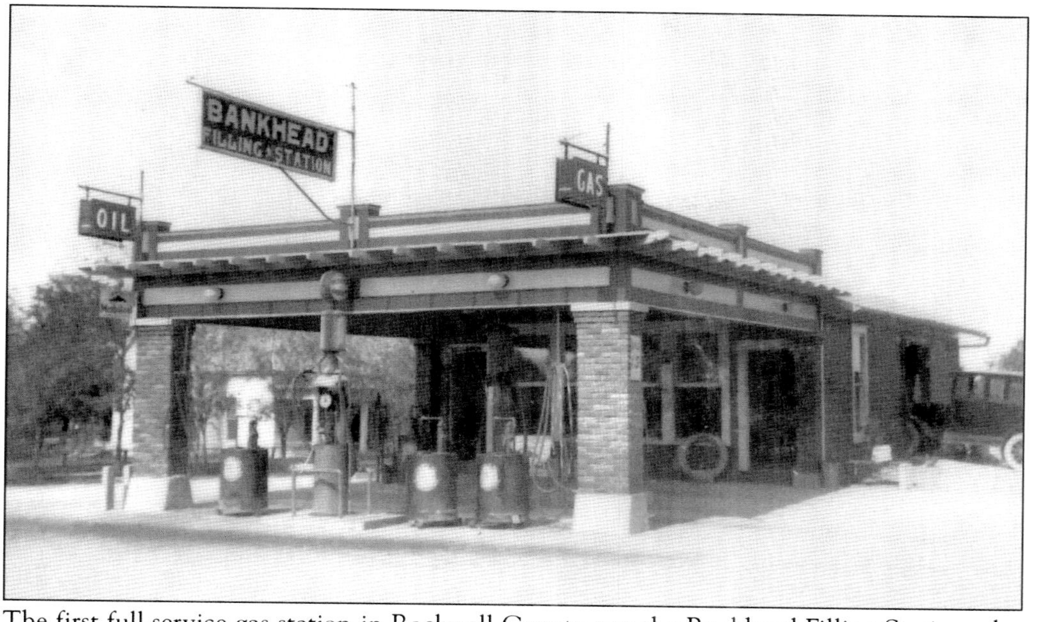

The first full-service gas station in Rockwall County was the Bankhead Filling Station, also known as the Lowe Filling Station. It was built around 1920 and was owned and operated by Jack, Woodie, and Henson Lowe. It was located at the corner of North Alamo Street and the Bankhead Highway (U.S. Highway 67), now known as State Highway 66. It was sold in the 1940s and demolished in the 1990s.

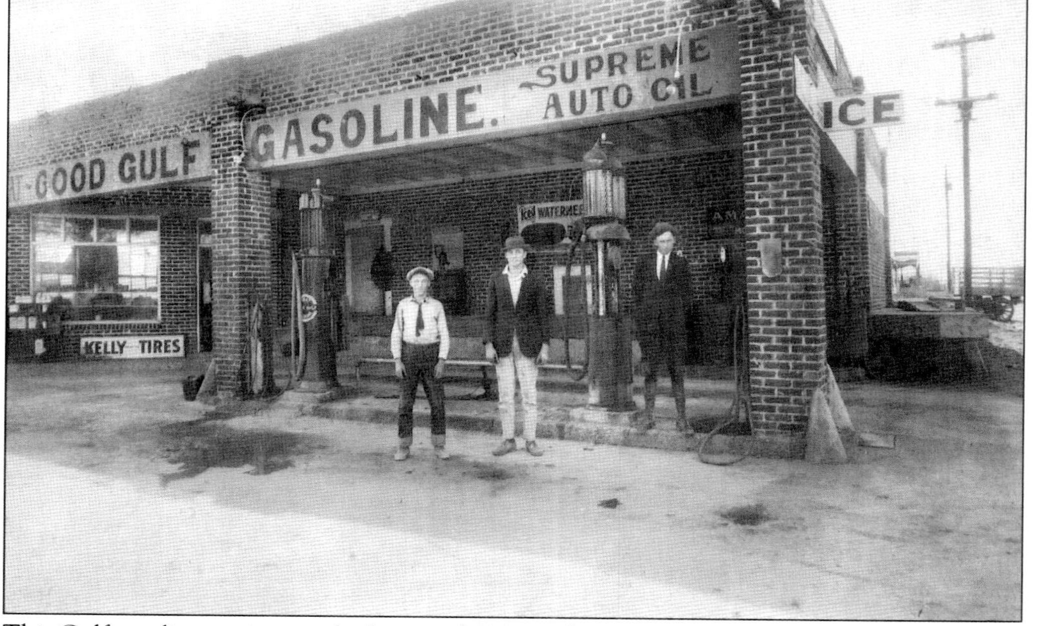

This Gulf gasoline station was built around 1920 at the corner of Fannin and Kaufman Streets. Its construction corresponded with that of the Bankhead Highway (U.S. Highway 67) that wound directly through downtown Rockwall. Pictured from left to right are O. D. Shoemaker, Herman Garrett, and Slatter Bourn.

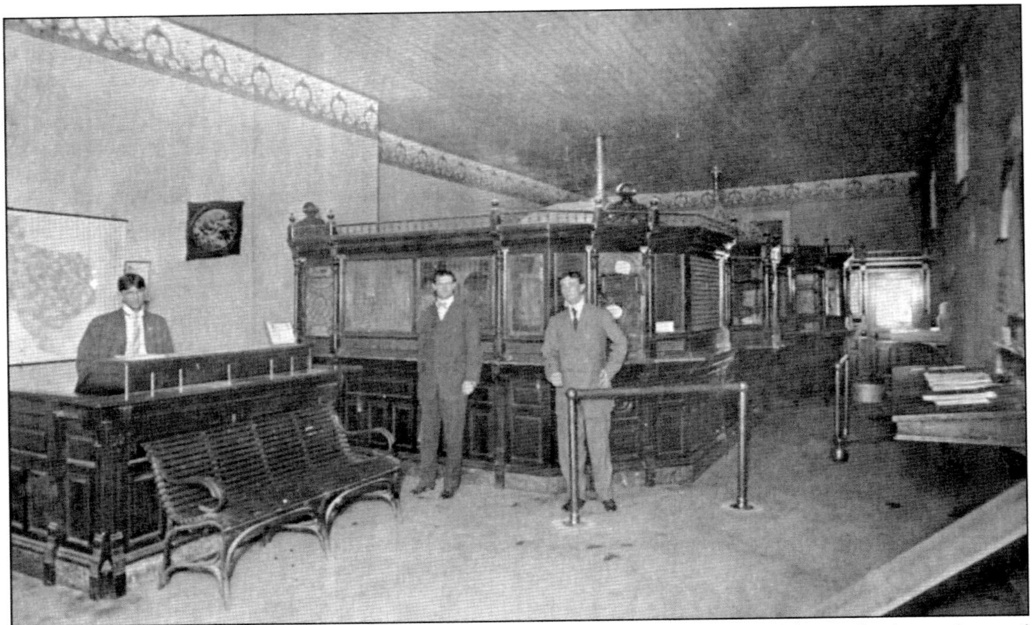

These two photographs are of the interior of the Farmers National Bank building, which was located at the corner of Rusk and San Jacinto Streets. Above, from left to right, are B. H. Wisdom, Frank Clark, and John Walker. Below (behind the cages from left to right) are bankers Lem Chisholm, M. H. McCoy, and George Adams. Local legend has it that famous outlaws Bonnie Parker and Clyde Barrow once stopped at the soda shop across the street from the bank in order to assess the ease with which it could be robbed. A newsboy who was a carhop in the afternoons recognized them. Apparently, the idea was abandoned because the bank was never targeted.

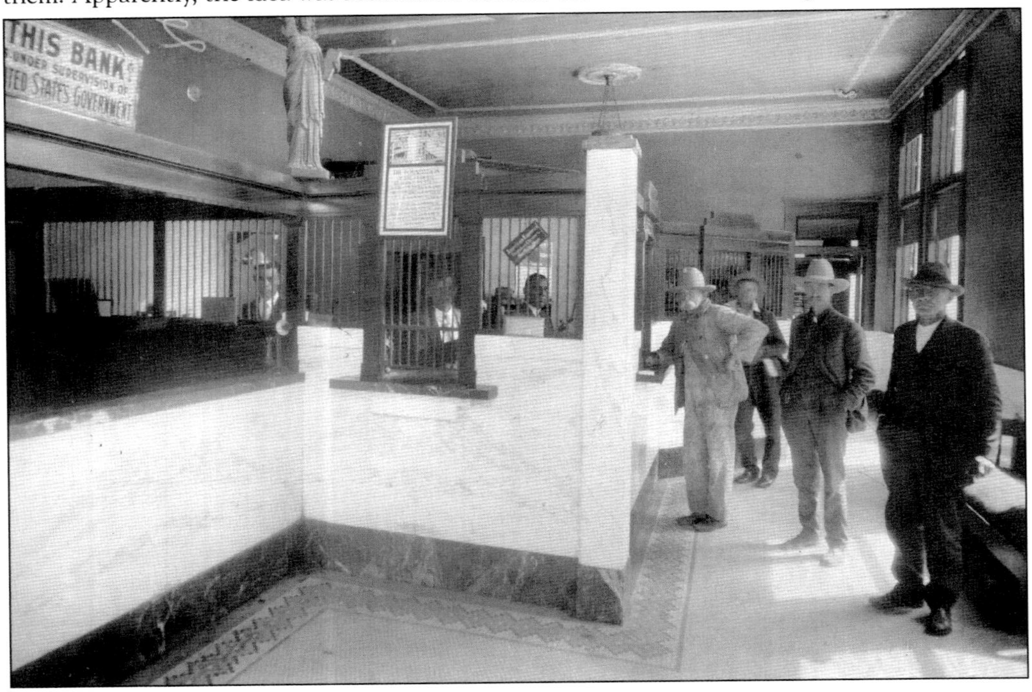

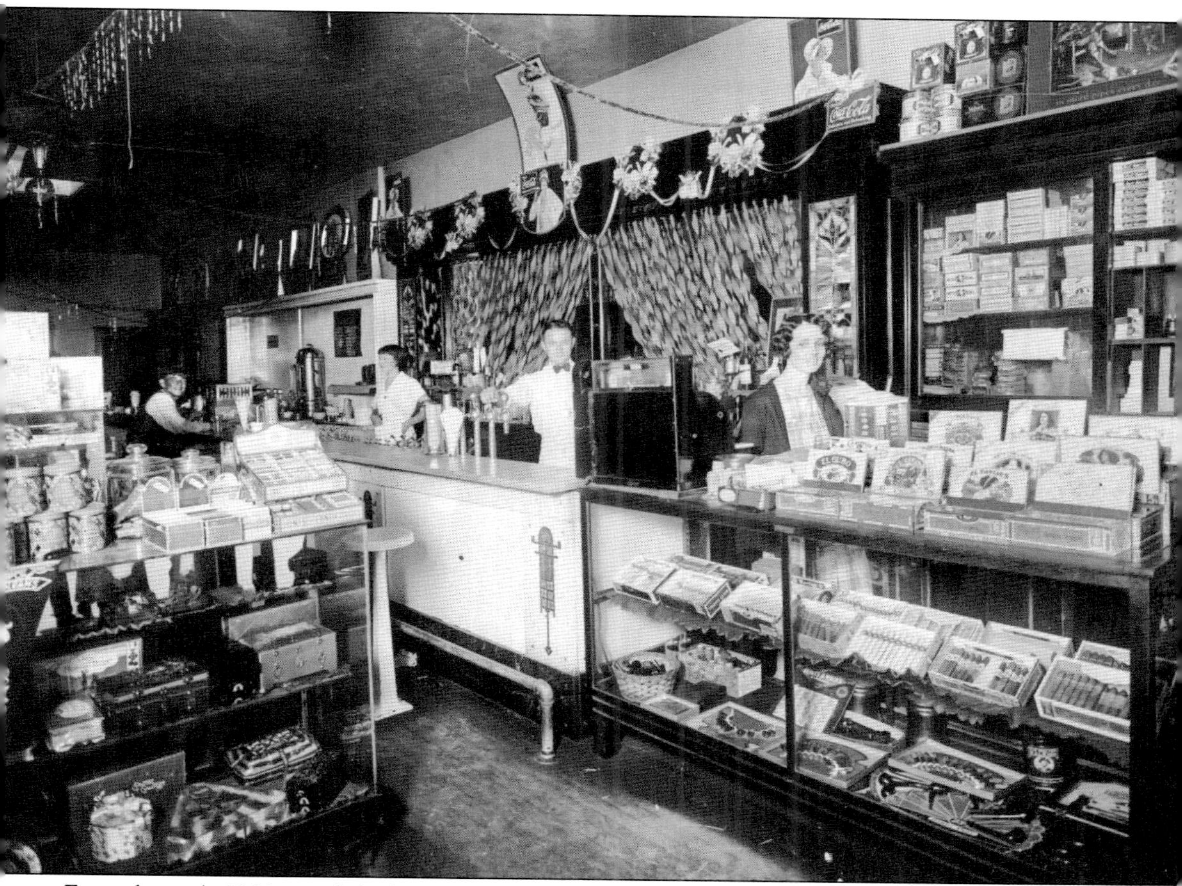

From the early 1900s until the late 1950s, Rockwall had a number of drugstores that offered soda fountain service for their patrons. The history of soda fountains dates back to the late 1800s when the curative powers of mineral springs were popular. Hoping to capitalize on the craze, drugstore owners offered artificially produced mineral waters for medicinal purposes. Sulfuric acid was combined with ground marble to produce carbonation, and the water was dispensed from metal urns. Counter service was introduced in 1903, and within a few years, the entire experience evolved from health-oriented to an enjoyable social activity that included newly marketed soft drinks and eventually ice cream concoctions. The popularity of the soda fountain waned with the introduction of prepackaged ice cream, bottled soft drinks, and fast-food restaurants. Pictured is Harvey Way, third from left, in one of Rockwall's soda shops.

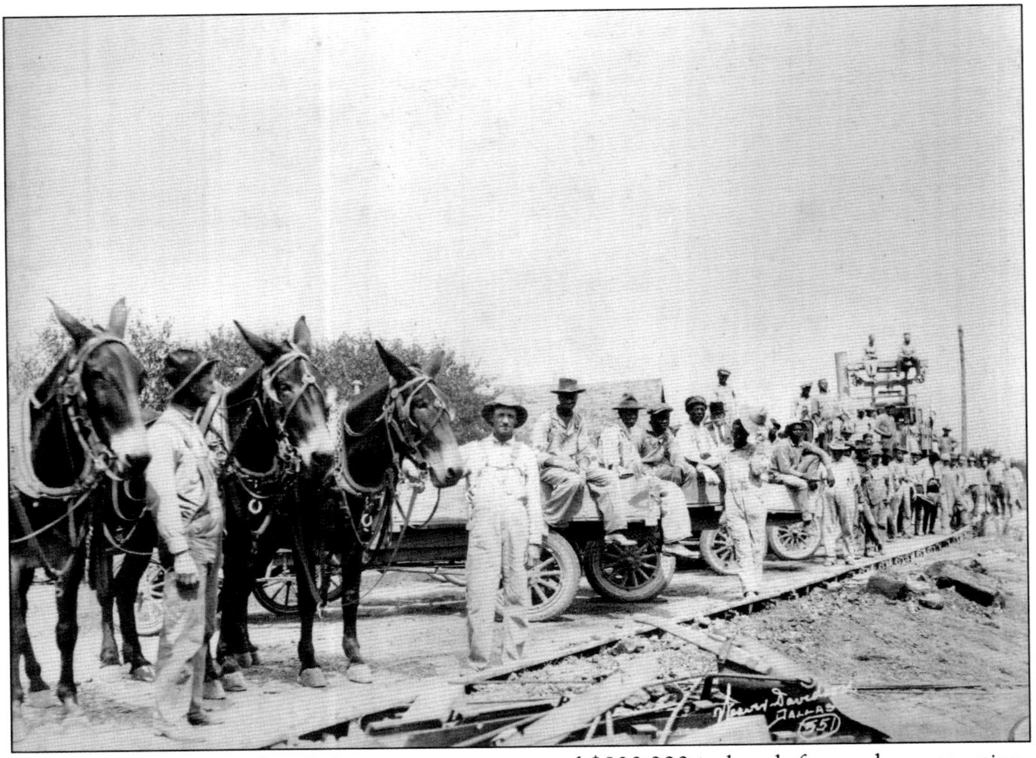

In the early 1920s, Rockwall County voters approved $800,000 in bonds for road construction. This included the Rockwall portion of the coast-to-coast Bankhead Highway No. 1 (later renamed U.S. Highway 67 and then State Highway 66). The bond money was also used to construct 9-foot lateral roads within the county. Above, the Bankhead Highway was under construction through Fate in 1922. Local resident Frank Dismore is shown on the left. Below, a public works crew is pictured around 1900 in early Rockwall County. Note the White Owl cigar advertisement painted on the side of the building. During the early 1900s, a number of Rockwall's buildings and barns rented out space for national advertising campaigns.

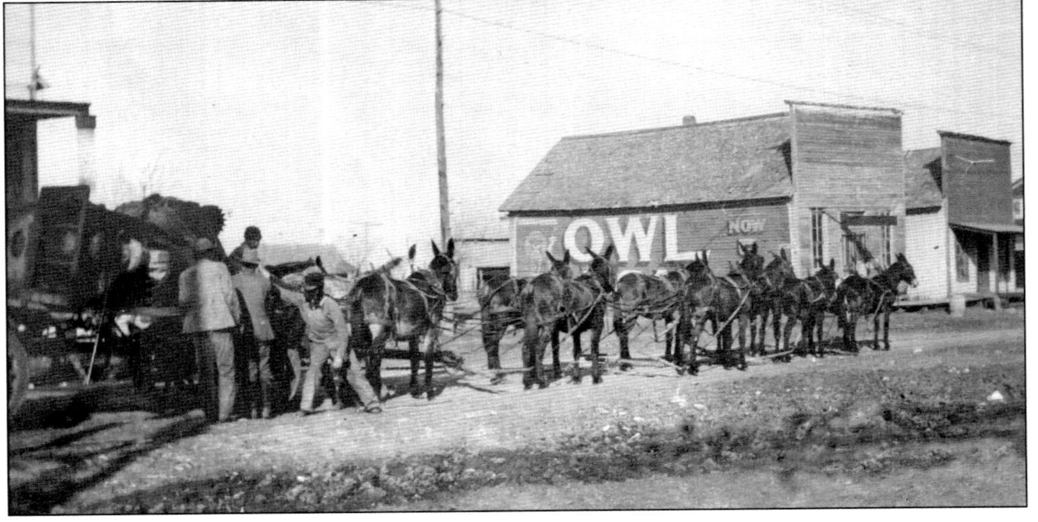

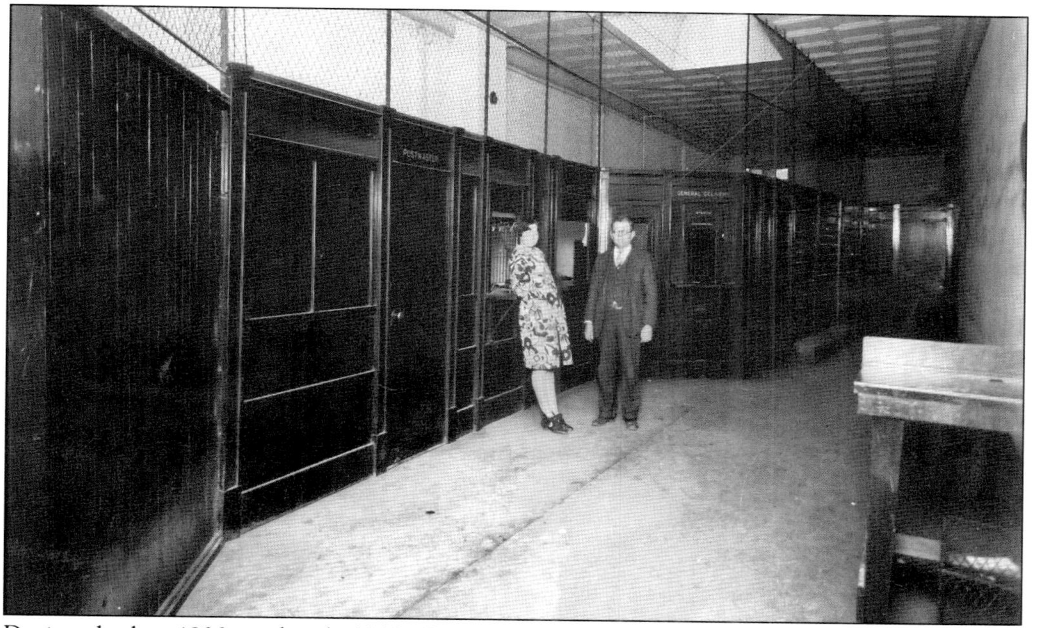

During the late 1800s and early 1900s, Royse City experienced steady growth. In fact, in 1900, it actually had the distinction of being the largest city in Rockwall County with a population of 1,245. That was slightly higher than the population of its nearby neighbor, the city of Rockwall. Above, Orpha Bailey, assistant postmaster of Royse City, is shown pictured with her father, Thomas Bailey, postmaster, in 1929. Below, post office employees pose for a photograph. From left to right are Homer Pierce, Roy Sisk, M. O. Flemmons, Tom Dowell, Tom Bailey, and Orpha Bailey.

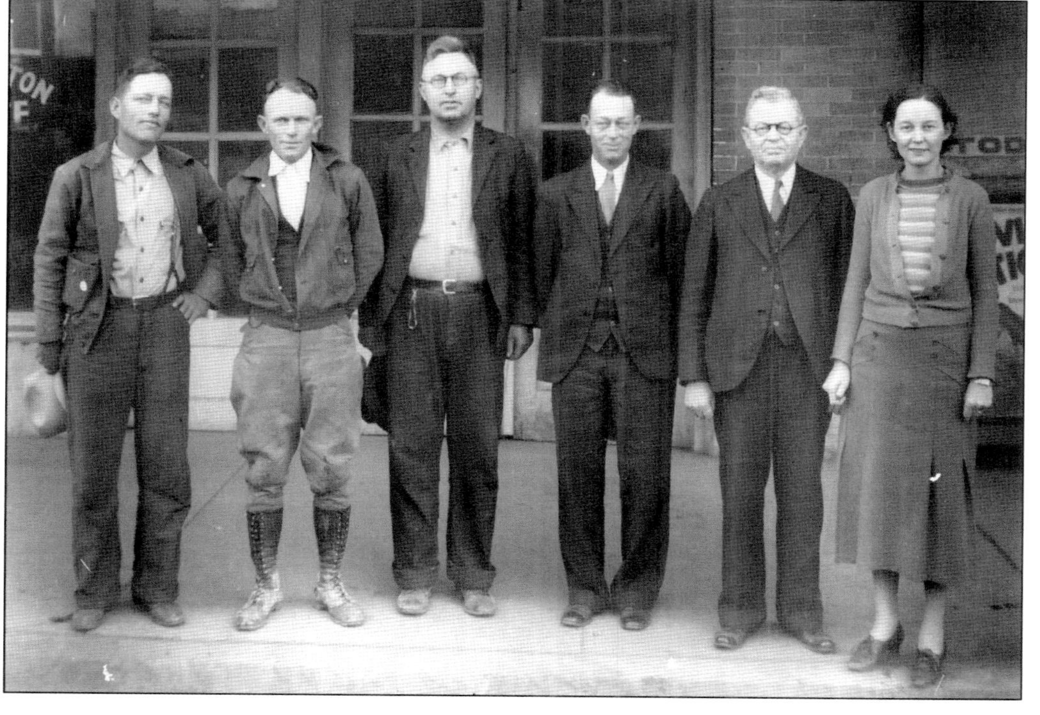

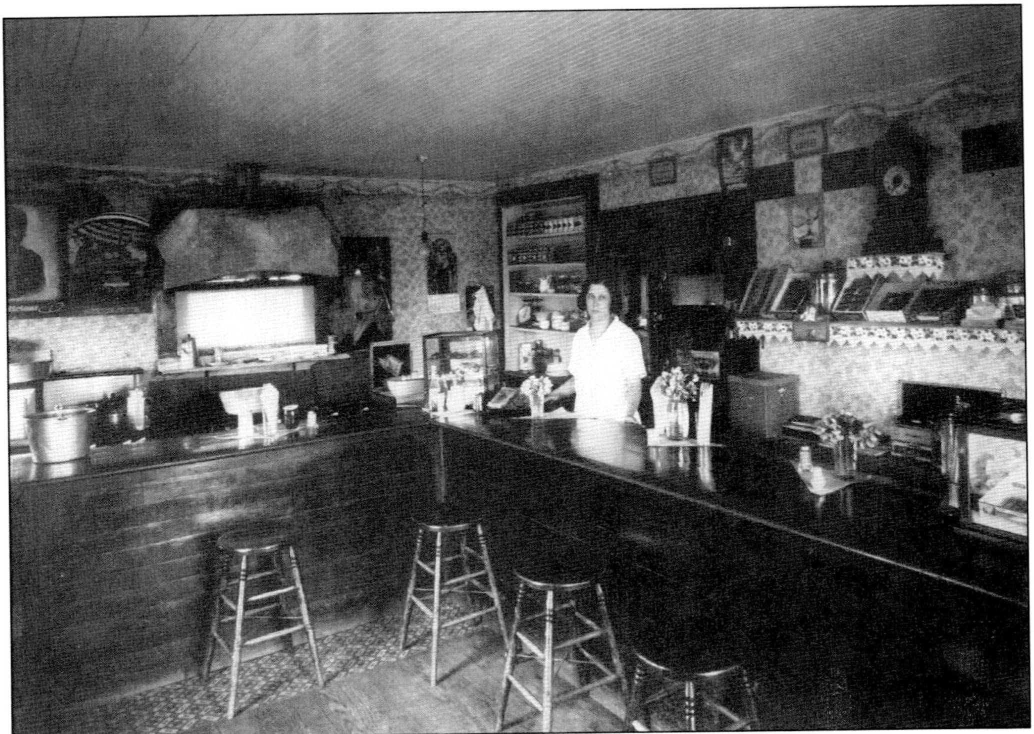

The Posey Restaurant, above, and the Posey Service Station, below, were located in an area of Fate commonly called Poseyville because it consisted of the James L. Posey home, the Posey Restaurant, and the Posey Service Station. Pictured in the restaurant is Flossie Posey Howell, daughter of James Posey and wife of Willis Howell. Poseyville was located on the Bankhead Highway, also known as U.S. Highway 67 (now State Highway 66). The Bankhead Highway was part of the National Auto Trail system. Marked with colored bands on telephone poles, these routes were set up to help travelers in the early days of the automobile. Many businesses sprang up along these heavily traveled roads.

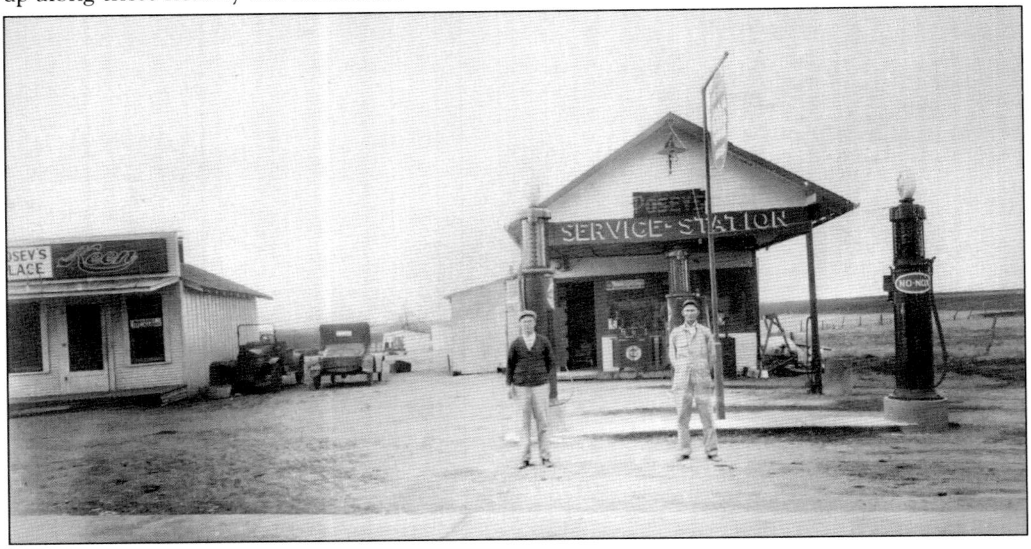

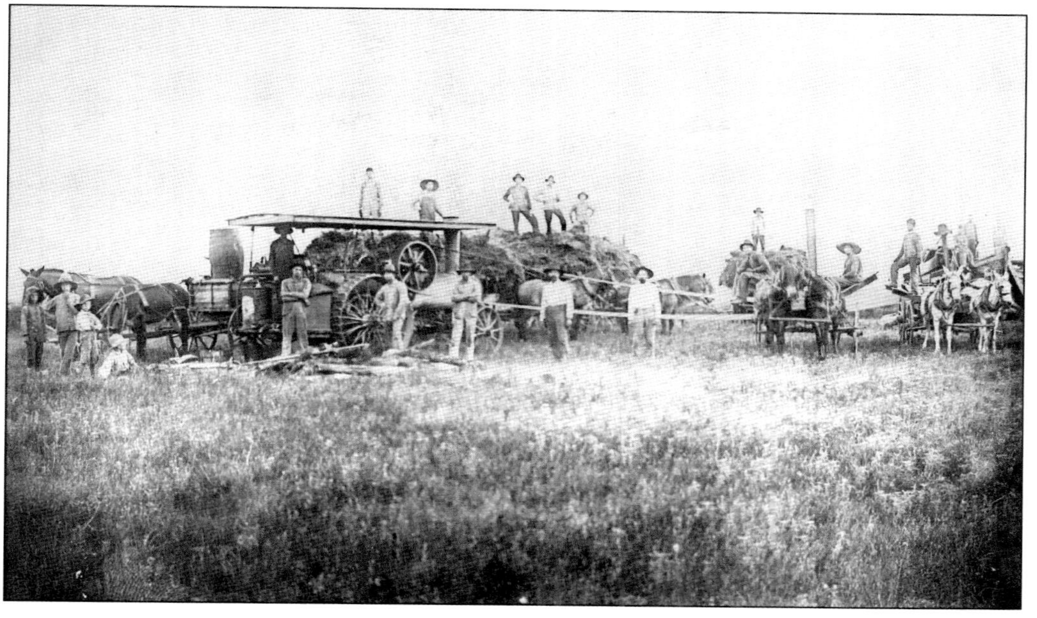

Prior to the Civil War, Rockwall's earliest settlers concentrated on crops consisting of corn and wheat with small amounts of cotton. Commercial agriculture remained at a minimum. As roads and production methods improved—heavily bolstered by the arrival of the railroad—cotton became the cash crop and remained so during the first half of the 1900s. Farming was not just a family activity; it was a community event. Neighbors would travel from farm to farm to help each other during times of planting and harvesting. Area farmers join together for a day of threshing (above) and a day of planting (below).

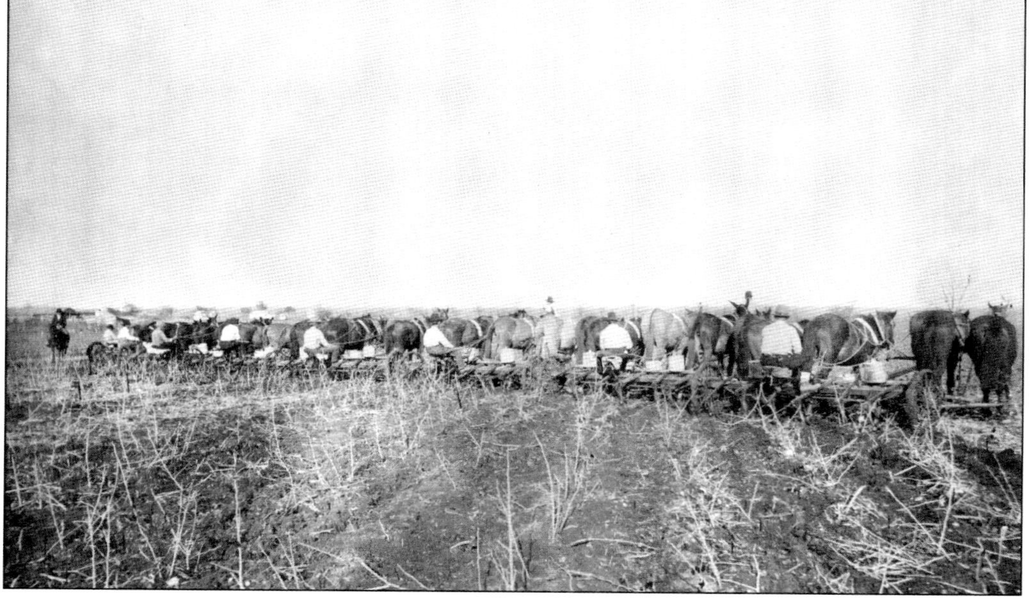

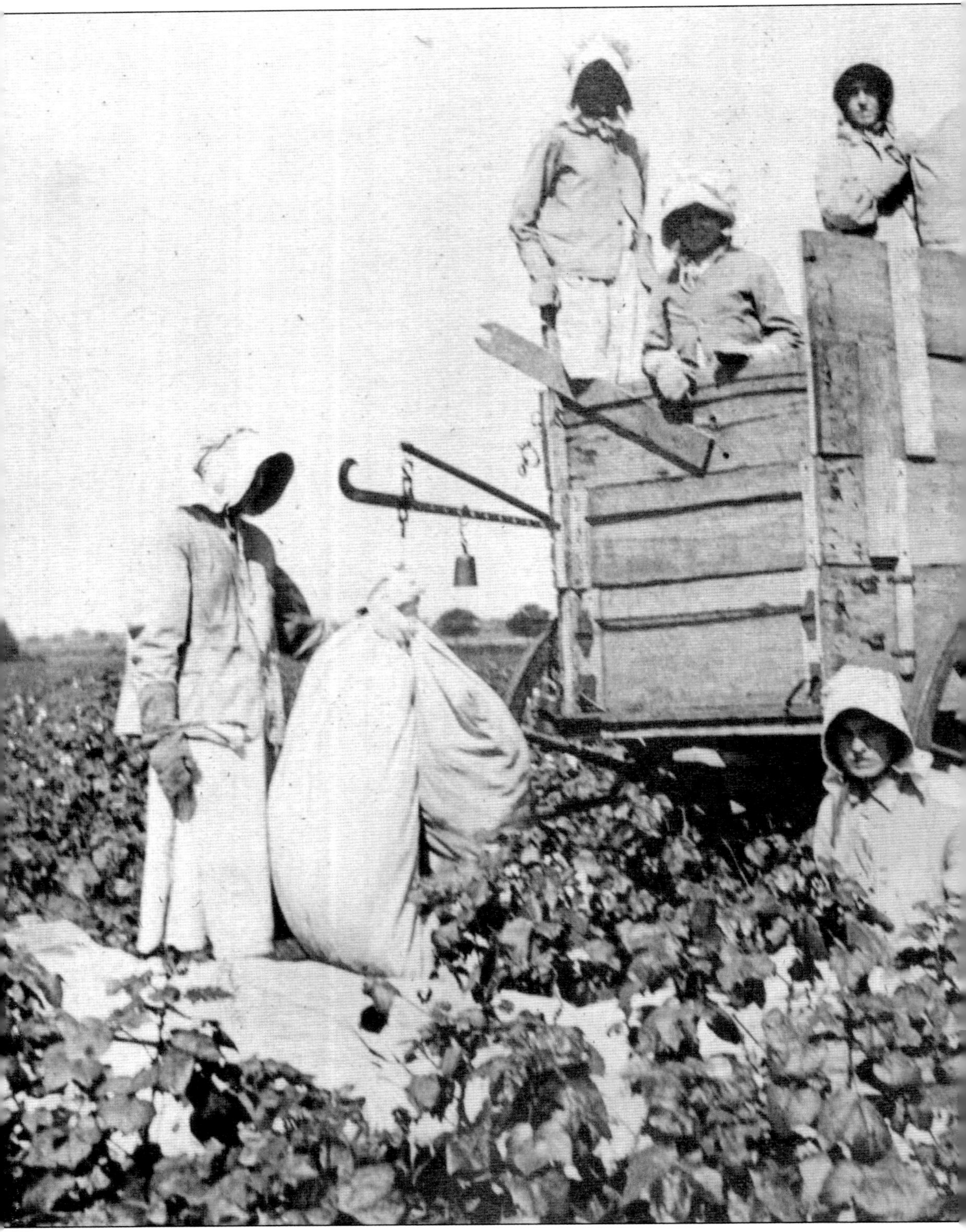

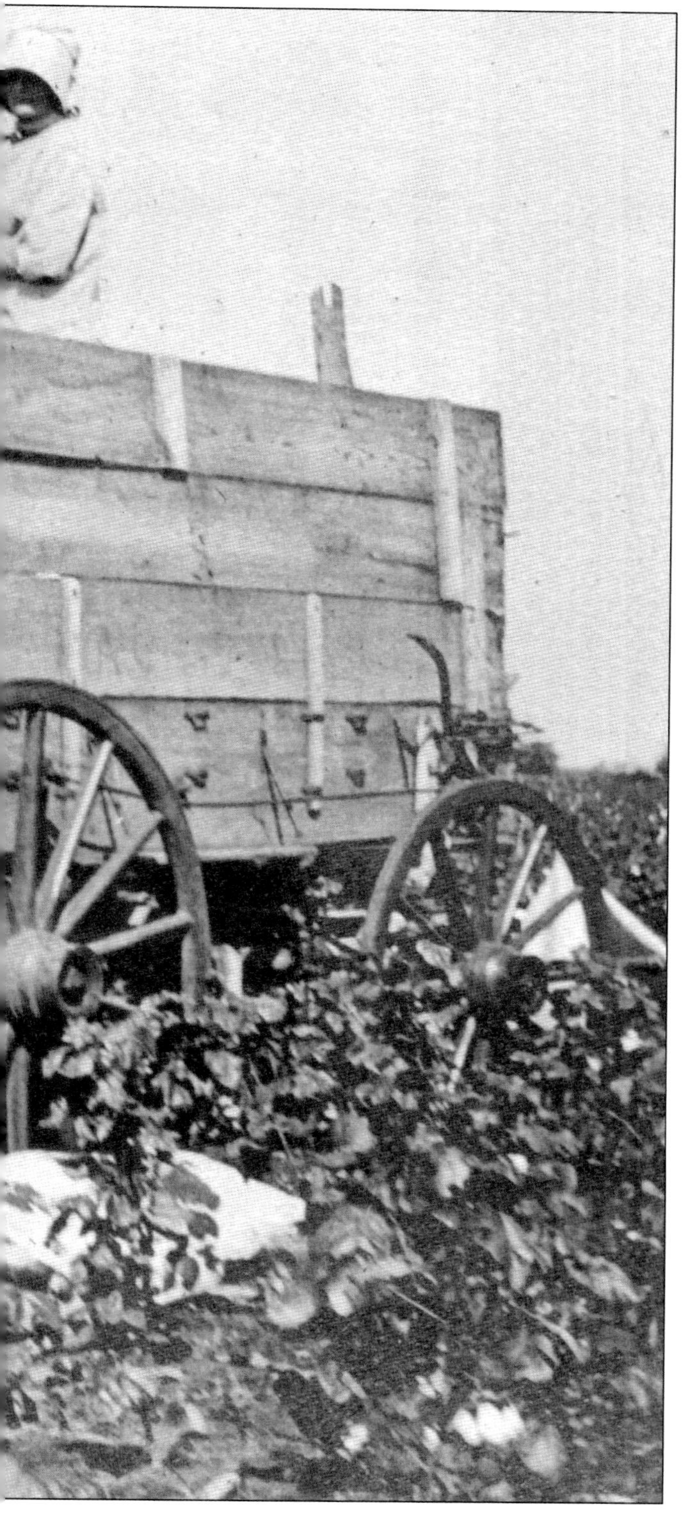

The Bourn sisters—Hattie, Leona, Mable, Marguerite, Marion, and Winnie—pick cotton at the family farm. Agriculture was Rockwall County's biggest business for almost 100 years after its founding. In 1900, there were approximately 1,000 farms in operation, mostly producing cotton. Although it decreased in popularity, farming remained an important occupation in the county well into the 1950s. During the first half of the 1900s, Rockwall's farming families were slowly getting to add the amenities that the area's city dwellers had enjoyed for a number of years. Most families started by retiring their horses and wagons and opting for an automobile. A telephone was usually the next purchase. But electricity and indoor plumbing were much longer in coming to the rural areas. In fact, some Rockwall County farmsteads were still using outhouses as late as the 1950s.

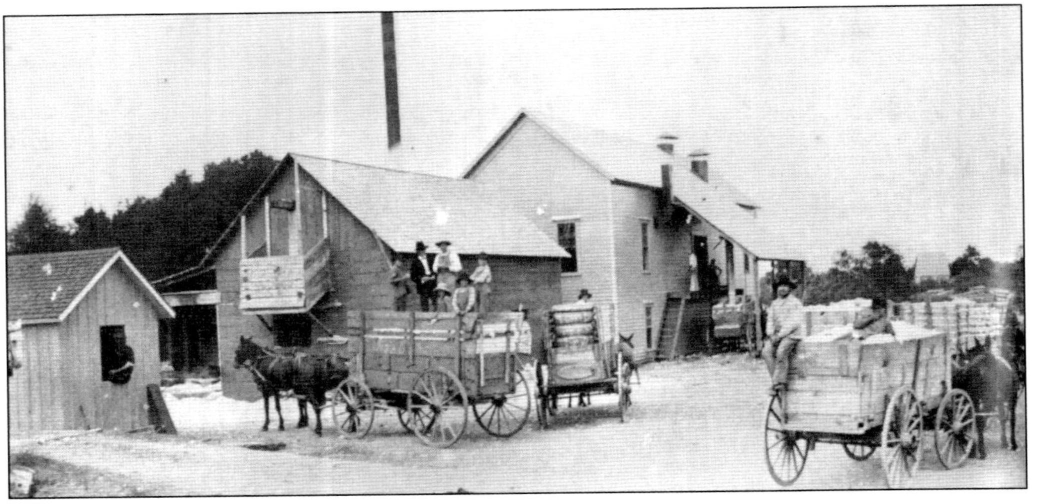

The area's first cotton gin was approximately 3 miles north of Rockwall at Locust Grove and was known as the Truitt Gin since it was built by the Truitt family in 1866. Many of the area communities built their own gins, and during the years of cotton farming, at least 18 gins operated throughout Rockwall County. Above is the gin in McLendon. Below is the Chisholm gin in the 1920s. Although today they stand as a combined community, McLendon and Chisholm began as two separate settlements, each named for prominent landowners in the late 1800s. McLendon bears the name of Preston Alexander McLendon, a farmer and a businessman. Chisholm is named after Enoch P. Chisholm, a farmer and a licensed preacher.

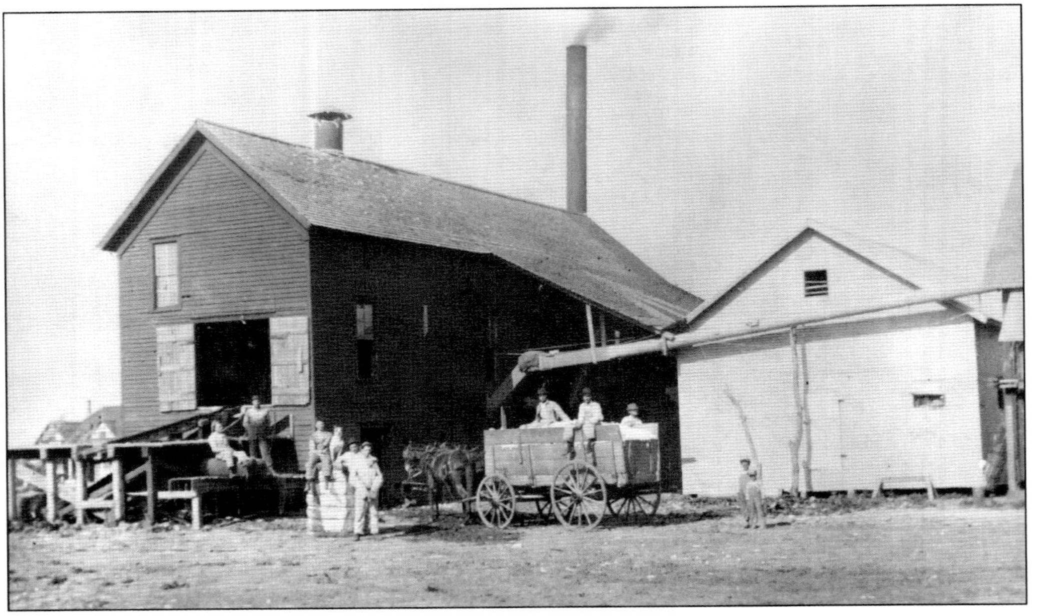

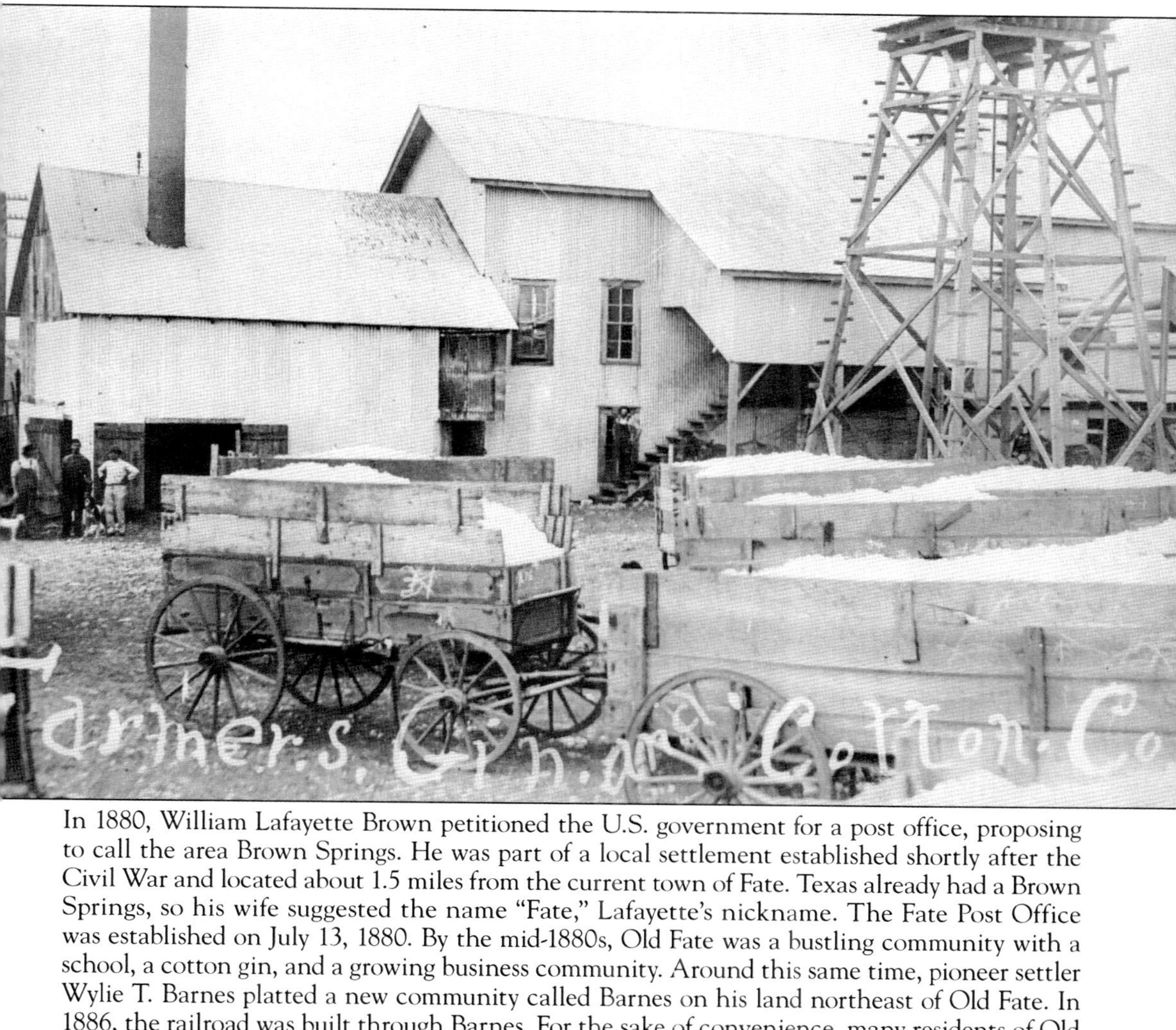

In 1880, William Lafayette Brown petitioned the U.S. government for a post office, proposing to call the area Brown Springs. He was part of a local settlement established shortly after the Civil War and located about 1.5 miles from the current town of Fate. Texas already had a Brown Springs, so his wife suggested the name "Fate," Lafayette's nickname. The Fate Post Office was established on July 13, 1880. By the mid-1880s, Old Fate was a bustling community with a school, a cotton gin, and a growing business community. Around this same time, pioneer settler Wylie T. Barnes platted a new community called Barnes on his land northeast of Old Fate. In 1886, the railroad was built through Barnes. For the sake of convenience, many residents of Old Fate—including postmaster Lafayette Brown—moved to Barnes. To avoid the application process for a new post office, residents of Barnes agreed to change their city's name, and on February 11, 1887, Fate permanently took up residence in its current location. Pictured is Fate's Farmer's Gin and Cotton Company.

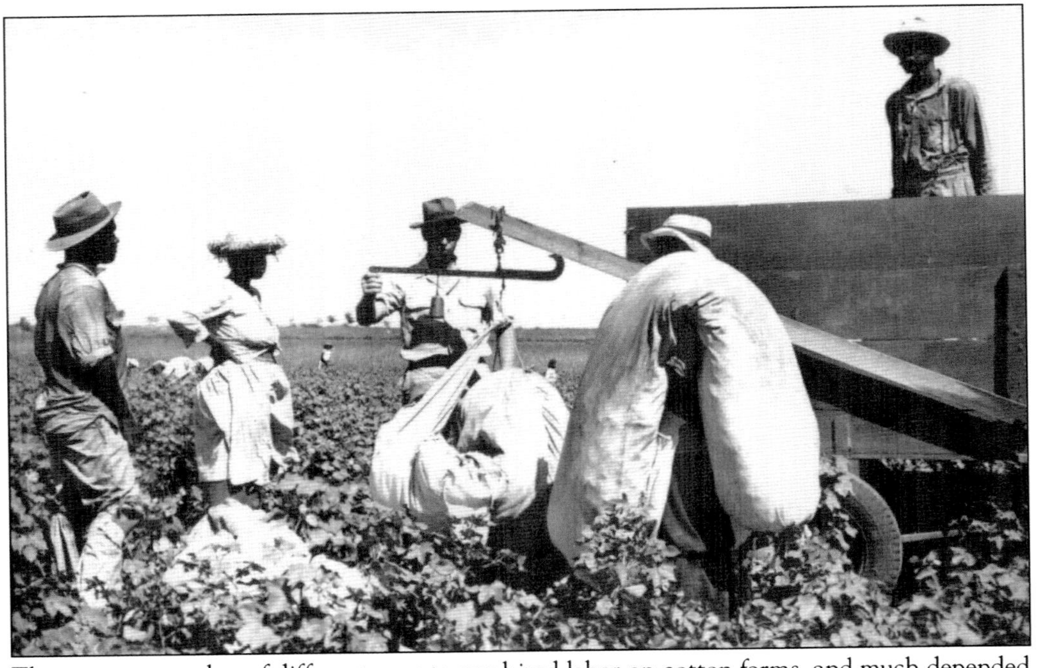

There were a number of different ways to pay hired labor on cotton farms, and much depended on whether the help were tenant farmers or hired hands who just offered daily labor. Some arranged shares of a crop while short-term labor was paid simply based on the weight of what they picked. Above, Jimmie Crawford weighs cotton at his family's farm, the Reagan Crawford Farm, in Fate.

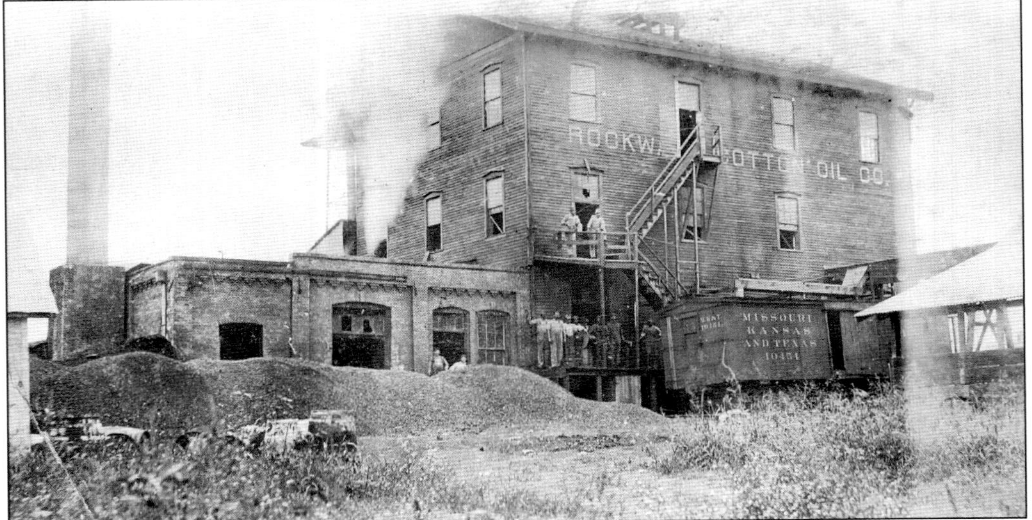

Due to a number of factors, including the increased ease of transportation and the outbreak of World War II, the economic structure of the county began to change dramatically in the 1940s. By the mid-1940s, almost a third of the county's population was commuting to Dallas for industrial jobs. Cotton still played a significant role in the county's economy, but production decreased during this time, and a number of gins in the area found business dwindling. Above, the Rockwall Cotton Oil Company gin is shown during its heyday.

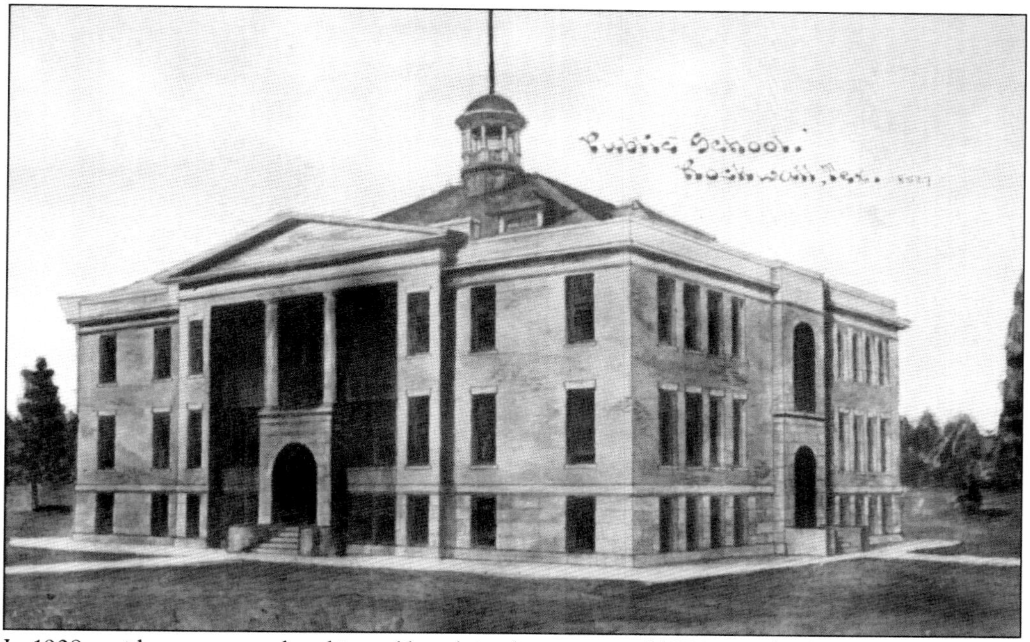

In 1908, residents approved and issued bonds in the amount of $25,000 to build a three-story brick facility for the Rockwall public schools. The building would house grades 1 through 11 and would be located on Fannin Street. The first floor was designated for elementary students, the second floor was designated for high school students, and the third floor held an auditorium.

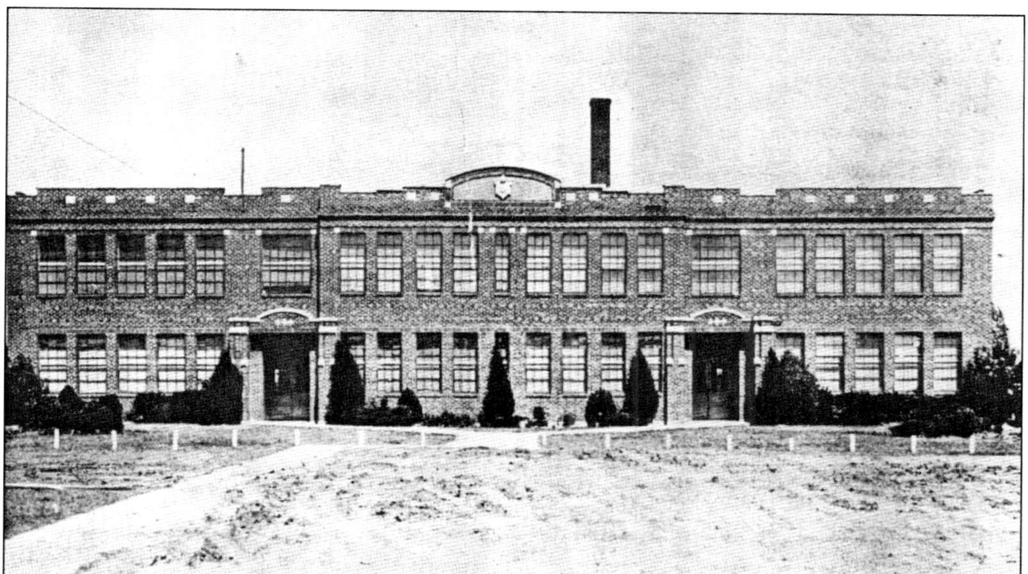

In 1925, a two-story high school was built on Clark Street for a cost of $50,000. There were 10 classrooms, an auditorium, and offices for high school and district personnel. It opened in the fall of 1925 and graduated its first class in 1926. The building remained in use as a high school until 1965. It was demolished in the mid-1970s.

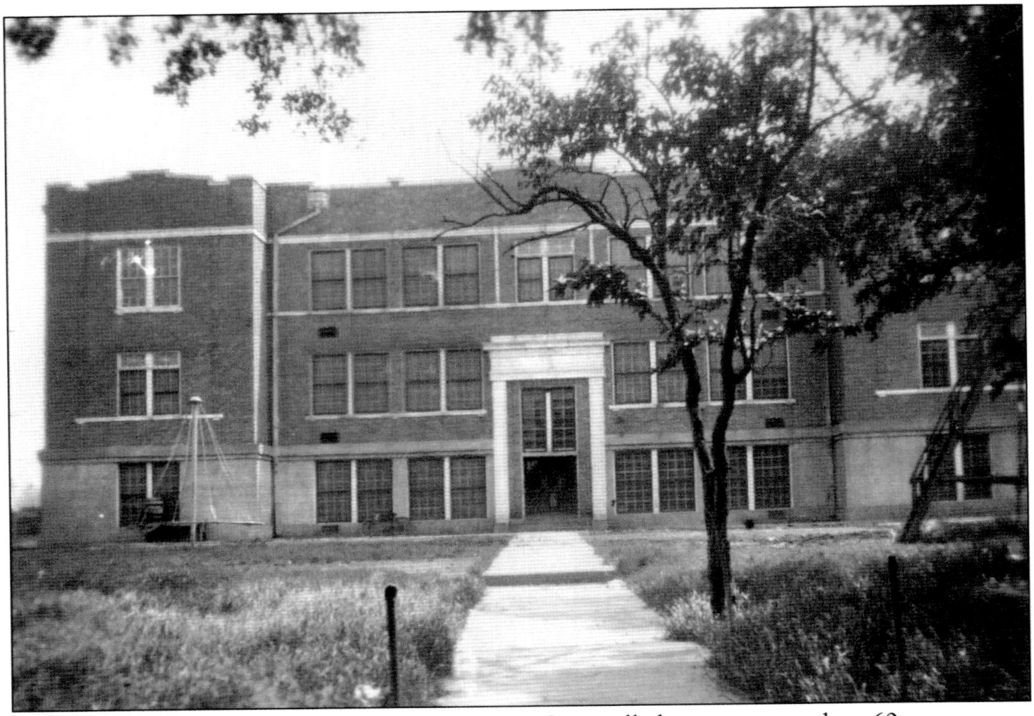

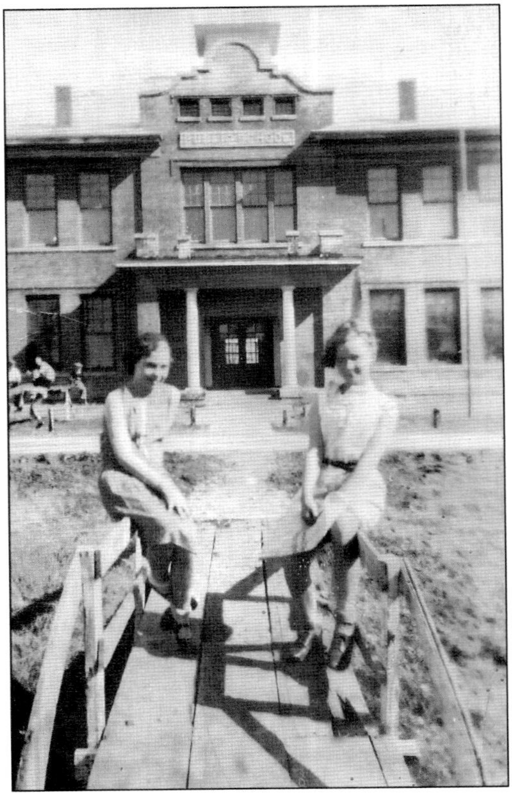

Originally home to more than 60 one-room country schoolhouses, Rockwall County now contains major parts of only two school districts—the Rockwall Independent School District and the Royse City Independent School District. But at the height of their population, many smaller communities had school systems that completely serviced their own students. In addition to Rockwall and Royse City, Fate, Heath, McLendon, and Chisholm all offered complete educations for their youth. As the population in the outlying areas declined, the grade levels offered in those schools decreased, and students were sent to schools in larger cities like Rockwall for the higher grade levels. By the end of the 1940s, the majority of the outlying schools had been consolidated into either the Rockwall ISD or the Royse City ISD. Above is a view of the old Royse City High School. At left, Marie Sewell and Martha Moore Vernon pose in front of the Fate public school.

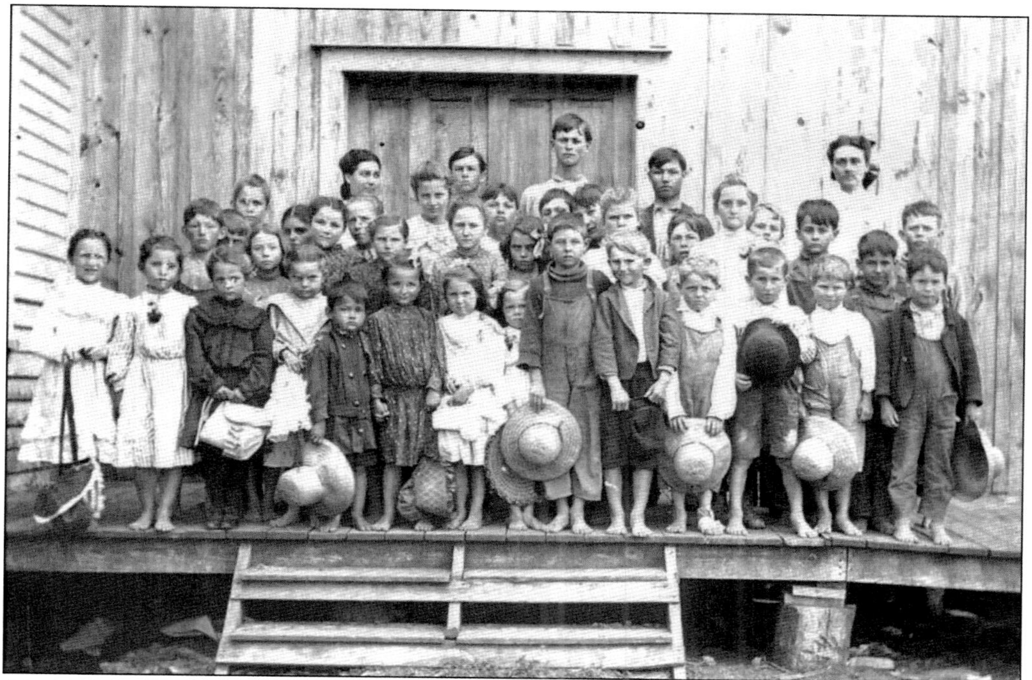

Above is picture day at the one-room Heath public school around 1901. Below, students pose in front of the L-shaped school building around 1910. The community of Heath was established when pioneers John O. Heath and Sterling Rex Barnes both brought their families to the area around 1846. The town was known as Black Hills and then Willow Springs before being officially named Heath in 1886. In the late 1800s, buffalo still roamed the prairie lands around Heath. Each day as the sun would set, children who played among the tall grass were called home by the ringing of a bell—a sign that the herd would soon cross the open land to drink at the nearby creek. That creek is known today as Buffalo Creek, a lasting legacy to the area's buffalo.

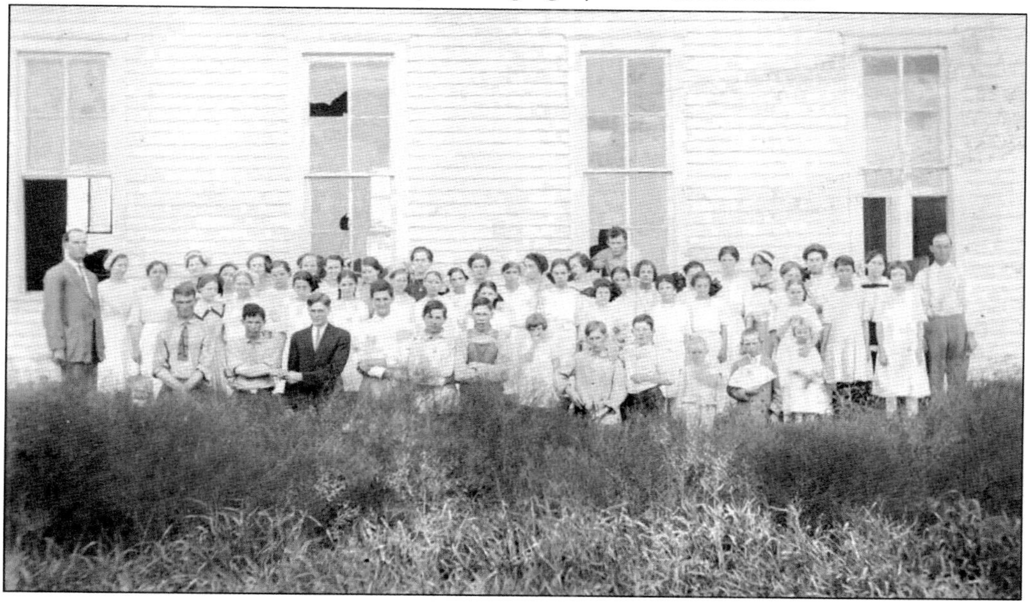

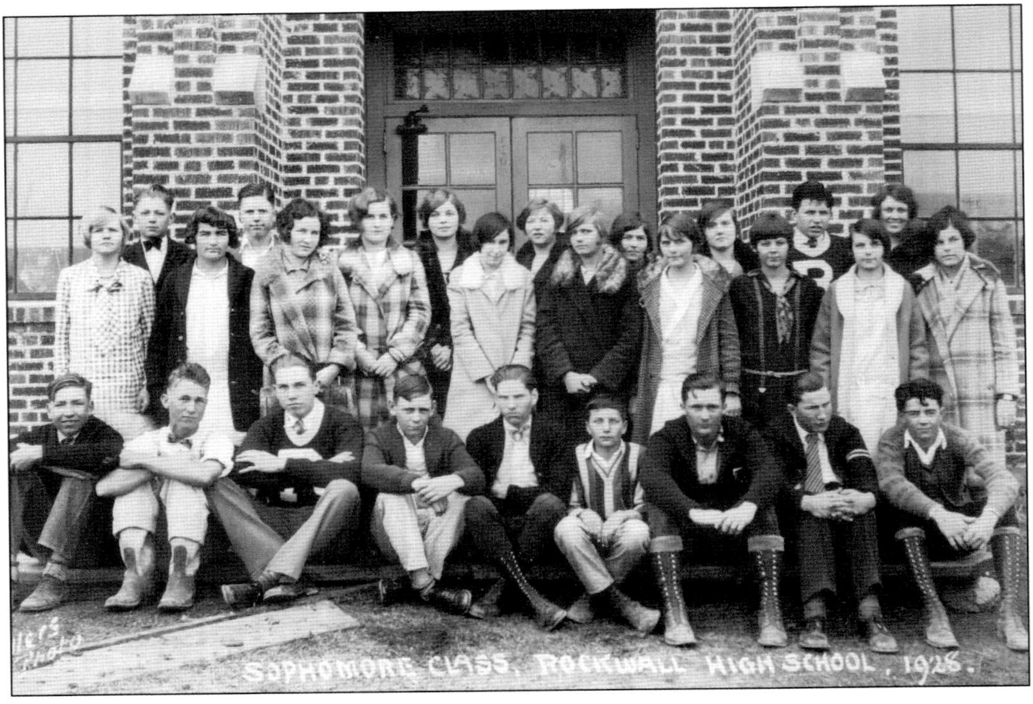

Here are the changing faces of Rockwall's high school students. Above is the sophomore class from 1928. A c. 1930 panoramic view appears below. Members of the class identified on the back of the photograph (spellings as they appear) are Dorothy Zuspann, Dorothy Lofland, Sybil Sebastian, Louise Spradley, Mary Agnes Moody, Rita Bell Williams, Ruth Hall, Rheba Payne, Hazel Hawks, Florence Hawks, Oleta Cannon, Blanche Lawerence, Margaret Piper, Madge Piper, Evelyn Evans, Ruby Willess, Muggins Lawhorn, Fay Basham, Frances Smith, Marjorie White, Fern Thompson, Lynn Peace, W. T. Estes, Earl Weant, Eathel Florence, Orville Sellers, Jake Smith, Lonnie Dawson, Linsey Townsend, B. F. Crawford, Burr Vernon, Woodrow Wilson, David Wallace, Skip Barnes, Paul Springer, Jim Thaxton, George Atkins, Jack Sauls, Dorothy Kimbrell, Nolan Williamson, John Hays, Hugh Shaw, Wade Canup, Joe Ed Deweese, and Dorothy Smith. (Below, courtesy of the family of Evelyn Lofland.)

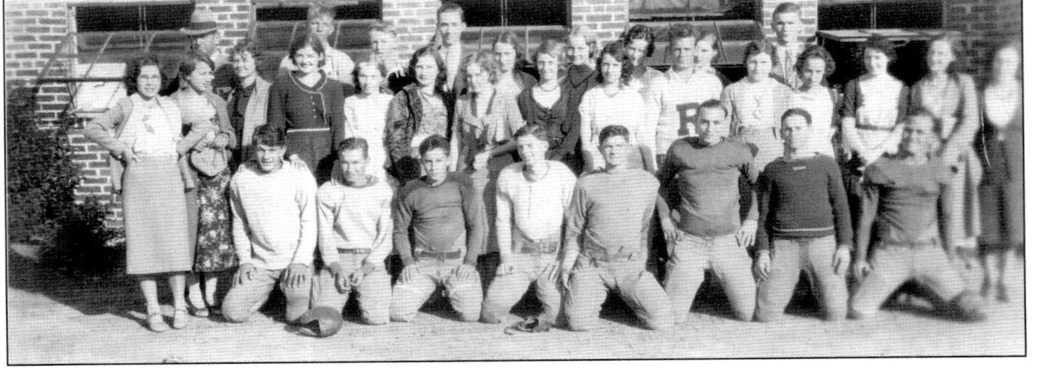

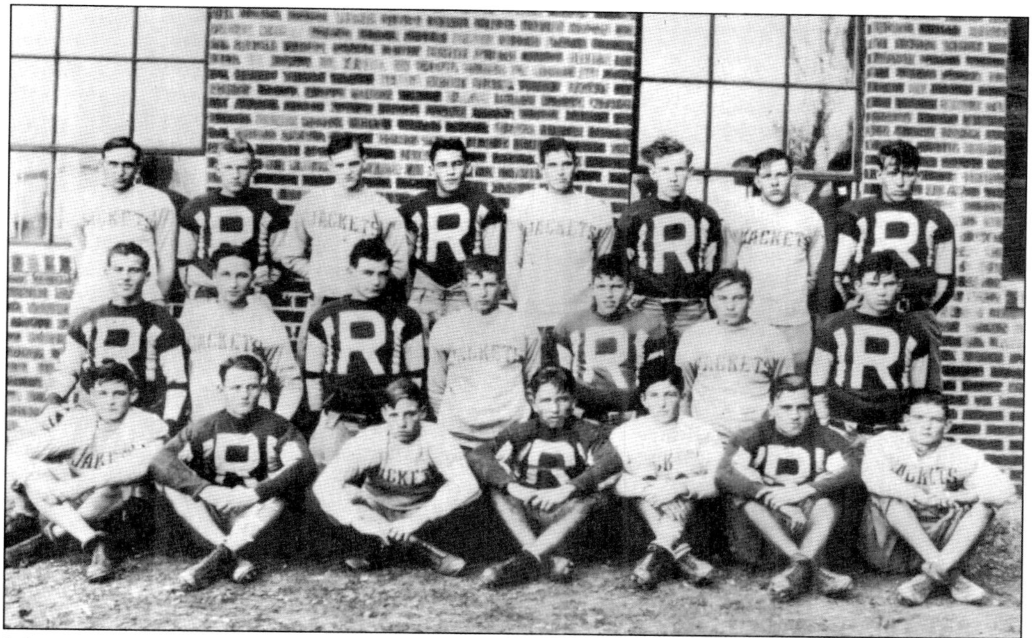

Like many small Texas towns, Rockwall has avid high school football fans. In the early decades of the 20th century, the most outstanding team for Rockwall High School was the 1933 Yellowjackets, a Class B-11 team. The 1933 squad (pictured above) had won 10 of 11 games in the regular season. For the third year in a row, the 1933 squad had won the bi-district title, and they would play Crowell for the regional title, the highest honor a team could achieve at that time. On December 15, 1933, Rockwall won with a score of 34-6. Below, a 1940s team includes Derwood Wimpee, no. 48, who would one day be elected county judge, and Ralph Hall, no. 46, who would represent Rockwall as an elected official at the local, state, and national levels.

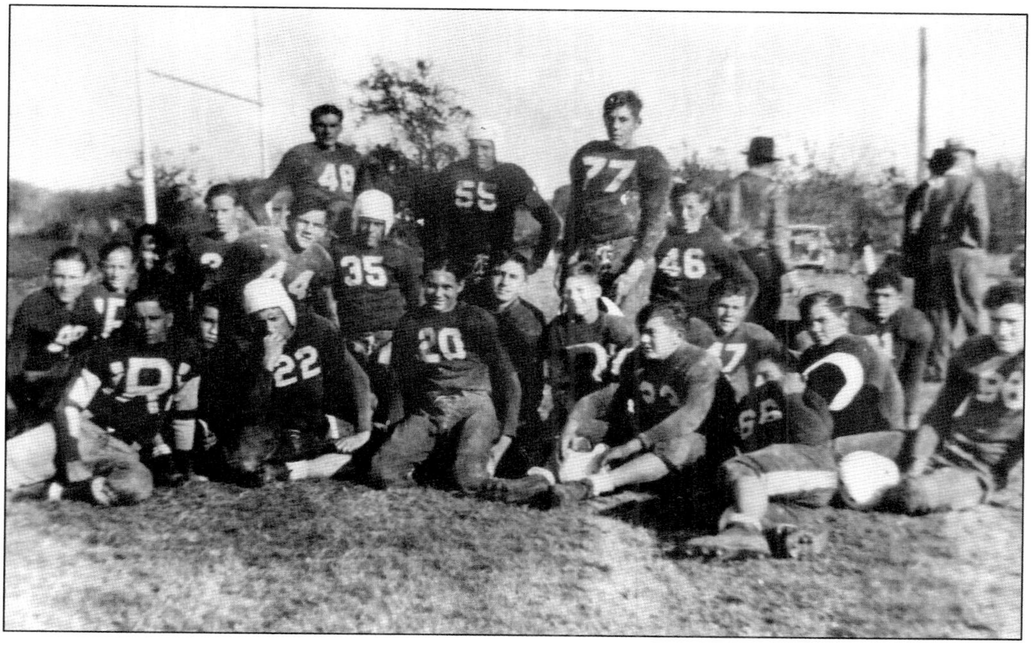

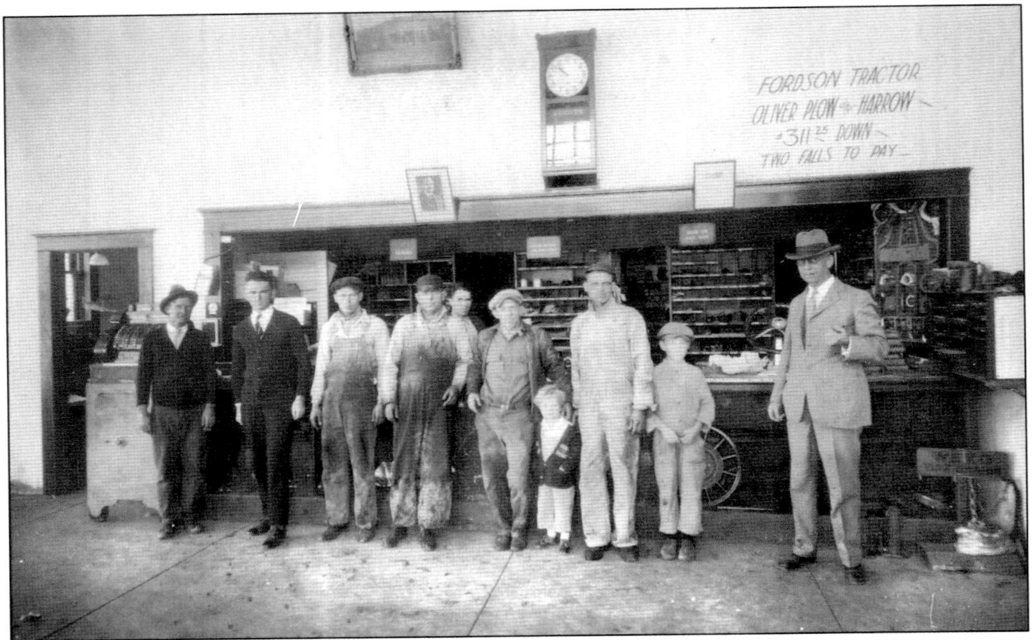

Rockwall's first Ford dealership was established by Dr. Paul Snow. In the early 1910s, pioneer automaker Henry Ford had invented the system of franchised dealerships, and in 1917, local resident Paul Snow built a brick structure on the corner of Fannin and Rusk Streets to house his fledgling Paul Snow Ford Motor Company. The building originally had a main showroom and an attached garage. The dealership operated through the 1960s under several different owners. Pictured above is the interior of the main showroom of the Snow Ford Motor Company. Below, Bill Sellers (left) and Bennett Shaw are shown in the service garage around 1923.

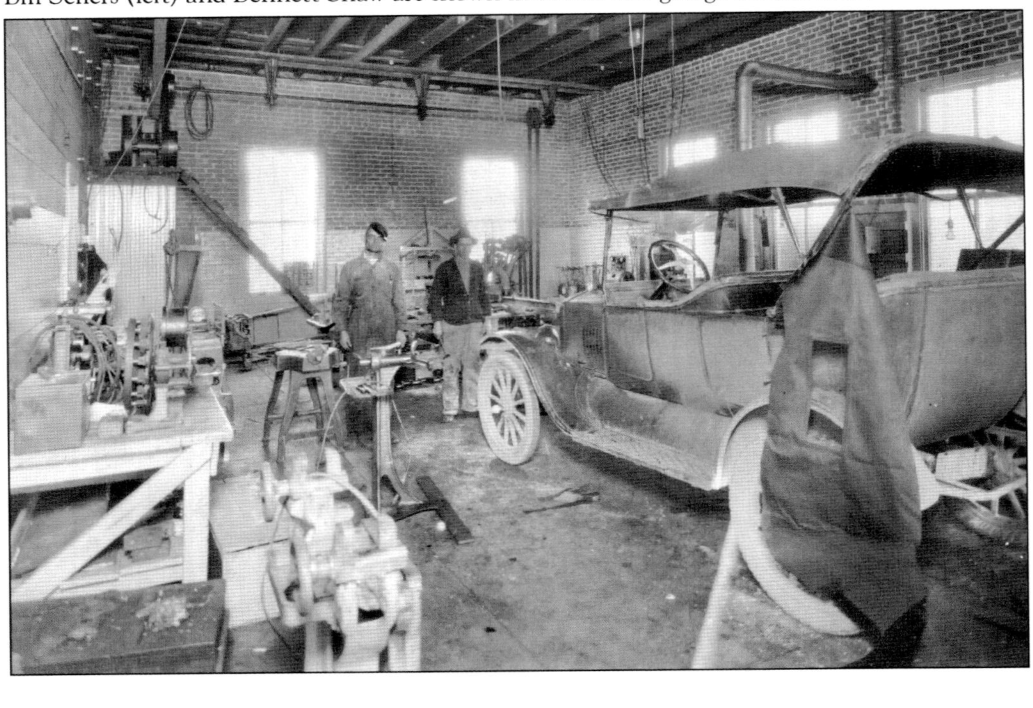

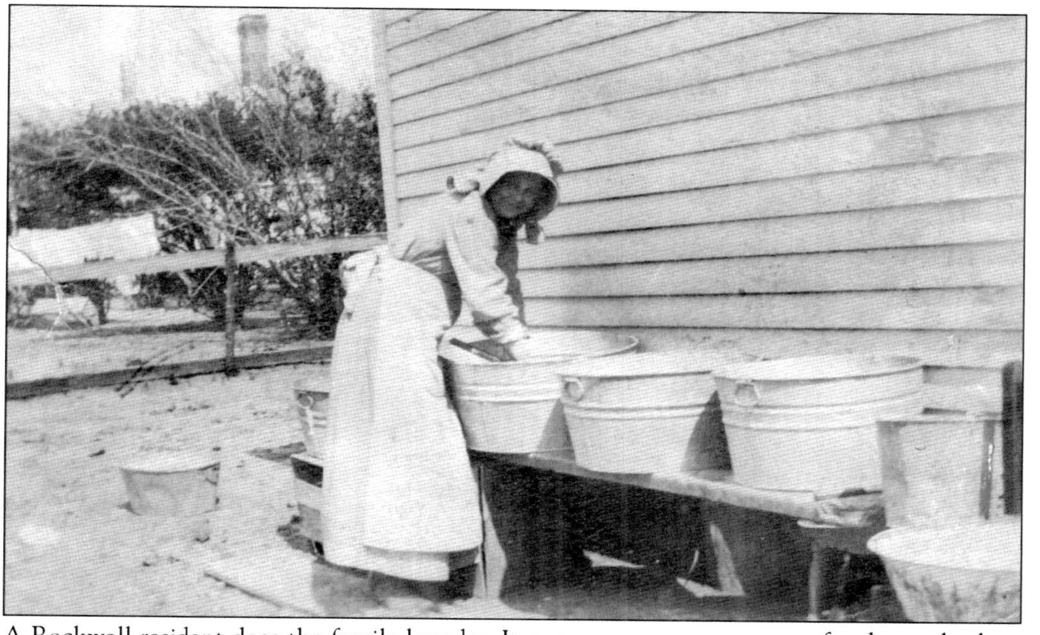

A Rockwall resident does the family laundry. It was a common occurrence for the washtub to double as the family's bathtub, especially on farms where well water was still common far into the 20th century. For the family bath, the same water was used for all family members, and the man of the house went first. Seniority ruled; thus was derived the phrase, "Don't throw out the baby with the bathwater."

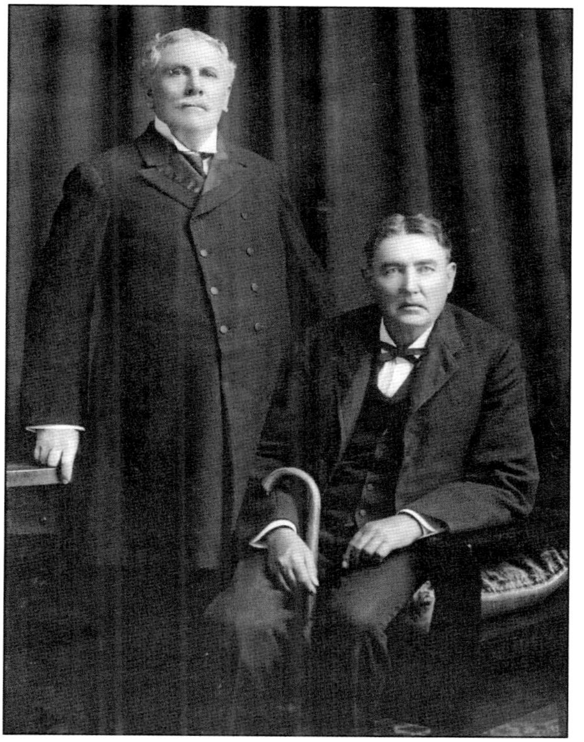

Dr. Hal Manson (right) was born in Tennessee in 1843, studied medicine at Cumberland University, served the Confederacy in the Civil War, and then moved to Rockwall County in approximately 1870. He counted Cyrus Scofield (left), author of the famous *Scofield Reference Bible*, as one of his close friends. They had served together during the Civil War and remained close until Dr. Manson's death in 1905.

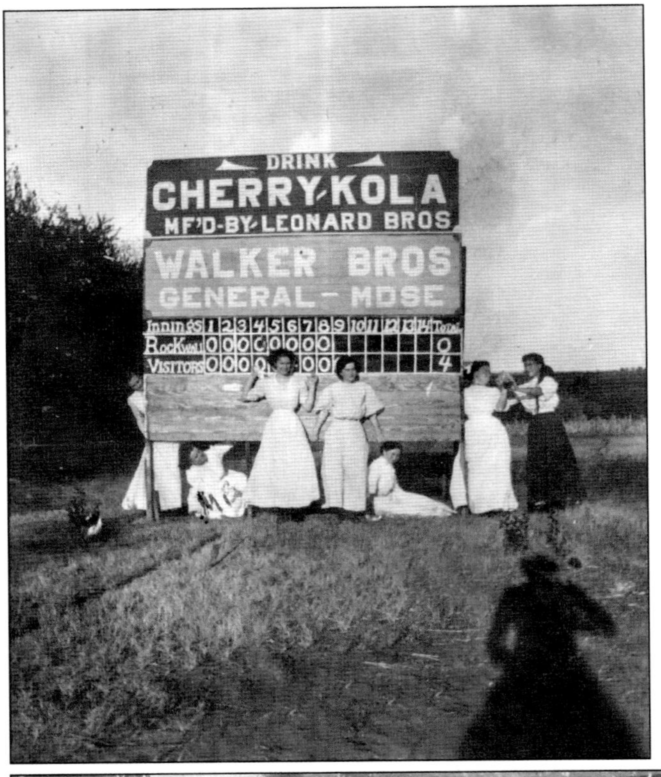

Beginning in the late 1800s and continuing well into the 20th century, many Rockwall County towns had their own baseball teams. Through the years, Rockwall, Royse City, Fate, and Heath all had traveling teams made up of local men. Fans and family members would follow the teams, cheering them on as they faced opponents from the surrounding areas. Different towns even had their own cheers. "Strychnine, Quinine, blue suits and fuss. What in the deuce is the matter with us? Nothing at all, nothing at all, We are the rooters for Fate baseball!" was one local refrain. At left, a scoreboard shows Rockwall down in the eighth inning. Below is a team of local Rockwall men in the early 1900s. (Below, courtesy of the family of Evelyn Lofland.)

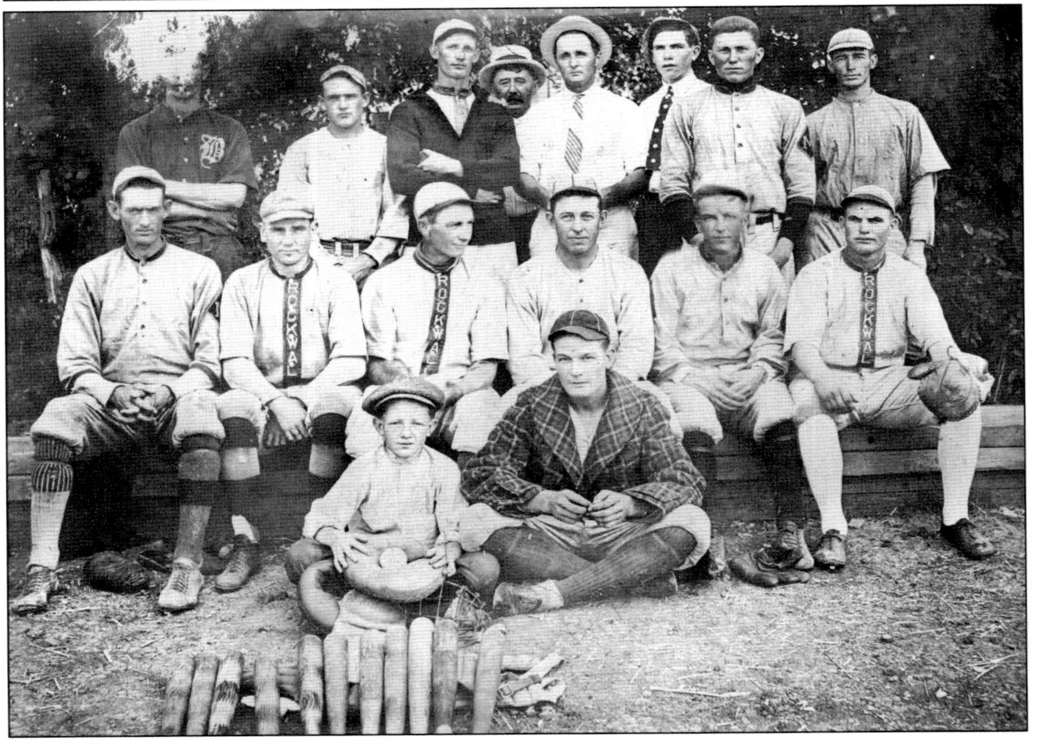

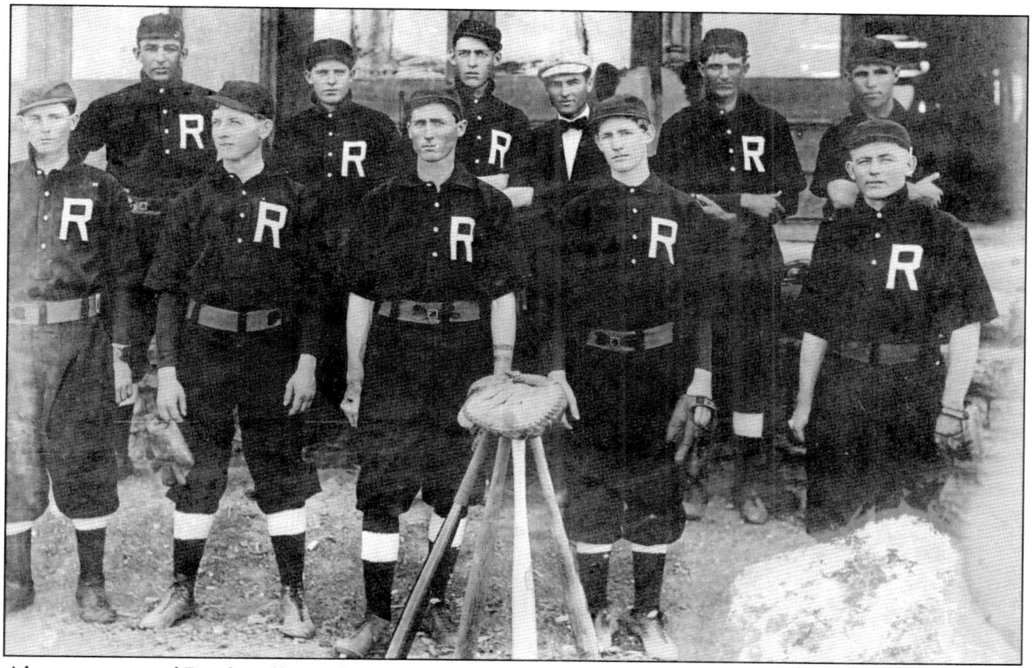

Above is one of Rockwall's early traveling baseball teams. Below, the 1909 Rockwall baseball team included, from left to right, (first row) Brown Walker, third base; Woodie Lowe, left field; Frank Clark, center field; Nig Johnson, catcher; and Milam, pitcher; (second row) Carl Wright, pitcher; Lester Walker, right field; Ernest Lowe, shortstop; John Gardenhire, first base; and Lee White, second base; (standing) Tom B. Ridgell, manager. The team manager, Tom Ridgell, was a prominent lawyer in town. He was married to Gay Bailey, one of the six children of T. W. Bailey, a well-known businessman and civic leader. (Above, courtesy of the family of Evelyn Lofland.)

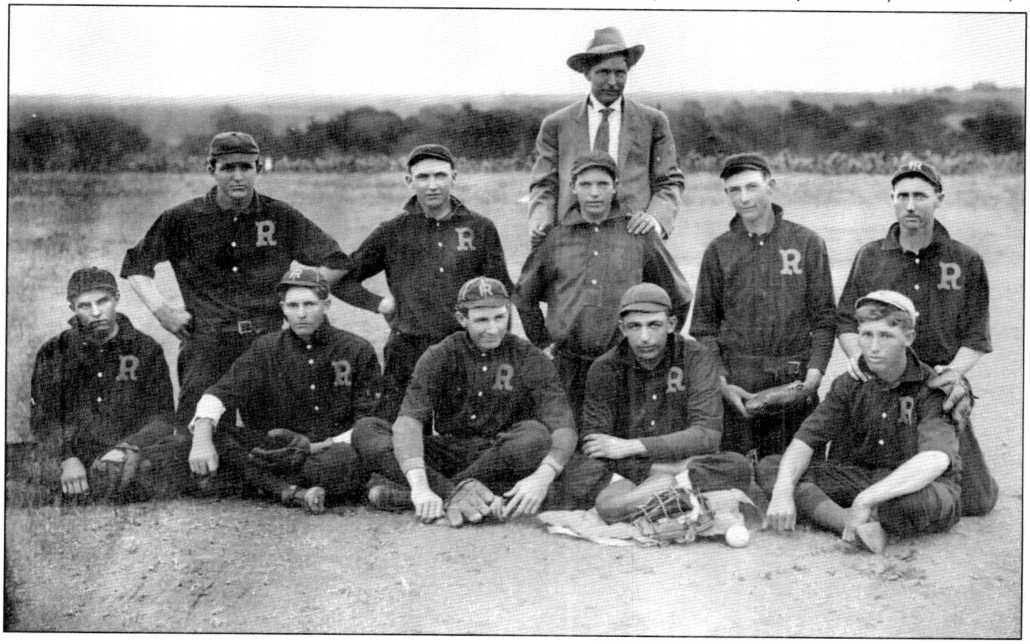

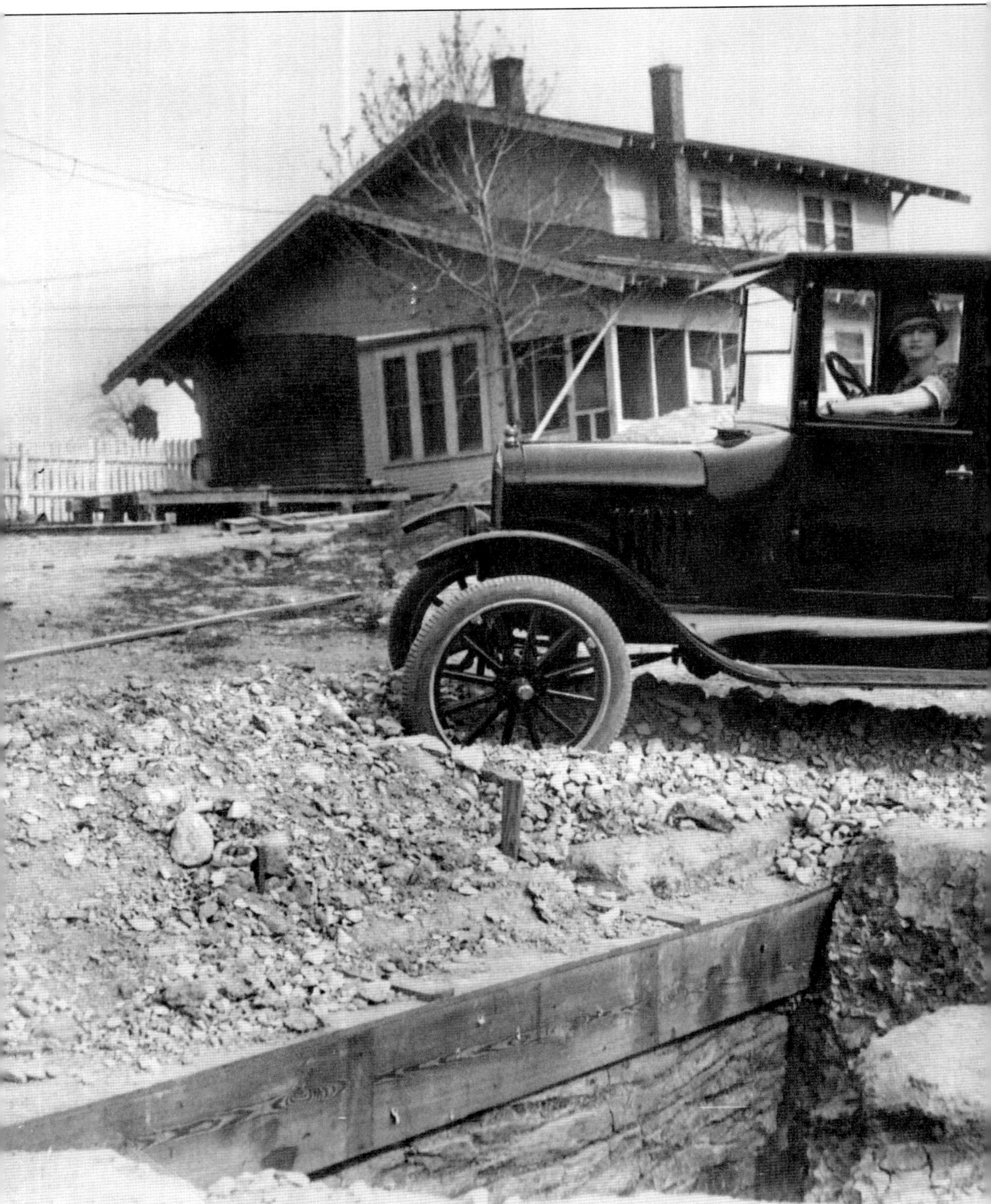

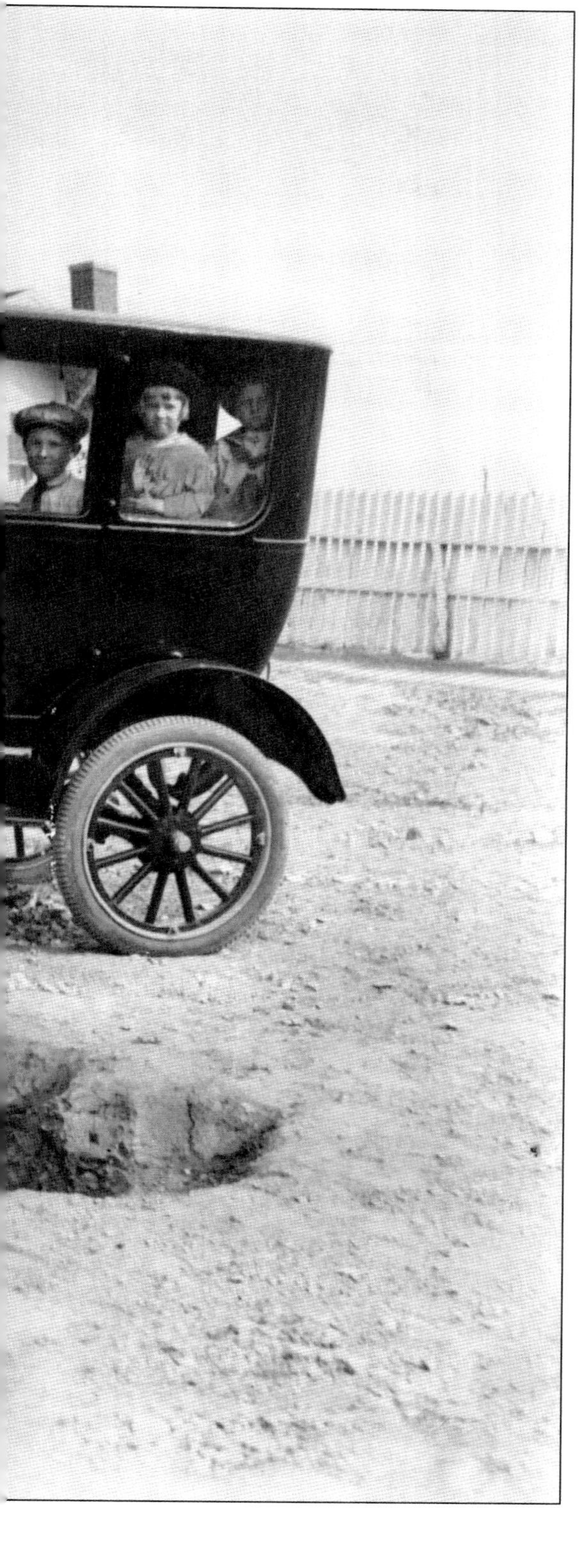

Since the time of its discovery, scientists, archeologists, geologists, architects, and laymen have studied the rock wall, the underground formation for which the city and county are named. Excavations have been dug at depths of up to 40 feet. Excavated rocks have been measured at 10 inches high, 18 inches long, and 24 inches thick; yet other individual rocks have been discovered that are small and more fragile. Coinciding with the 1936 Texas Centennial, a section of the wall was excavated and opened for viewers for a small admittance fee. In the first few months, the attraction averaged 70 visitors a day. In this photograph, Golden Shaw takes the children of Dr. and Mrs. Paul Snow to see the rock wall. This excavation was on property belonging to the Canup family.

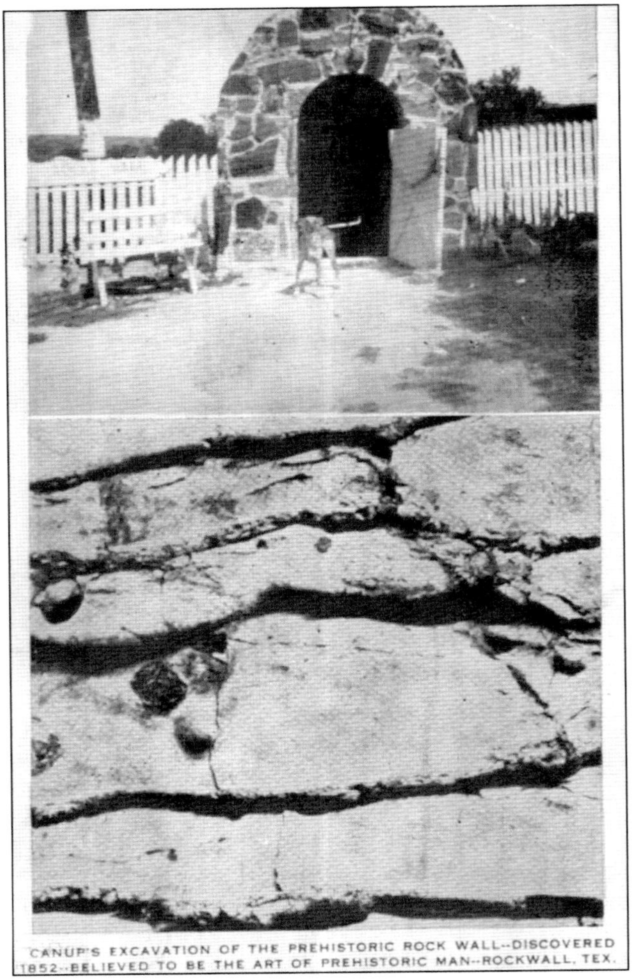

In the 1940s, a rock wall viewing site was opened to the public. Visitors could pay a quarter to see the underground formation for which the city and county are named. This souvenir postcard shows the entry to the viewing site and a section of exposed rocks. It touts the popular local opinion that the wall was the handiwork of prehistoric man.

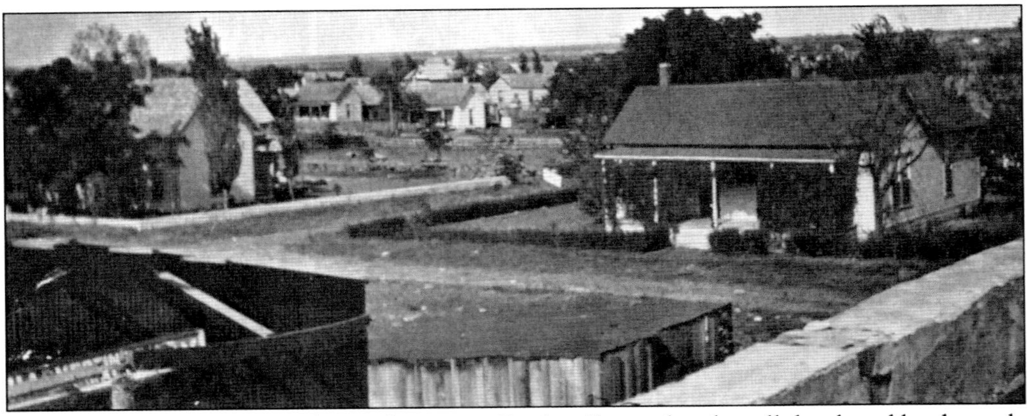

The residential area just bordering downtown Rockwall was already well developed by the early 1900s. This photograph, taken around 1910, shows a neighborhood near downtown. Most of these homes were built in the late 1800s and reflect what was known as the national, or folk, style of American architecture. They were mostly L-shaped or square homes with few flourishes.

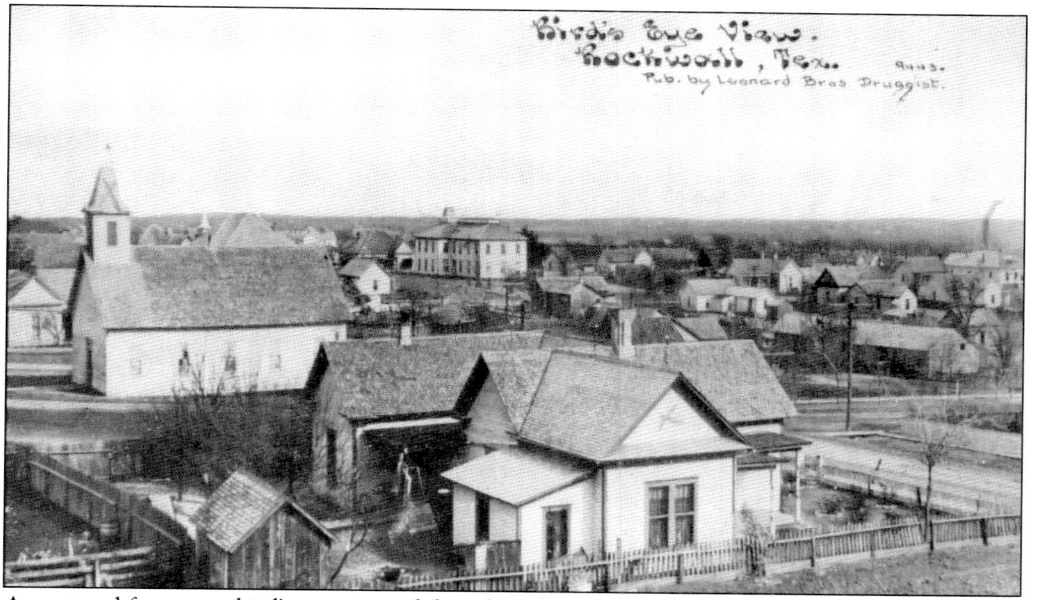

A postcard features a bird's-eye view of the edge of town. The large building in the background is Wells College. Wells College, also known as Rockwall College, was organized in 1893 by J. K. Wells as a private elementary and college preparatory academy. Wells advertised that Rockwall had a "conspicuous absence of vices and pernicious influences." The first session was held on January 1, 1894, and the doors closed in 1912.

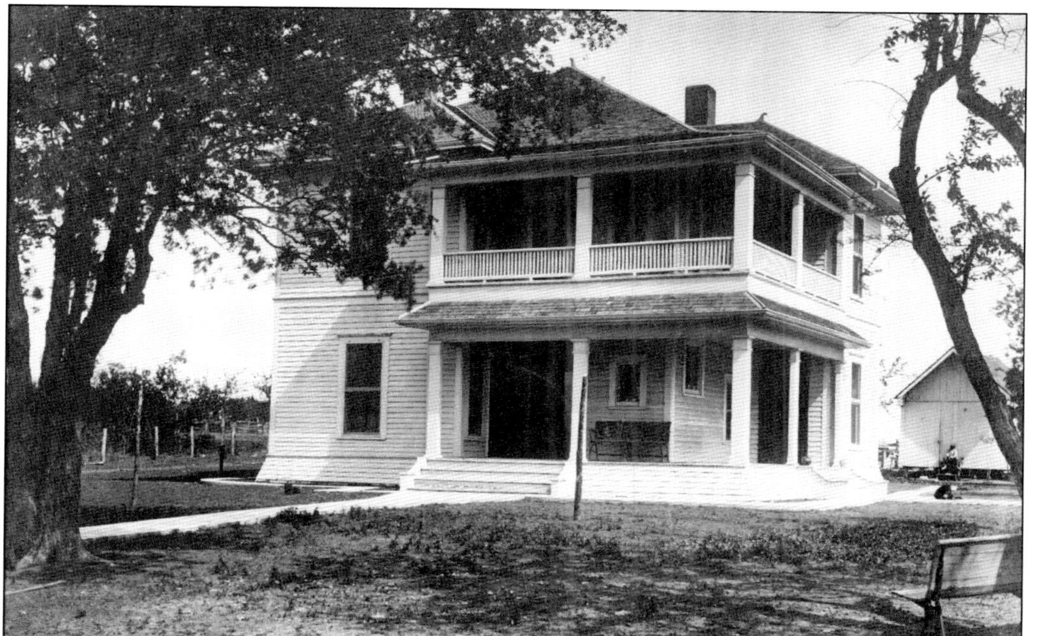

A Dallas County native, E. D. Foree first came to Rockwall and began his civil law practice around 1892. He served as county attorney from 1894 to 1898 and was the county judge from 1898 to 1902. Around 1900, Judge Foree built this home at the corner of Clark Street and what is now State Highway 66. It was later destroyed by fire.

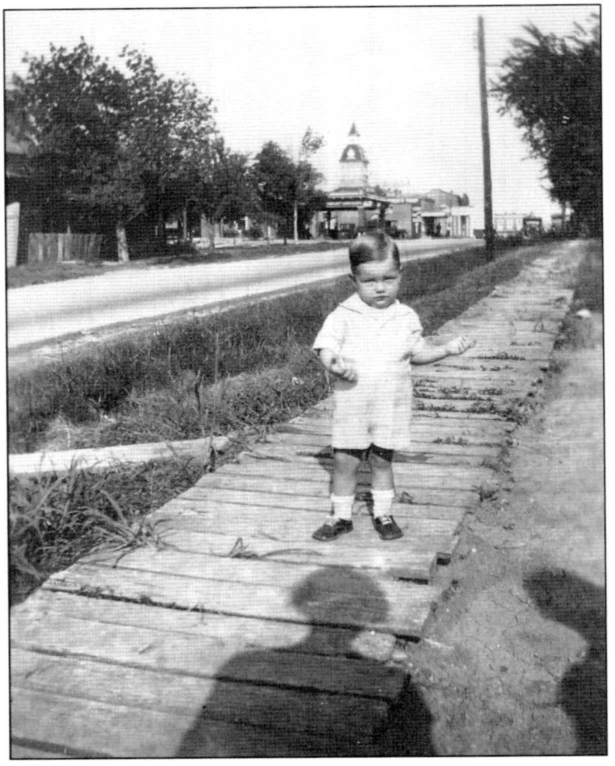

As Rockwall's population grew, the city's residential area expanded. At left, wooden sidewalks were built in neighborhoods near the downtown square to keep shoes and hems clean on the walk to town. Below, Jewel Reese is in front of the family home, considered by many to be Rockwall's first true mansion. In 1911, Wes Martin of Royse City was commissioned to build this Greek Revival home for Judge James Reese and his family. The home originally sat on a 25-acre tract of land with large trees, gardens, and orchards. It was located on a hill, which locals called "Reese Hill," just a short distance from the downtown square.

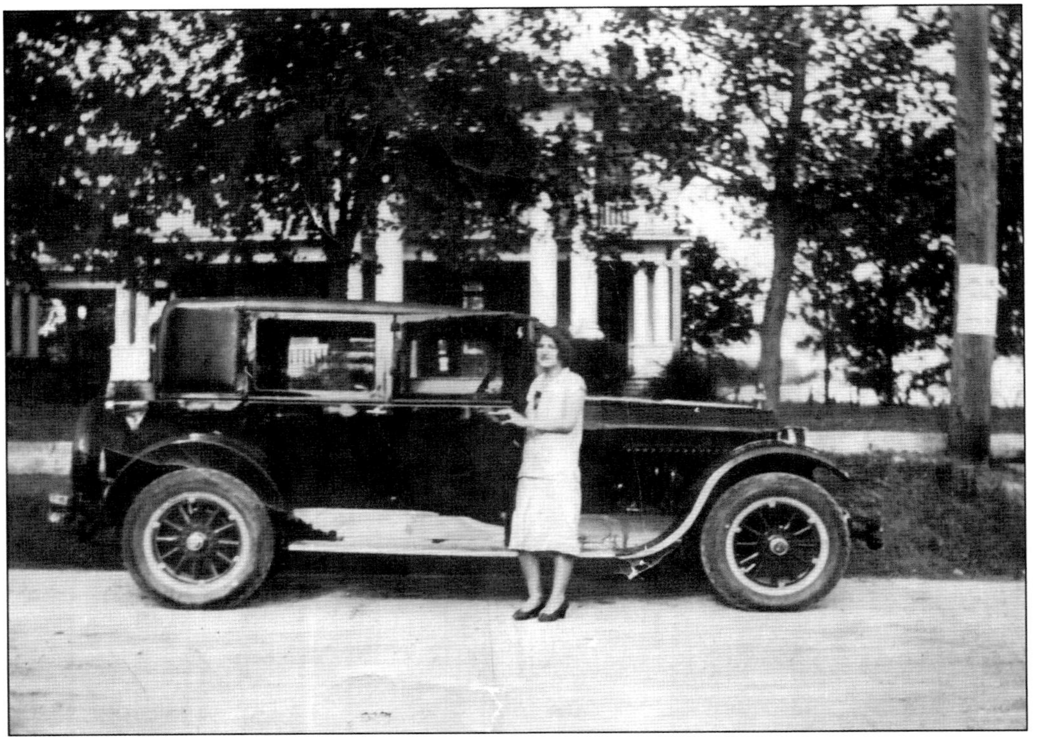

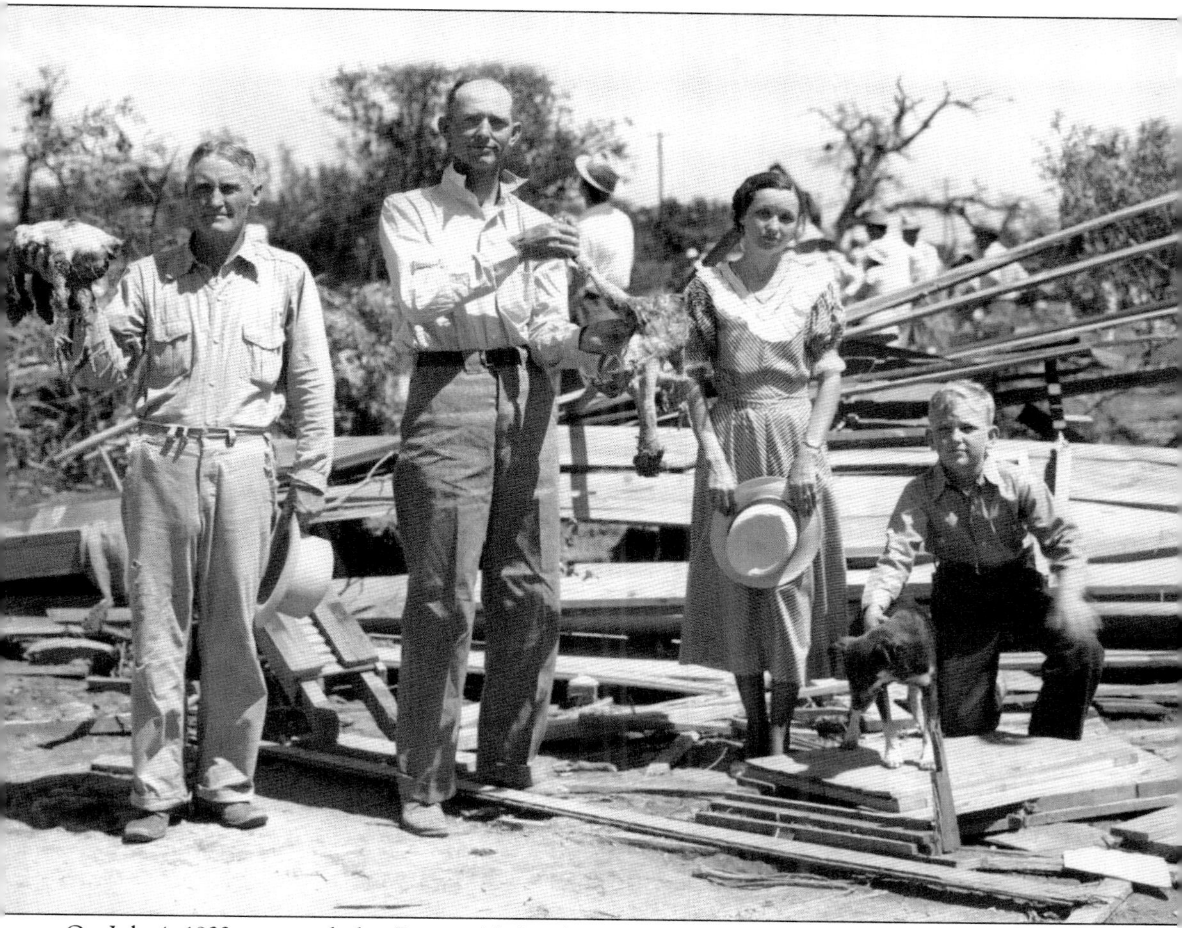

On July 4, 1933, a tornado hit Fate and left a devastating path of destruction. Miraculously, no one was injured, but the twister left behind extensive damage. Livestock were killed, and houses were literally flattened. In this photograph, a family poses in front of the remnants of their home. With a total population of less than 200 people and with money sparse in the aftermath of the Great Depression, the city was slow to rebound. During the 1930s, the high school dropped to a grade school. By the 1940s, the population had decreased to such a point that even the churches consolidated—all community members met together in the same church building, and each of the four represented denominations took one Sunday of the month to conduct the service.

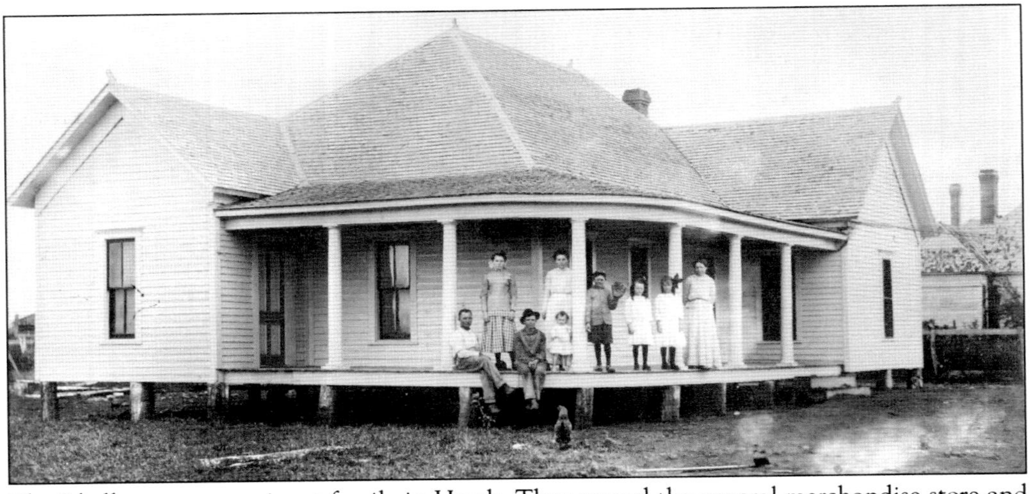

The Isbells were a prominent family in Heath. They owned the general merchandise store and an interest in the gin and the bank. In this photograph, family members pose in front of the family home in 1911. Pictured from left to right are Matthew Knox Isbell, Fay Isbell, Grady Isbell, Grace Isbell Vaughn and her daughter Lena, Frank Isbell, Mary Isbell, Anna Isbell, and matriarch Emma Lena McLendon Isbell.

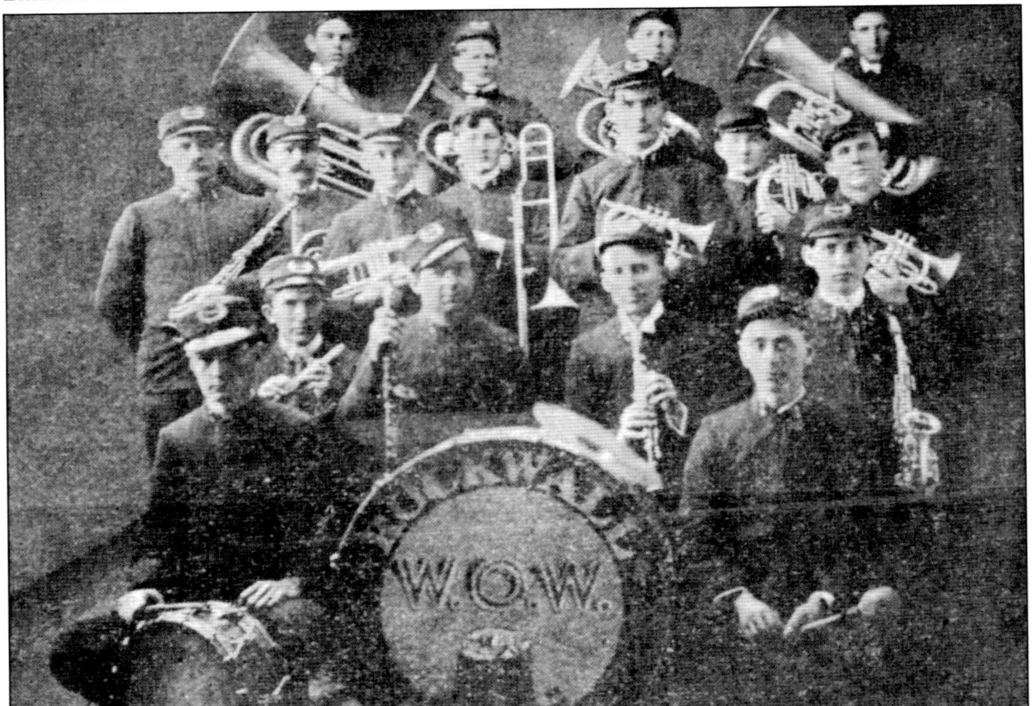

Fraternal organizations were popular in the early 1900s, and Rockwall had a growing chapter of Woodmen of the World (WOW). WOW was a fraternal group that offered life insurance benefits to its members and encouraged community service. In addition, it offered a social outlet through regular meetings and participation in activities such as the Woodmen of the World band. Pictured is a postcard photograph of Rockwall's WOW band around 1900.

Although the transition to automobiles was already on the horizon by the early 1900s, the long-tenured tradition of courting via horse and buggy was still being used throughout Rockwall County. At right are Olen Wallace and Evelyn Brown in their courting days, around 1908. On this particular day, a number of courting couples had lined up in their horse and buggy and waited in line for a professional photographer to take their picture. Below, a couple rides through the open roads of Rockwall, an umbrella shielding them from the heat of the sun. By 1920, the concept of the horse-and-buggy ride had been completely replaced with the idea of the Sunday drive. (Right, courtesy of the family of Evelyn Lofland.)

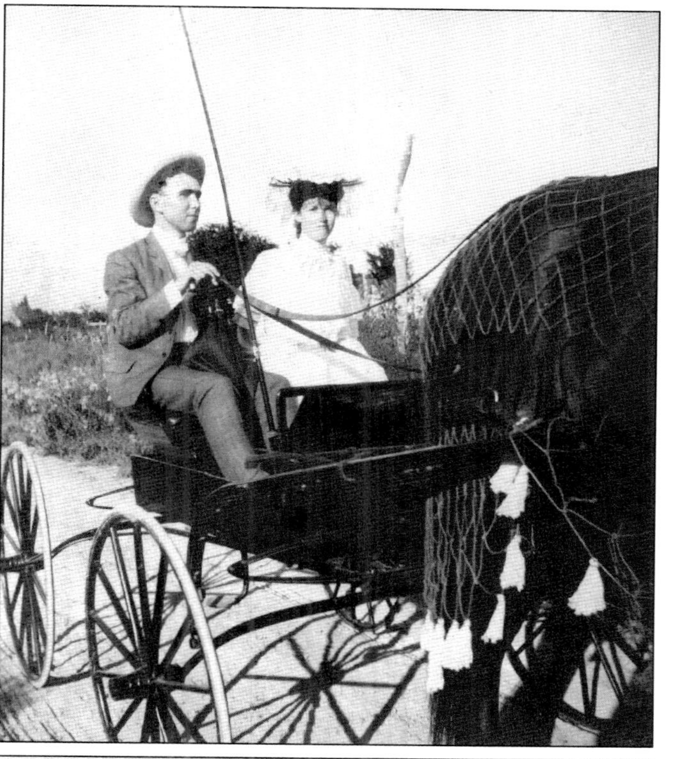

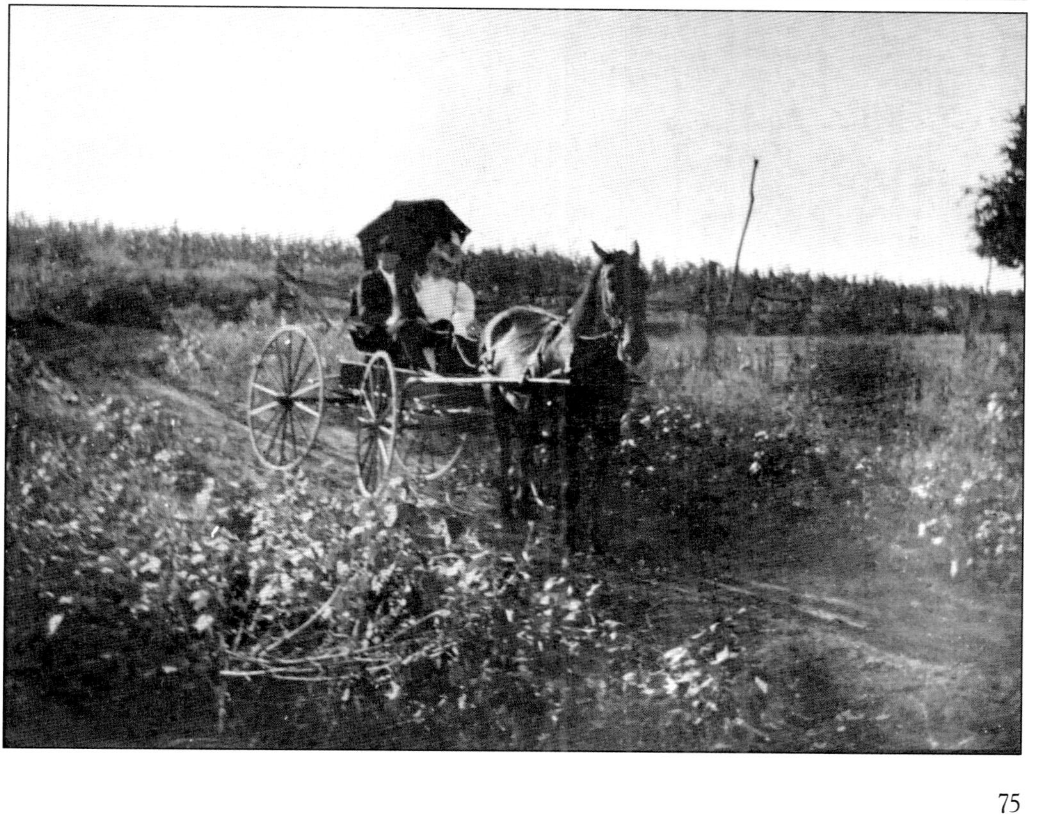

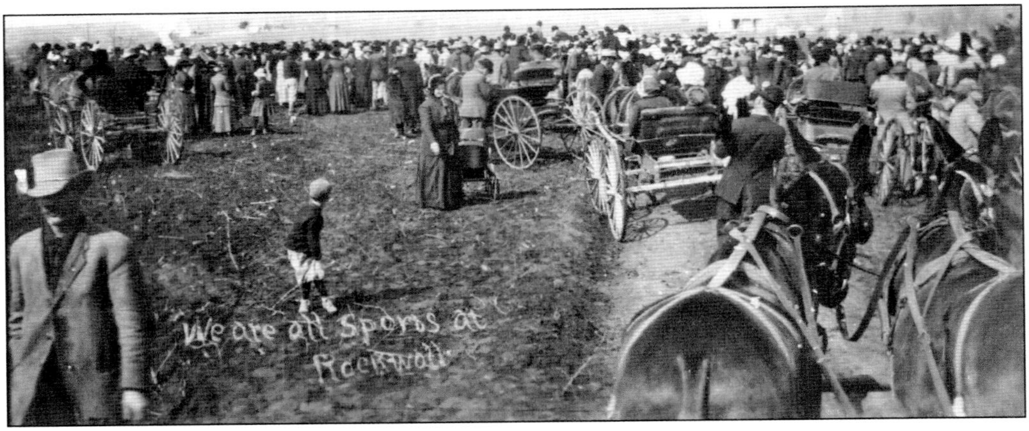

According to family history, in addition to donating land for a school and building the first cotton gin in the area, pioneer settler James Truitt also owned a racetrack north of Rockwall. A number of gentlemen in the area raised blooded horses, and in the late 1800s and early 1900s, racing was a popular spectator sport for families. Above, this picture postcard shows the crowd at the track on race day and bears the inscription, "We are all sports at Rockwall." Below, horses, jockeys, and other track personnel pose for a professional portrait in front of the stables around 1910.

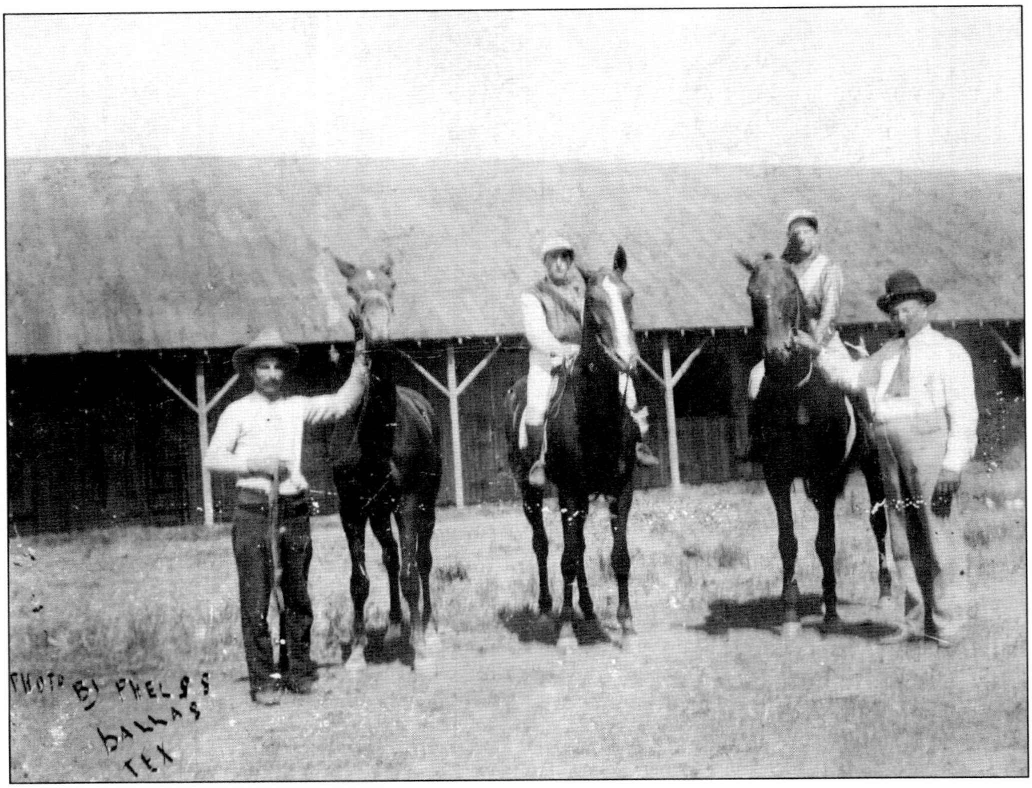

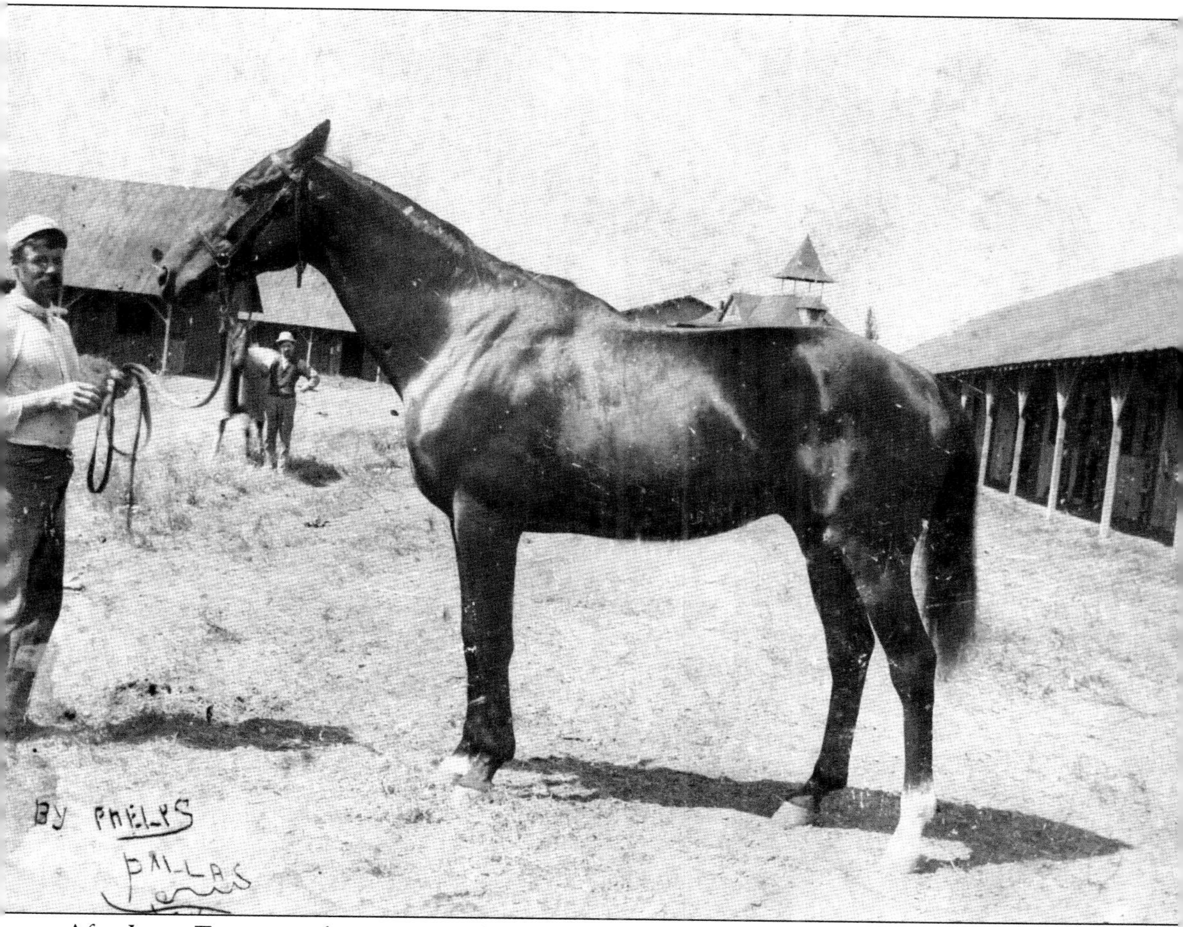

After James Truitt passed away in 1903, handwritten documents refer to the racetrack as the Hays track. Dave Hays was James Truitt's son-in-law, having married the Truitts' youngest daughter, Fannie, in 1895. (Fannie has her own place in Rockwall history—she is the first recorded birth for the county, having been born not long after its official formation in 1873.) By the time this c. 1910 photograph was taken, the track was well developed with stables, a grandstand area, and a devoted following of breeders who brought their horses to race. While the main duty of the horse in the time of pioneer expansion and well into the first part of the 20th century was working the land, sprint races did become popular entertainment, and some farmers and ranchers saw an opportunity for economic gain. As a result, a number of local men began breeding horses for racing.

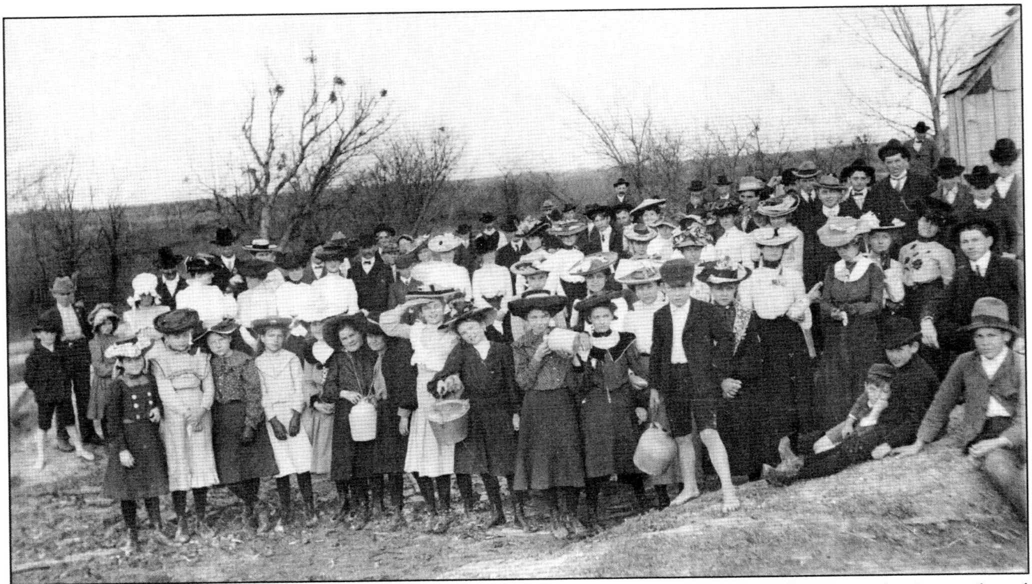

Here are two views of dinner on the grounds. Above, a *c.* 1900 group photograph shows local residents in their Sunday finest. Below, a congregation from the small community of Munson enjoys a potluck lunch around 1940. Historically, dinner on the grounds originated in a time when Sunday services were held in both the morning and evening, and transportation methods prevented members from traveling all the way home between services. Instead, they packed food for their family, spread cloths under trees on the church grounds, and all ate together between the day's scheduled events. As roads and transportation improved, dinner on the grounds evolved into a social and celebratory event.

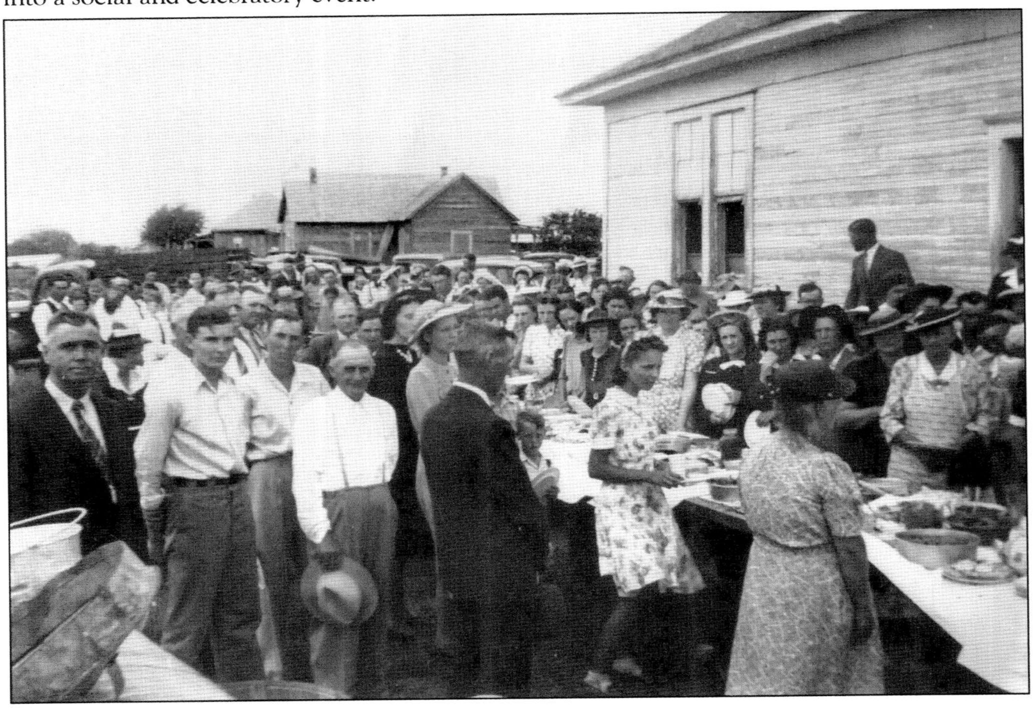

Three

The Fabulous 1950s and the Decline of King Cotton 1945–1965

World War II had caused more than 1,000 people to leave Rockwall County, either to serve in the war effort or to find industrial jobs. By the late 1940s, some of that population had been recaptured, but the area continued to see a pattern of stagnant growth. Between 1950 and 1960, the population of Rockwall County hovered right around 6,000.

By 1959, the county's cotton crop was only 7,466 bales, half of the 1940 production. Farmers were moving away from cotton and investing in livestock. In 1948, five-and-a-half times as much land was being used as pasture throughout the county as it had been in 1925. The number of farms dropped from 1,031 in 1930 to 320 in 1959.

In the 1950s, there were a number of developments that poised Rockwall for its future. Lake Lavon, designed for flood control, conservation storage, and recreational purposes, was completed in 1953. Roads continued to improve and provide easier transportation. The interstate highway system connected Dallas to Rockwall via I-30 (or, as some old-timers called it, the "super slab," referencing the old slab roads of the 1920s).

Those who grew up in Rockwall in the 1950s often recall the images of an idyllic existence—soda shops on the town square, pep rallies for the Friday night football games, blue jeans and bobby socks. Future Homemakers of America and Future Farmers of America were popular extracurricular clubs, and Rockwall offered all the advantages of a small town sitting just outside the shadow of the big city.

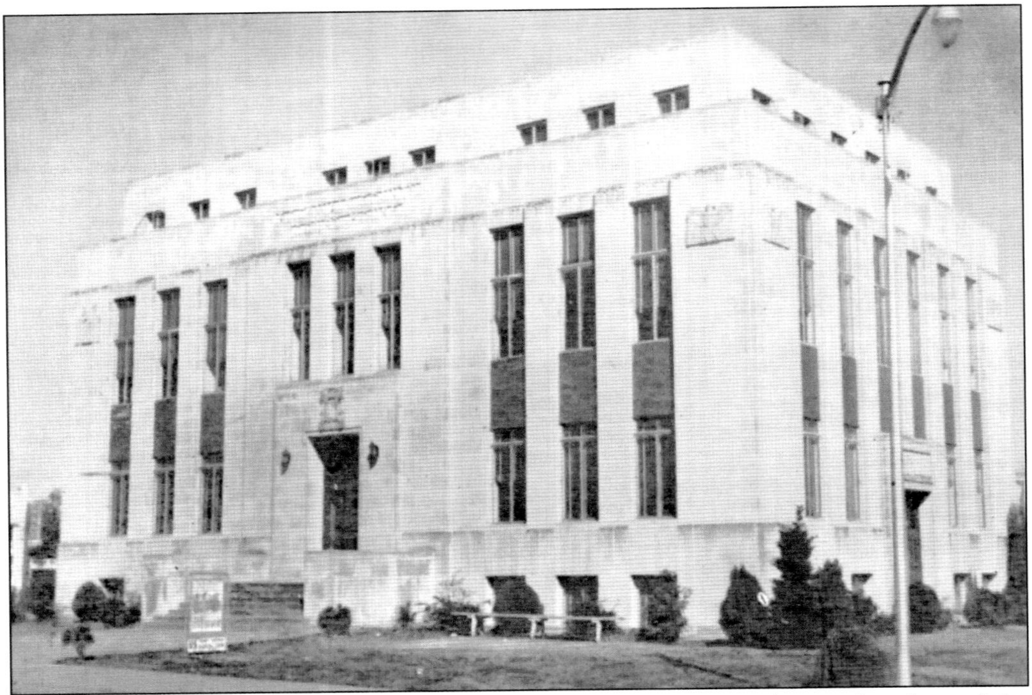

Above, a picture postcard shows the Rockwall County Courthouse. The top floor housed the Rockwall County jail. The jail had individual cells as well as common areas, and depending on where inmates were, at times, they could call down and converse with passersby on the sidewalk. Below, the view east on Rusk Street shows the old Highway 67 sign (on the sidewalk at right), the First United Methodist Church (center rear of photograph), and the Magnolia Oil Company Gas Station (left of church). The Magnolia Oil Company constructed this gas station after the Bankhead Highway was built through Rockwall. Magnolia leased the building to several different local operators, including Marvin Young and Ted Cain.

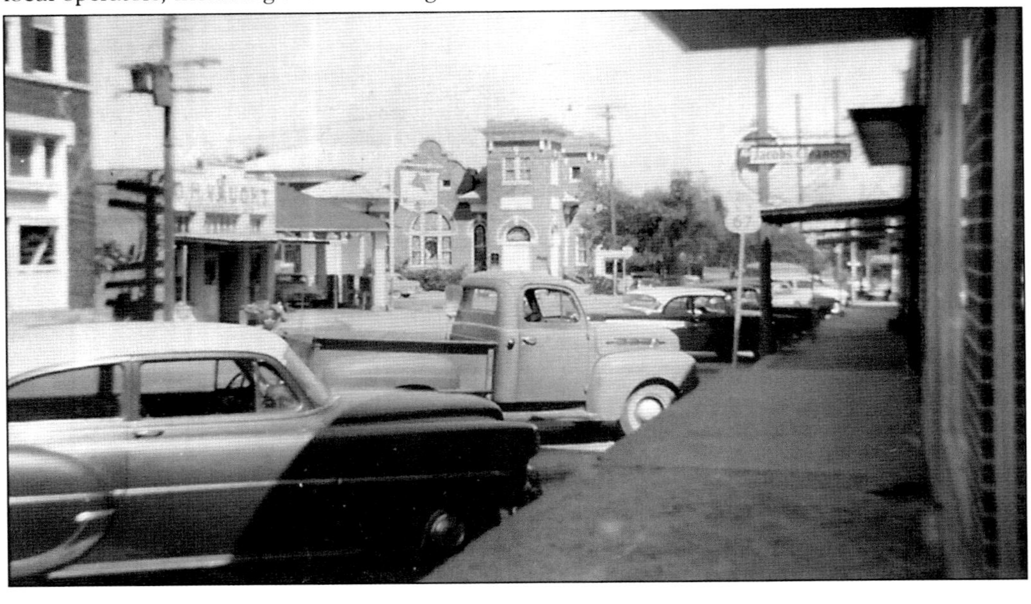

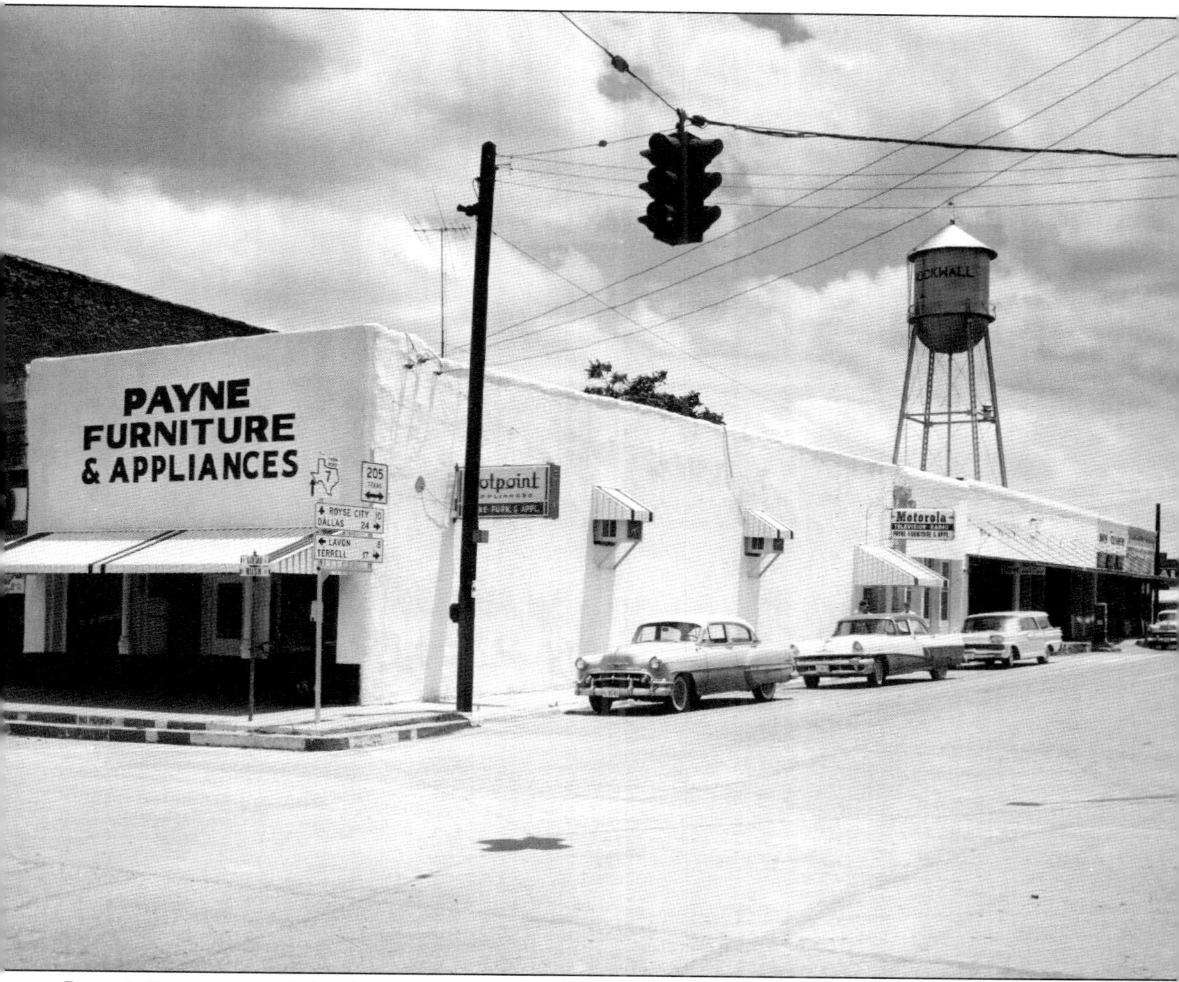

Payne's Furniture and Appliances was a fixture on the Rockwall square for more than 30 years. It was owned by local residents D. E. and Paralee Payne. At a time when television was new, Payne's displayed one of the few sets in the county in the front window. For months, the store became a gathering place for residents eager to watch the moving images on the small screen. Even after regular business hours, D. E. Payne would leave the set running so those who had brought folding chairs and set them up on the sidewalk in front of the store could watch into the evening hours. Payne would return later—after his guests had gone home—to shut down the television for the night.

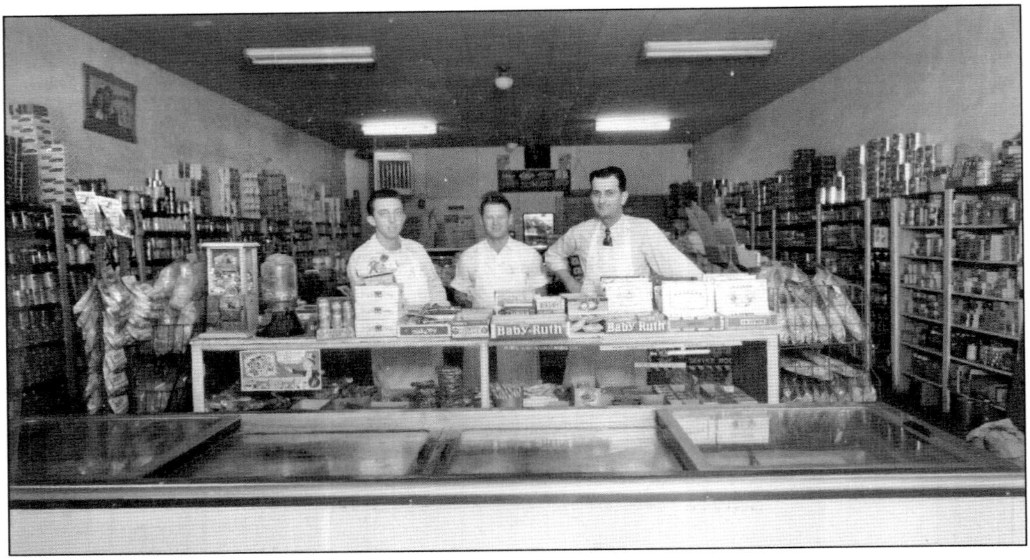

The Deaton Grocery and Market was located on the east side of the square. Pictured behind the counter are, from left to right, Roy Gene Mitchell, M. J. Rodgers, and Clyde Maxwell. Below is the eclectic interior of the Jack Lowe Newsstand. Playing pinball are, from left to right, Richard Dawson, Carl Smith, and Jess Sheffield. Proprietor Jack Lowe stands facing the camera. Lowe stocked popular magazines of the day such as *Look* and *Life* as well as local and regional papers. He also kept an array of snacks and sodas on hand for patrons waiting their turn at the popular pinball machines.

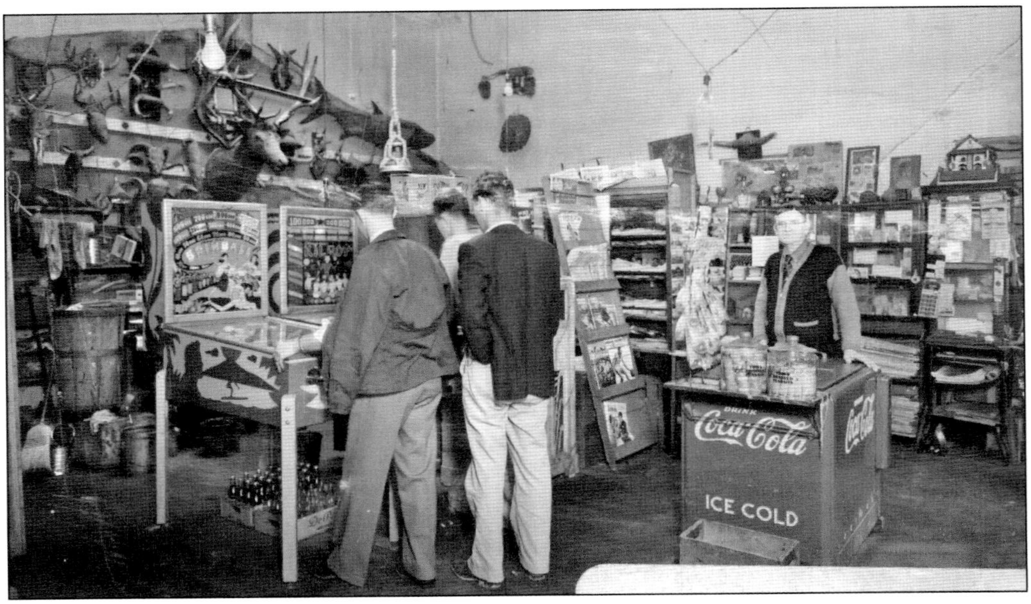

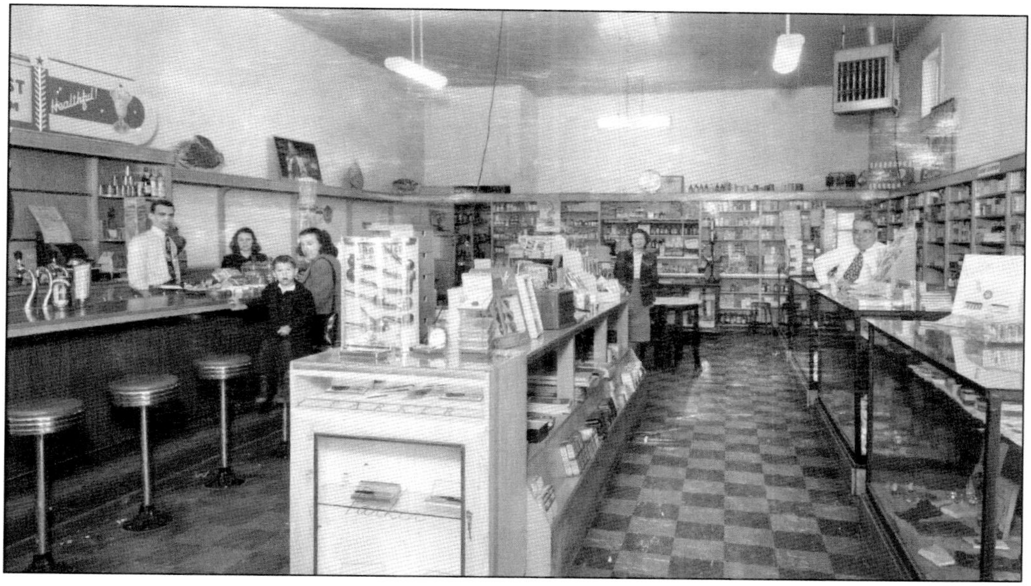

Cunningham's Drug Store was located on the southeast corner of the square. Identified (on the back of this photograph) are, from left to right, Richard Dawson, Ida McIntire, Mrs. Earlie Darr and son Vernon, Mrs. Jack Cunningham, and Jack Cunningham. Although operated under different owners, this building on the corner of Rusk and San Jacinto Streets was home to a drugstore for more than 80 consecutive years. Occupants included the Corner Drug Store, Bailey's Drug Store, Rochell and Canup, DeVaney Drug Store, Cunningham's Drugstore, and the Rockwall Drug. Below, a 1950s-era view of the soda fountain shows the waitress serving two local policemen.

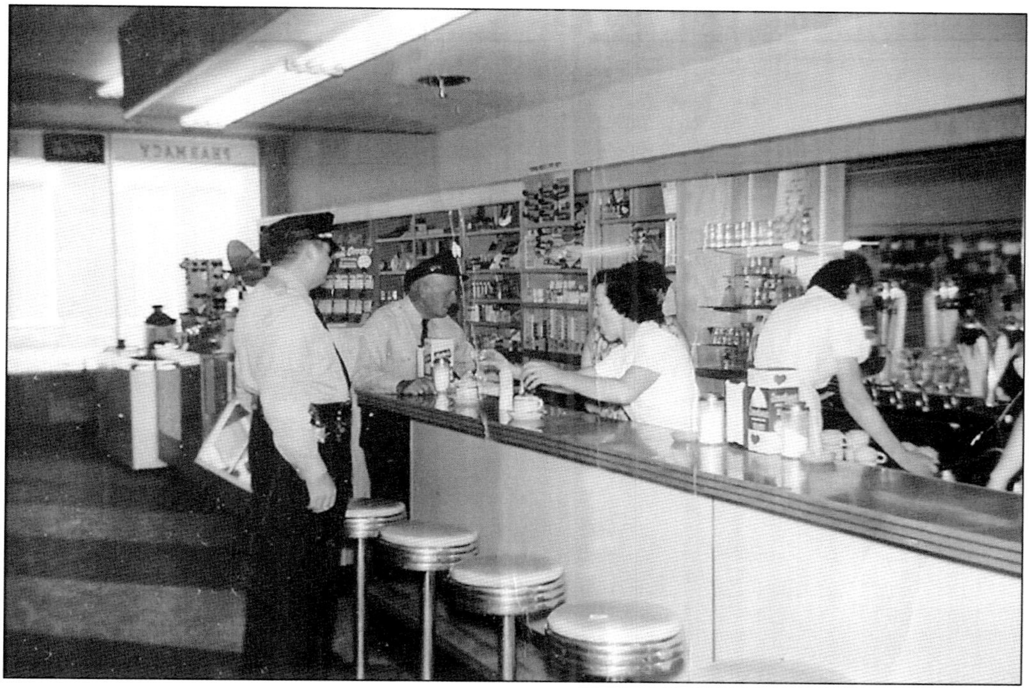

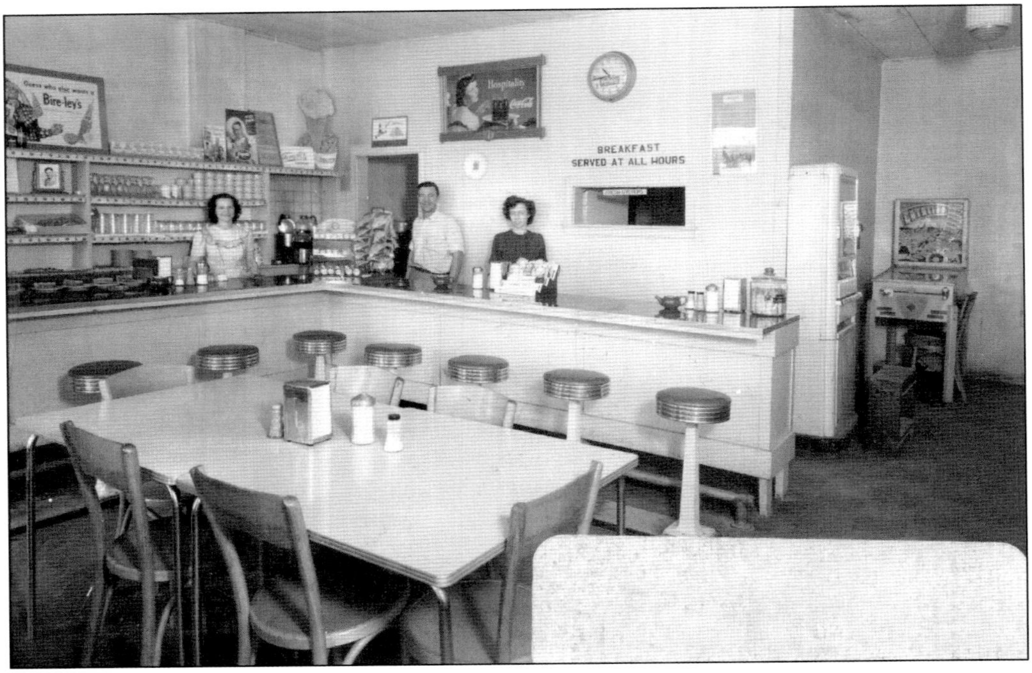

The Dawson Café was located on the Bankhead Highway (U.S. 67). Identified on the back of the photograph are, from left to right, Mrs. Leon Dawson, Leon Dawson, and Mrs. Richard Dawson. (It is interesting to note that prior to the 1960s, notations on the back of photographs often identified women by their formal married names, as in "Mrs. Leon Dawson.") Below, the Andrew and Martin Hardware Store was located on the east side of the square. Pictured from left to right are Rolater Bourn, Harry Martin, Jay Andrew, and Andrew Gray. Andrew and Martin occupied not only a storefront building along San Jacinto, but also operated a storage/warehouse building next door to the main showroom. This second location was used to store overstock and also to make direct sales of larger items.

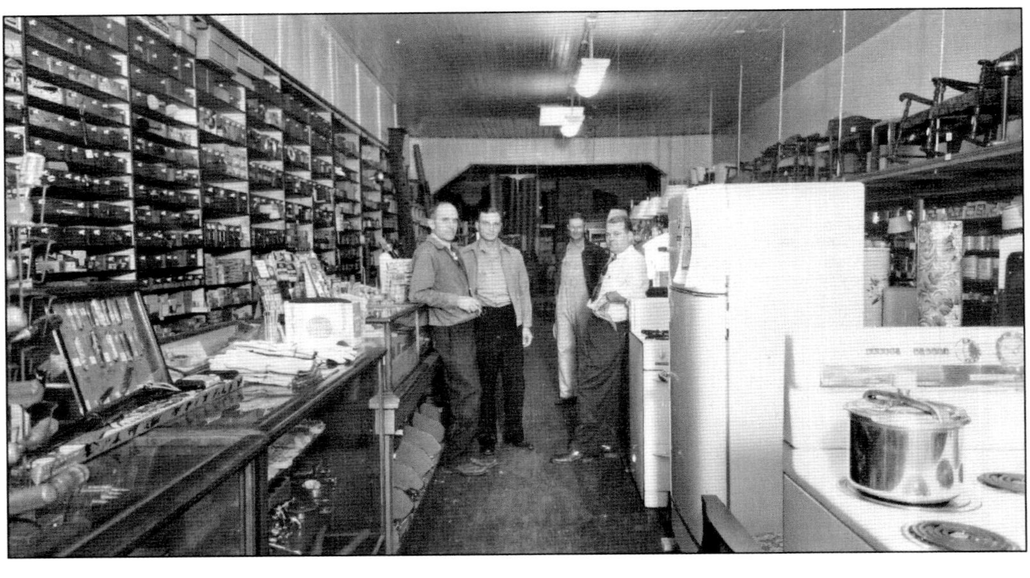

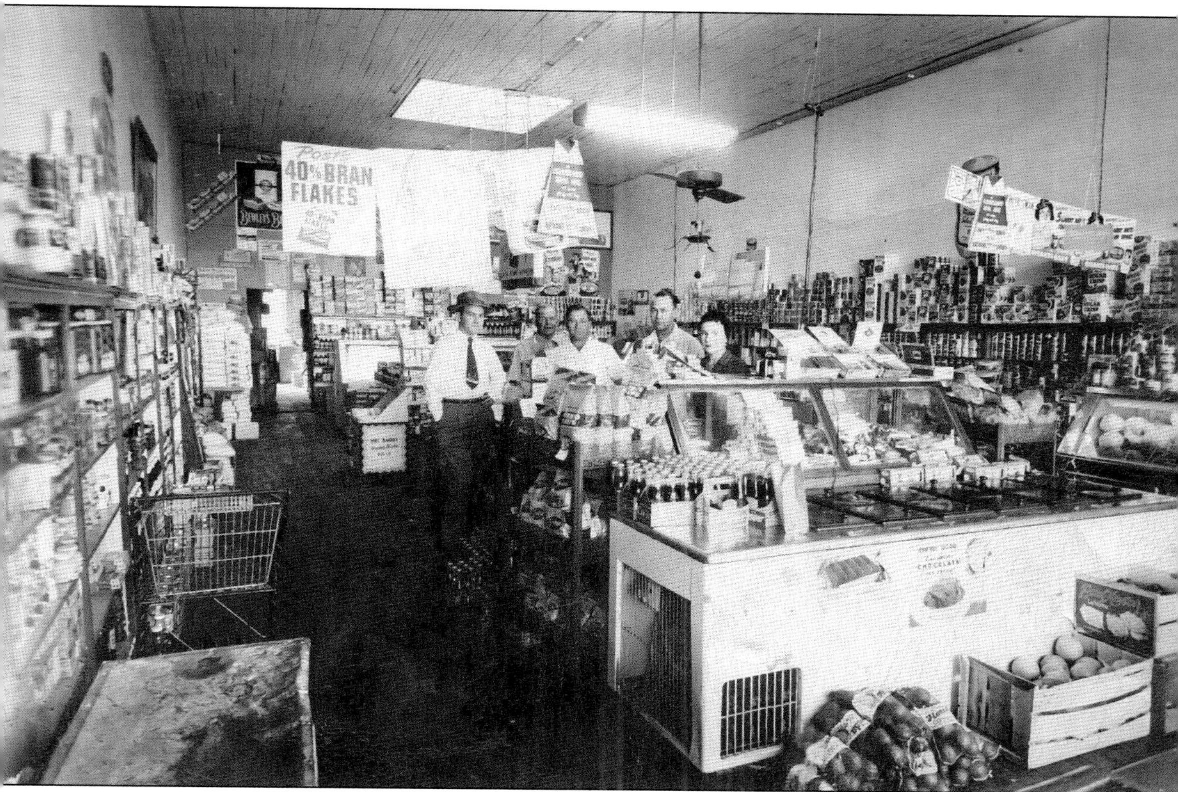

The Holt Grocery Store was located on the south side of Rockwall's downtown square. In this 1950s photograph, a White Swan salesman (in tie) pitches his wares to, from left to right, Charlie Jefferson Holt, butcher Buford Yeagher, owner J. D. Holt, and Winn Lowe. In those days, theft was hardly considered a problem, and produce and product deliveries were made to the store in the night. Delivery personnel left the orders outside the store, and merchants would bring in the orders when they arrived for work the next morning. Although the crime rate was not naturally high, the fact that a night watchman patrolled the square helped curtail deviant youngsters who might want to add thievery to their list of pranks. The night watchman system was in place for years. Arvel Gray, who served as the weekend watchman for 10 years, recorded memories of a system where he "had to walk the square turning keys at regular intervals along the way" in order to make sure the town square was secure.

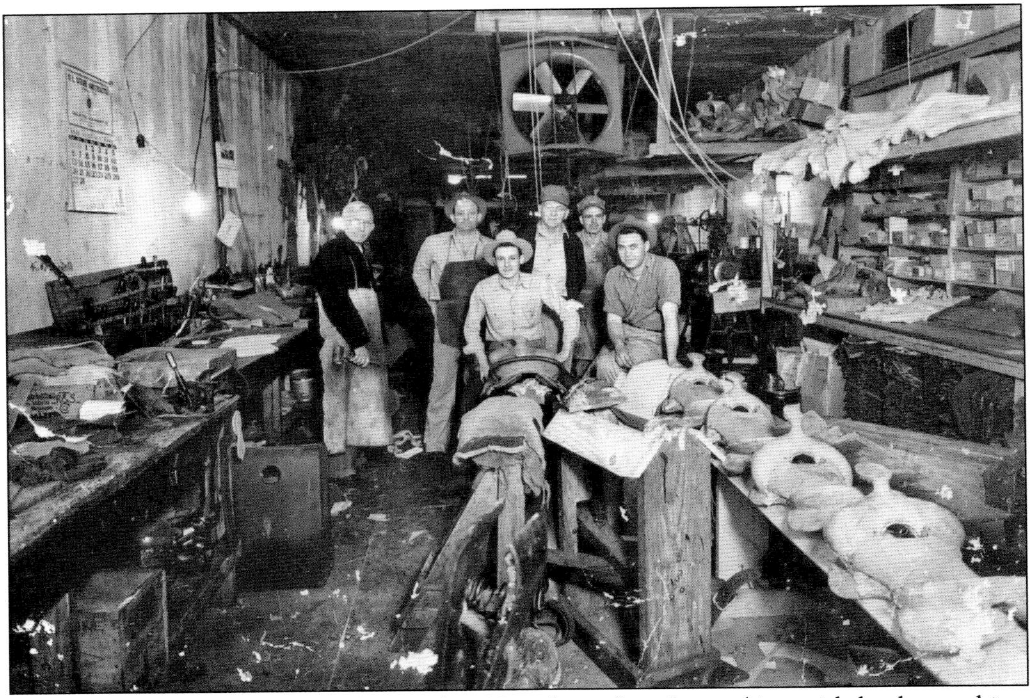

G. H. Vaught came to Rockwall around 1900 with a talent for working with leather and just $16 in his pocket. He opened a harness shop, and business boomed. Soon the Vaught Harness and Saddle Shop was operating not only as a local storefront operation, but also as a national mail-order business. Pictured above in the downtown Rockwall shop in 1952 are, from left to right, (seated) Billy Cook and Lloyd Compton; (standing) George Huse, Roy Whitlock, Henry McCrary, and W. A. Mahler. Below are, from left to right, Henry McCrary, G. H. Vaught, Jim Lofland, Roy Whitlock, Louise Whitlock, and two unidentified workers.

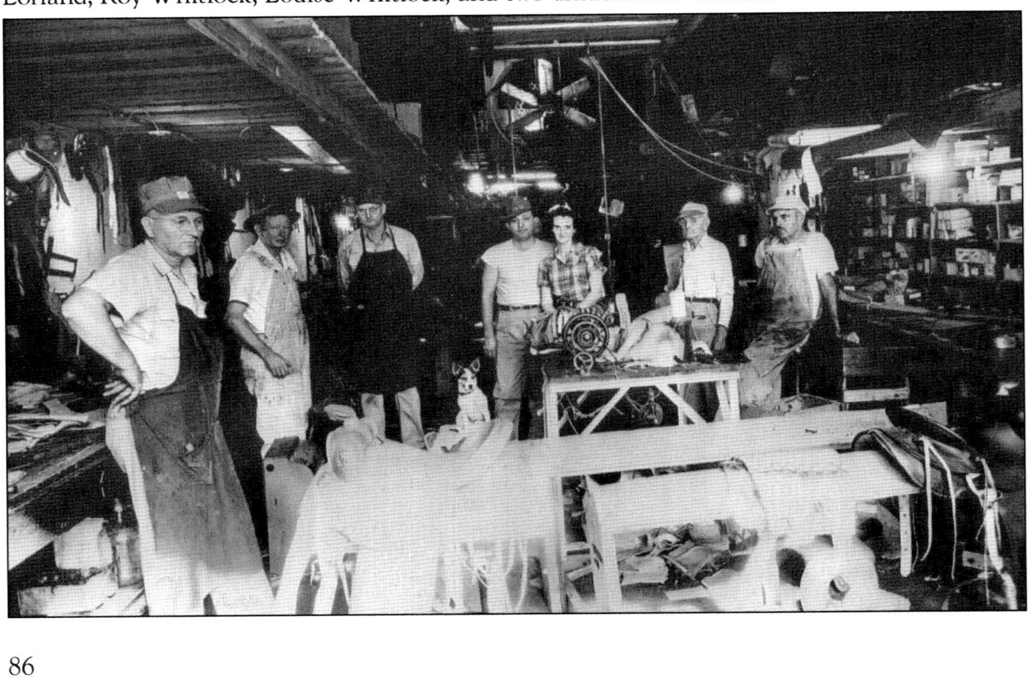

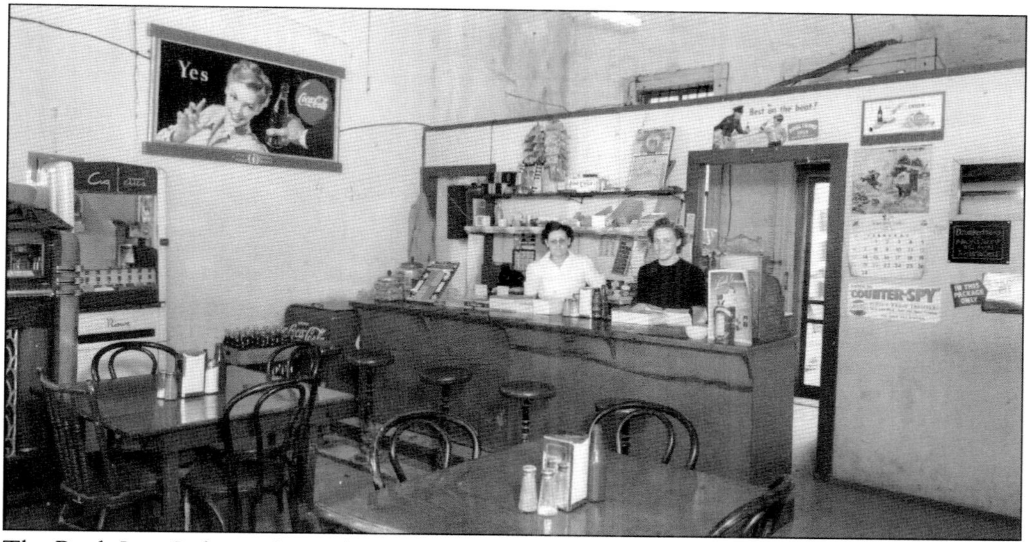

The Rock Inn Café was located on State Highway 205. Pictured are (as noted on back of the photograph) Inez Horton (left) and Mrs. "Boots" Mooney. Below, the building on the northeast corner at Rusk and San Jacinto Streets played an important part in Rockwall's early banking industry. Since the beginning of the 20th century, at least four different banks have occupied this corner. This interior view shows daily business in the 1950s. Pictured third from left is O. L. Steger Sr., a civic and business leader, area historian, and former mayor. Steger lived his entire life in Rockwall County except for the 16 months he served his country during World War I. Steger passed away on November 11, 1972, but left behind detailed written accounts of growing up in Rockwall.

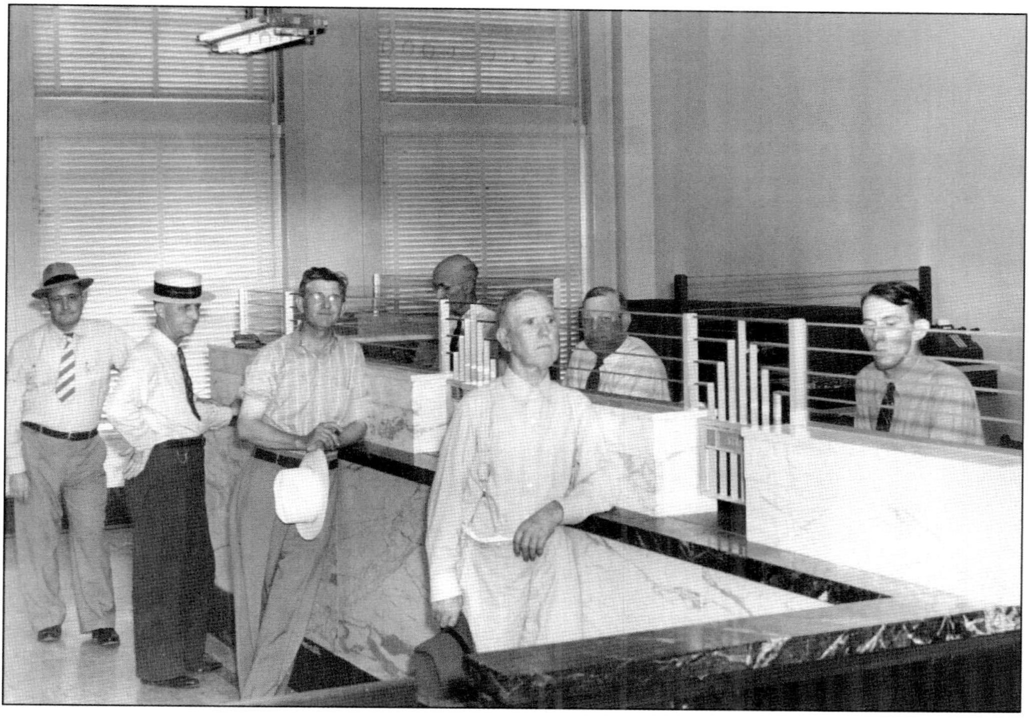

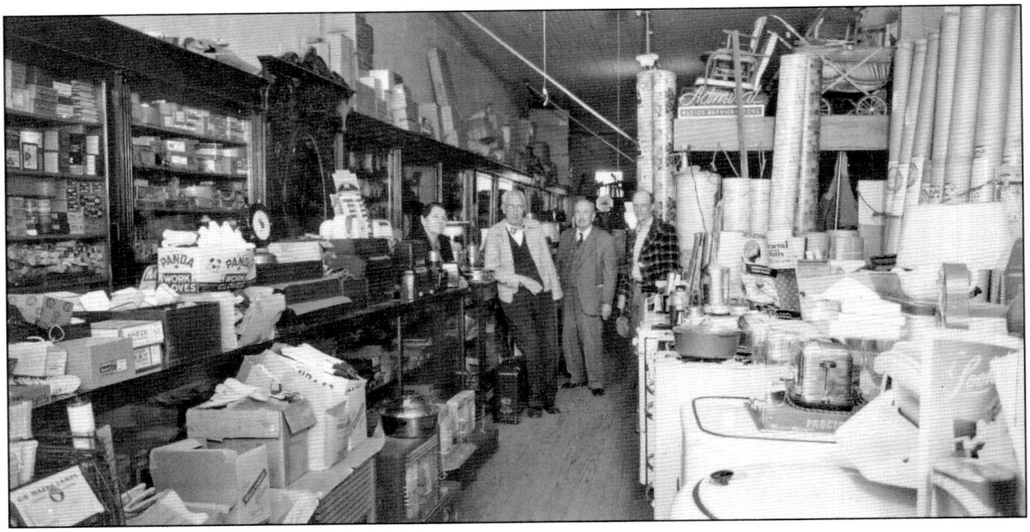

Following World War II, many women who had been out in the workforce filling jobs came back home and began raising families. It was during this time that the image of the typical 1950s homemaker emerged. The economy prospered, and advertisers pitched their wares toward women striving to make a picture-perfect home life. Above is the McDonald Hardware Store on the south side of the square. From left to right are Mrs. J. D. McDonald, J. D. McDonald, Dr. J. F. Corry, and Hershel Hobbs. McDonald's carried everything the 1950s-era female could want—a bevy of small appliances, the latest linoleum patterns, and even children's rocking chairs and baby carriages (top of the photograph). Below, a dry-goods store on the square carries striped shirts for boys, bolts of fabric, and other 1950s-era family necessities.

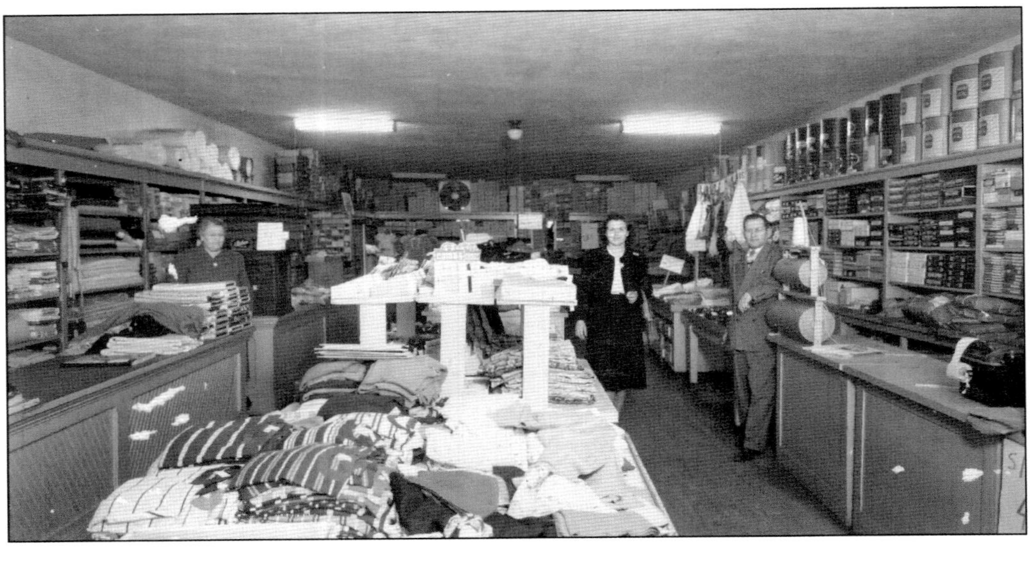

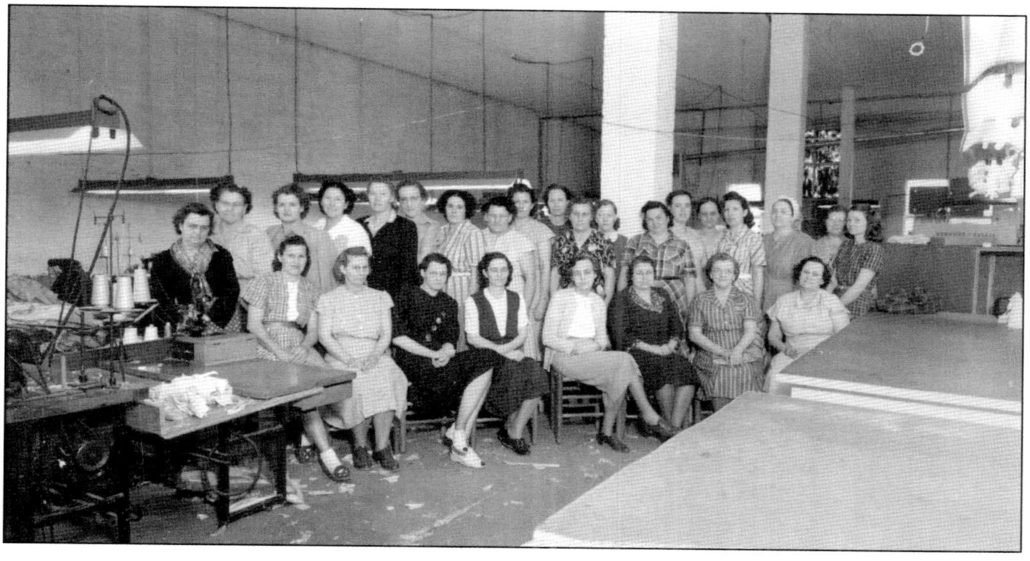

These are two views of Rockwall women in the 1950s. Above are workers at the sewing room, a local manufacturing business located on the west side of the square. Below is the organizational meeting of the Rockwall Business and Professional Women's Club. The organization was formed in 1955 with 65 charter members as a local chapter of the National Federation of Business and Professional Women's Clubs. Mary Belle Miller served as the first president. Through fund-raising efforts, the group raised more than $40,000 to help build the community building and pool at Harry Myers Park.

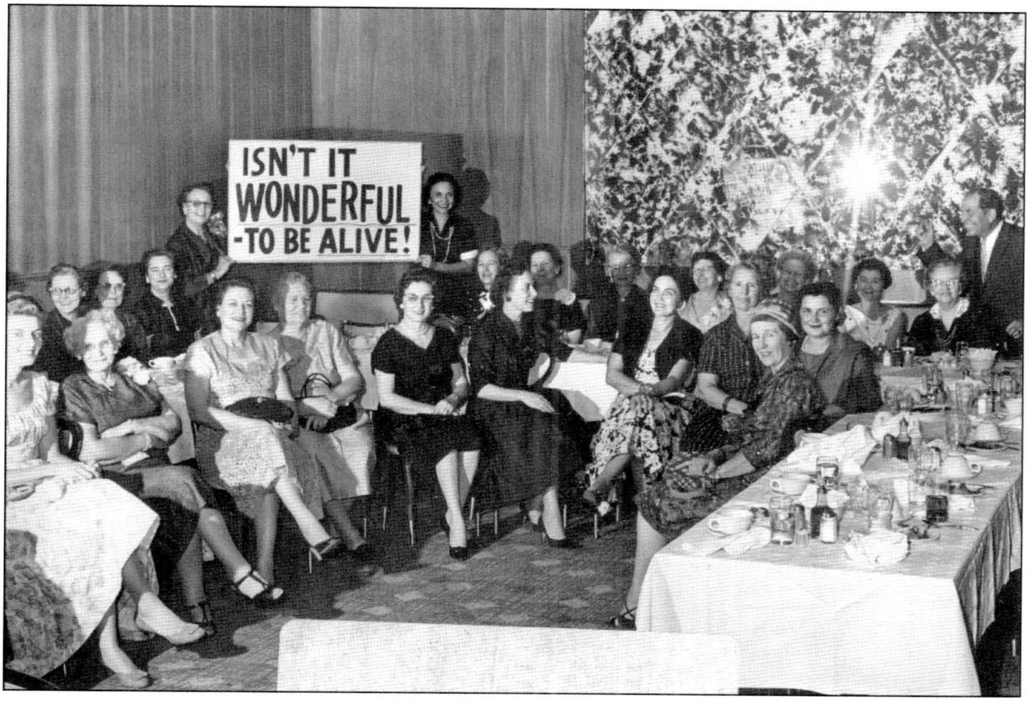

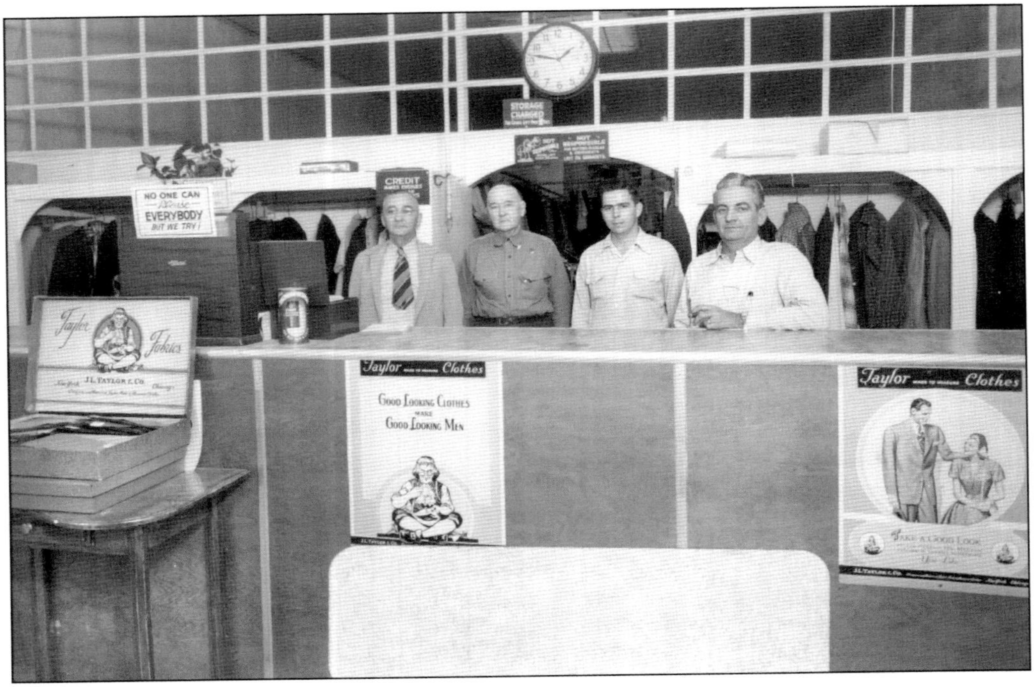

Jacobs Cleaners was located on East Rusk Street. Minding the shop above are, from left to right, Fred Hathway, Dan Smith, James Jacobs, and Vivian Jacobs. In addition to laundry services, Jacobs was a vendor for J. L. Taylor and Company, a custom-made clothing company. Taylor Clothing had been in business since the early 1900s, operating on a slogan that said, "Let Taylor tailor you once and Taylor will tailor you always." Below, in the interior of the Peck Garage and Paint Shop, are, from left to right, Opal Hunnicutt, Reagan Hall, Willis Kimmons, Paul Crawford, and Robert Peck, as he takes a break from a paint job.

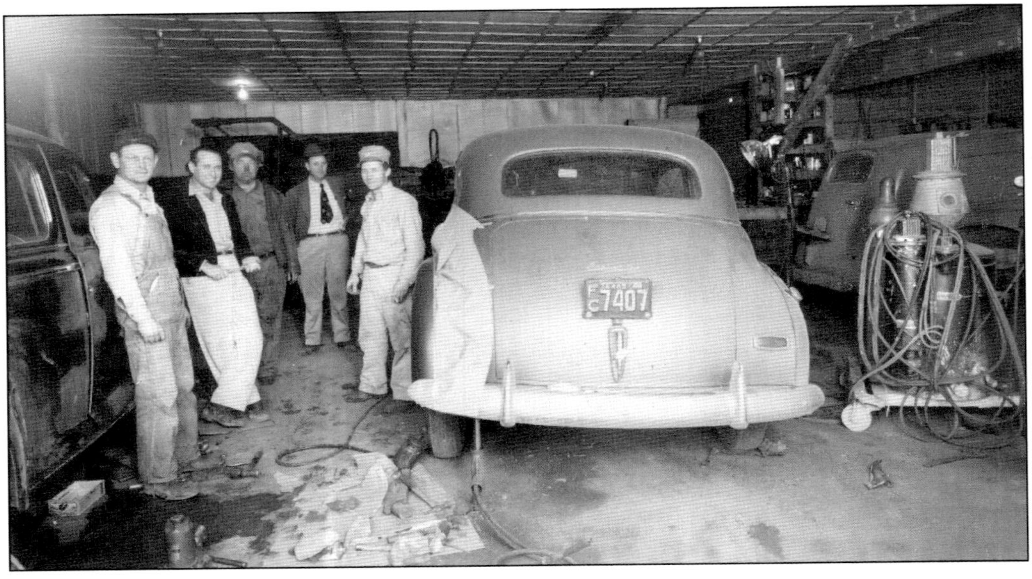

A movie theater was located on the northeast corner of Kaufman and San Jacinto Streets in downtown Rockwall for almost 40 years. For much of that time, it was called the Ritz. The Ritz theater played serials and first-run movies. The segregated theater reserved the lower floor for white patrons only; African American moviegoers were relegated to the balcony.

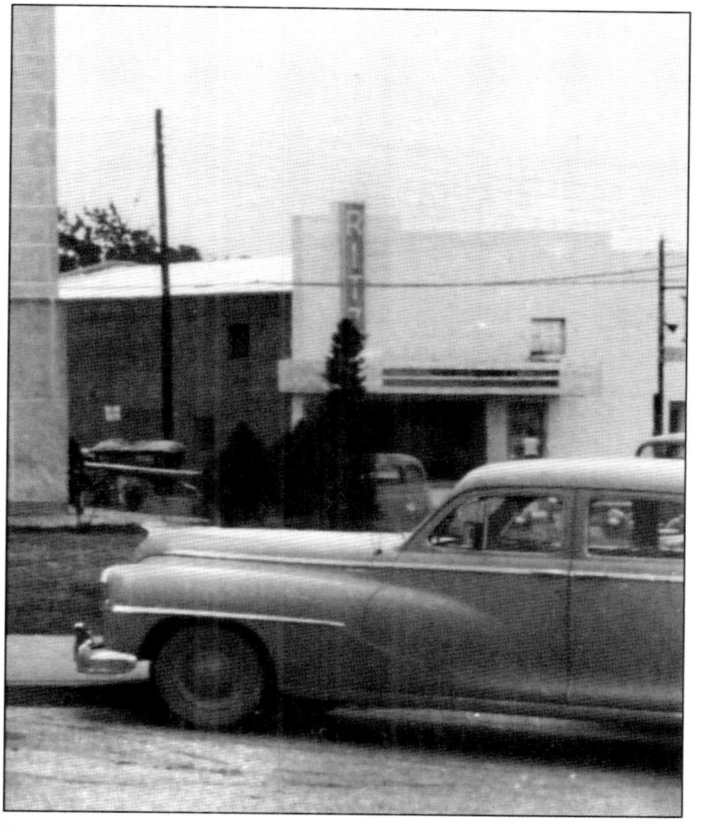

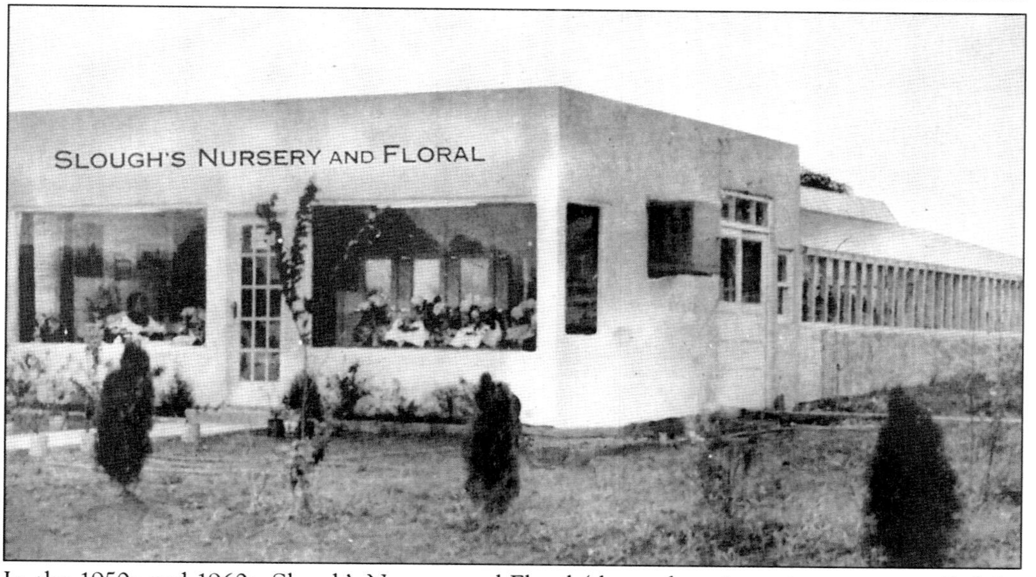

In the 1950s and 1960s, Slough's Nursery and Floral (shown here in a picture postcard) did a booming business. The storefront with attached nursery was located on the west side of Clark Street between Munson and Storrs Streets. The building was demolished in the mid-1970s to make room for new home construction.

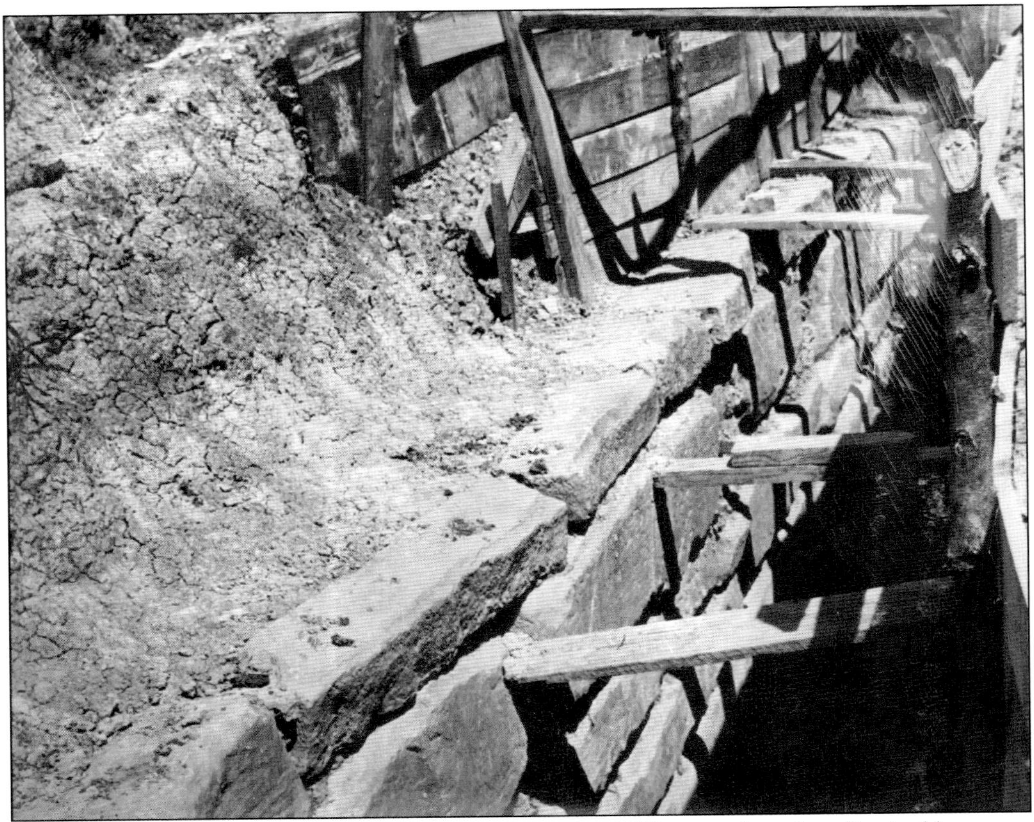

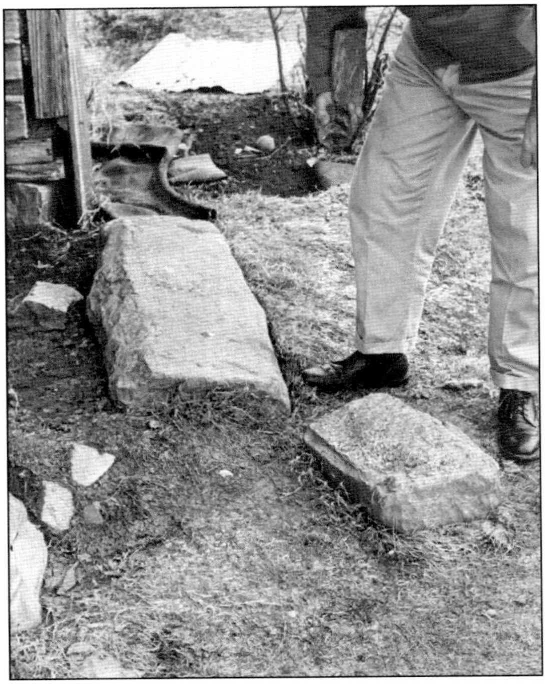

By 1950, a number of studies had been conducted regarding the origins of the rock wall, but Rockwall residents still seemed to find the conclusions controversial. In 1874, geologist Richard Burleson called exposed sections of the wall "igneous occurrences." In 1901, geologist Robert Hill classified the rocks as sand dykes. In 1909, *Science Magazine* published an article by Sidney Paige classifying the rocks as "disconnected sandstone dykes." In 1925, physics professor and former Southern Methodist University (SMU) president R. S. Hyer concluded the formation was natural. In 1927, geologists L. W. Stephenson and J. W. Fewkes (both associated with the Smithsonian) concurred. By 1950, the only dissenting voice was Count Byron de Prorok, who had examined exposed sections of the wall in 1925 and concluded it was constructed by prehistoric man. Above is an excavated section of the wall. At left is an example of a large rock.

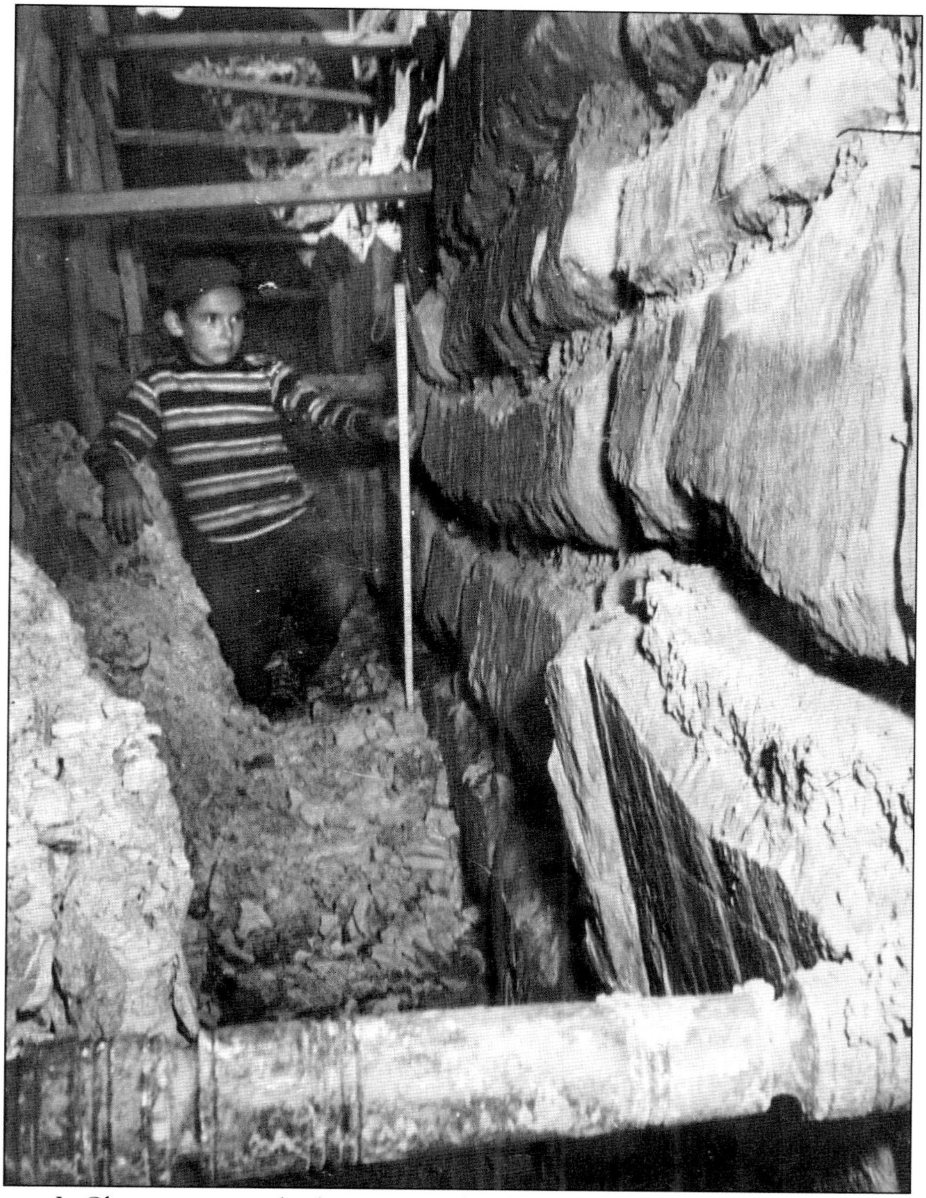

Dr. James L. Glenn was a civic leader, active in the chamber of commerce, and the pastor of the First Presbyterian Church in Rockwall. He was also interested in the origins of the rock wall, and in 1950, under the auspices of the Rockwall Chamber of Commerce, he prepared a report entitled, "Photographic Essay on The System Of Rock Walls At Rockwall, Texas." Dr. Glenn's thorough report gives a summary of the study of the system of rock walls, including the theory that a natural fault line runs through the county and has resulted in this underground formation. At the time of publication, 11 known outcroppings of the wall had been recorded. A map of these locations is included as well as numerous photographs. Among his personal observations, Dr. Glenn states, "The fact that there is a natural fault here does not preclude the construction of other walls by a prehistoric race within the same region." Above, a boy walks beside an excavated section of the rock wall in a photograph appearing in Dr. Glenn's report.

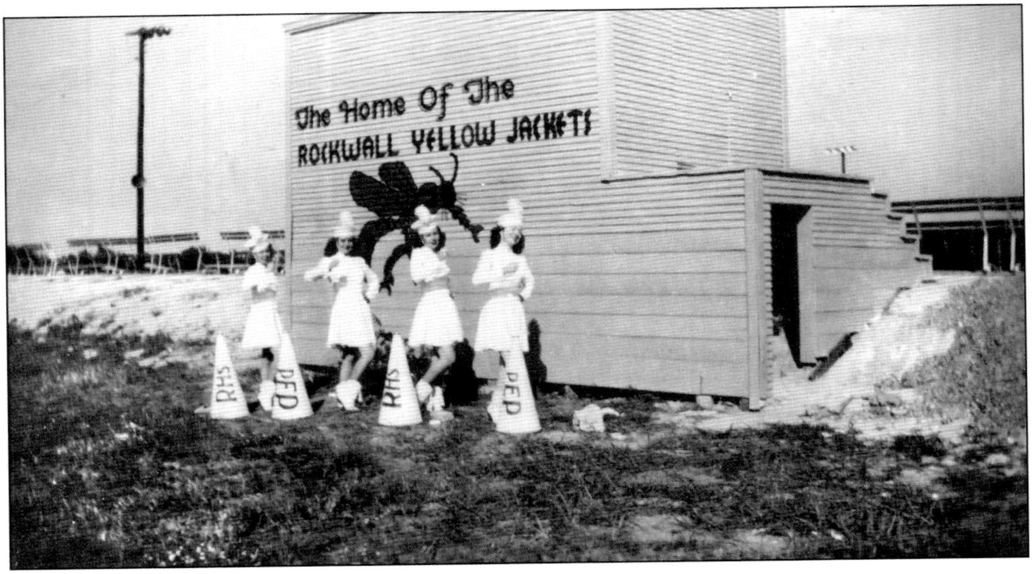

The Rockwall High School class of 1948 had four cheerleaders who rooted their football team to victory. Pictured above are, from left to right, Nancy Maynard Holt, Mary Sue Bryan, Anna Wade McCoulskey, and Sammie Jean Wylie. This cheer squad was as significant for its fashion firsts as it was for its finesse on the field—it was the first squad allowed to wear skirts with hemlines above the knees. Below, a young Paulette Lofland was the cheerleader mascot for the 1947–1948 school year. She accompanied the regular cheerleaders to the games, wore a matching uniform, and helped cheer on the sidelines.

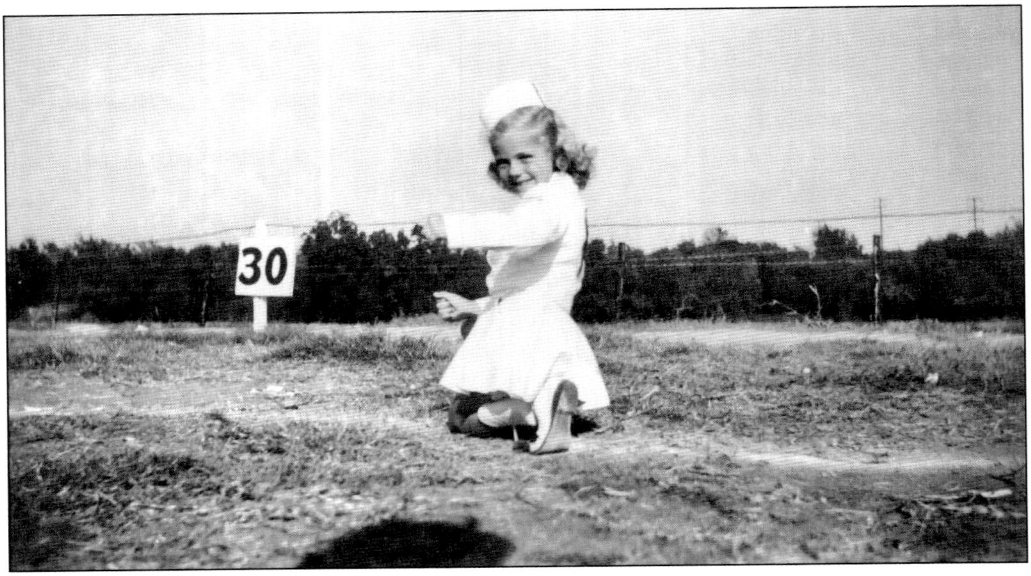

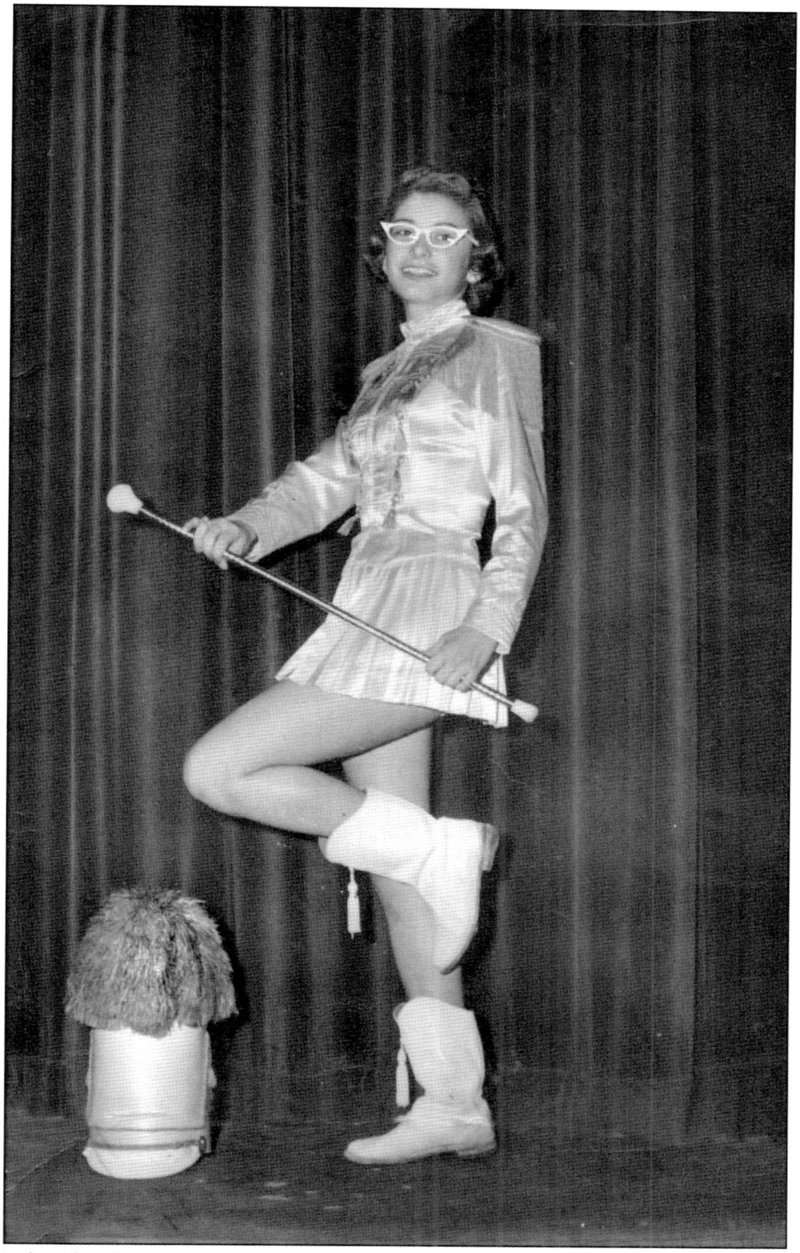

Rockwall High School majorette Mary Sue Reinhardt shows support for the Fighting Yellowjackets. From the 1920s through much of the 1940s, a simple football field was located by the old Rockwall High School near downtown off of Clark Street. Wooden bleachers lined the field, and the biggest rivalry was when Rockwall played neighboring Royse City. During the 1940s, then-superintendent J. A. Wilkerson, who also served as a math teacher and coach during his tenure, guided the construction of a new field with tiered seating and a field house. Thirty years later, when Rockwall ISD constructed a new stadium on Townsend Road, it was named after Wilkerson and Harvey Sanders, an avid fan, volunteer coach, and local restaurant owner who often let the football players eat at his sandwich shop—regardless of whether or not they could pay.

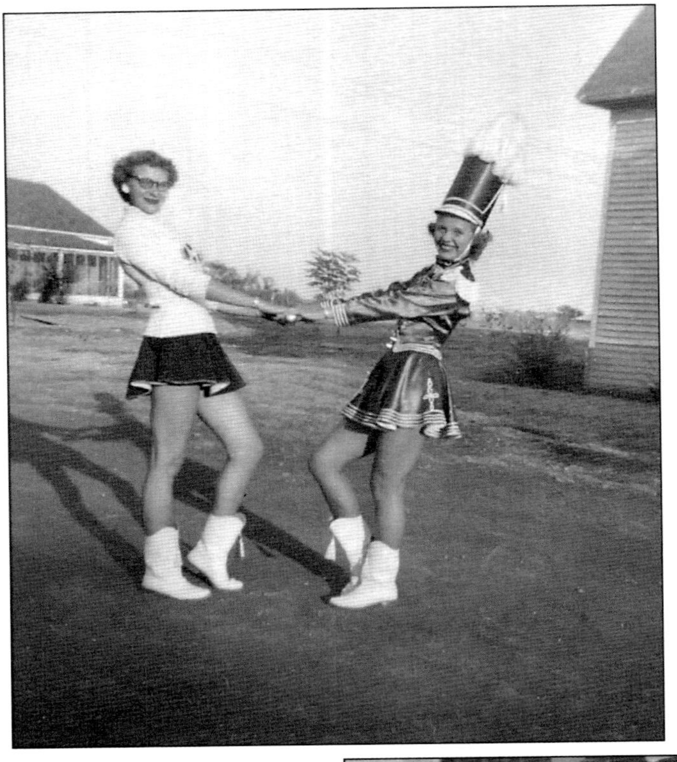

At left, Heath natives Patsy and Tommie Hall show their Rockwall High School team spirit in 1952. Patsy was a cheerleader, while younger sister Tommie served as a majorette. Their mother hand-sewed the sequins on her costumes. Both girls had various claims to fame: Patsy played on the RHS girls' basketball team and was valedictorian of her graduating class; Tommie was voted the Future Farmers of America Sweetheart for the school, the surrounding FFA district, and the regional FFA Area Five. In 1978, by then a published poet and a career English teacher, Patsy was appointed poet laureate of Texas by the state legislature. Below are Rockwall High School bobby-soxers, a typical 1950s scene around Rockwall High School.

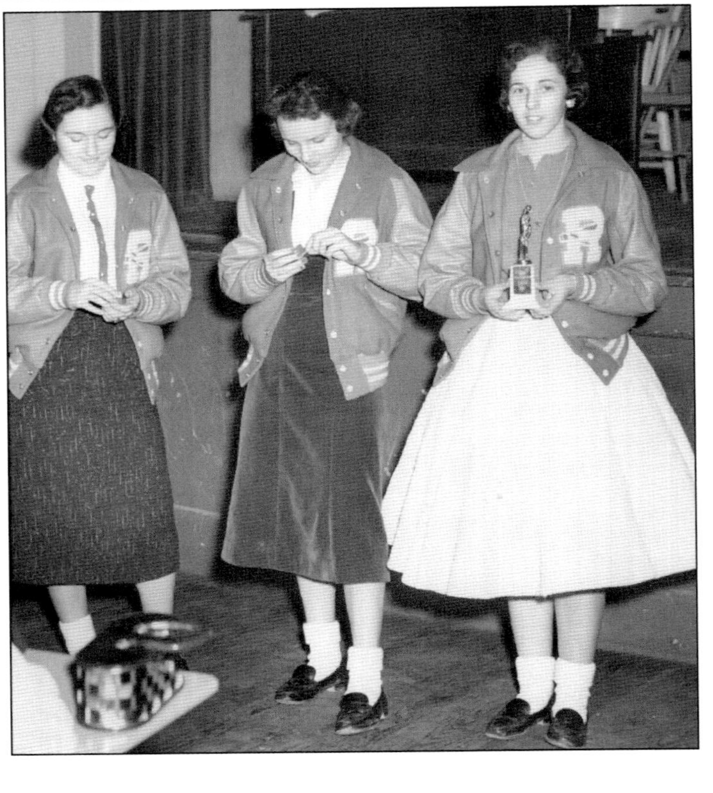

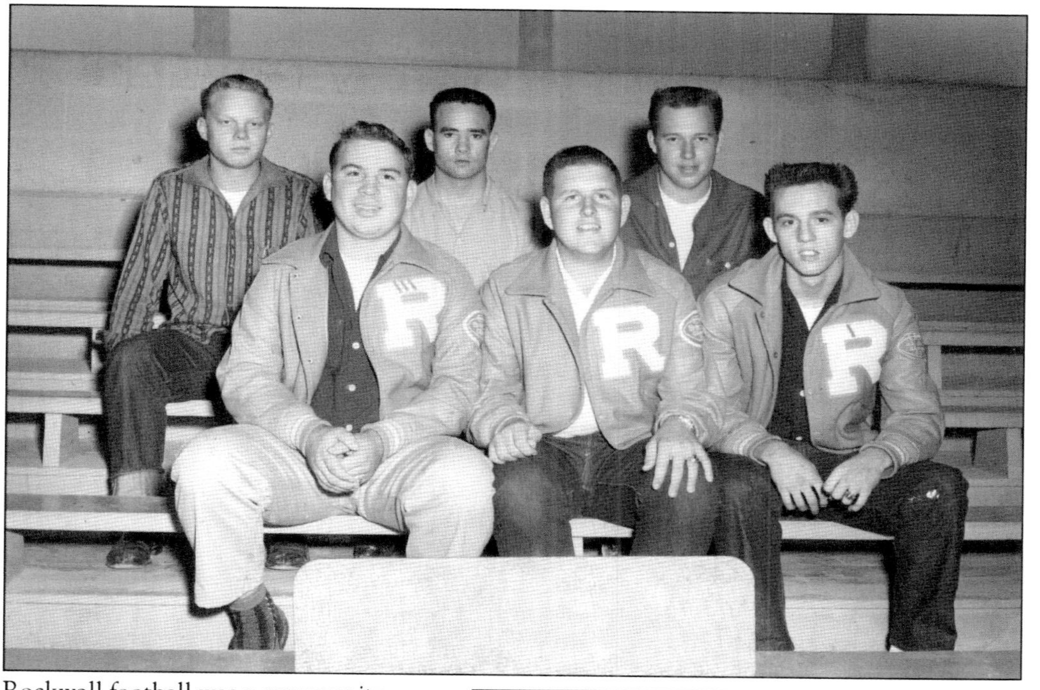

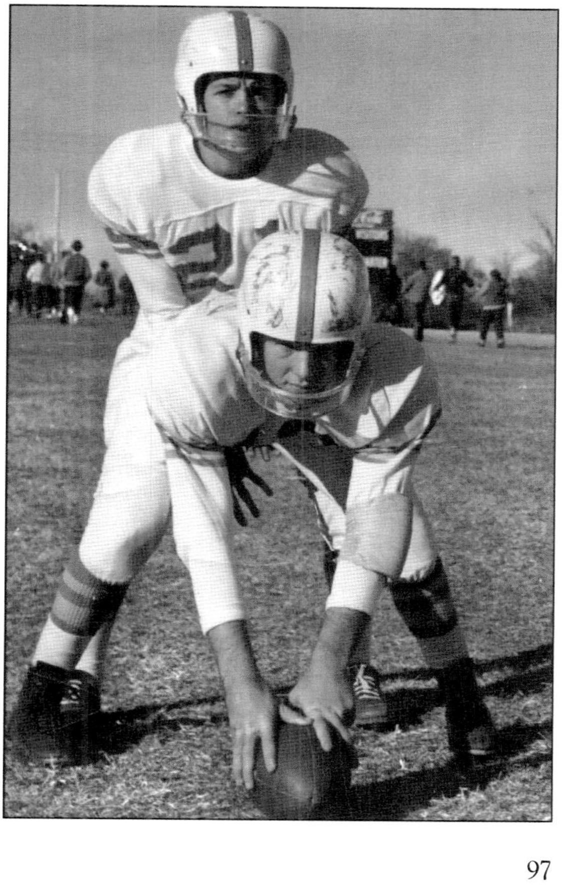

Rockwall football was a community event in the 1950s. Pep rallies were held on the town square, and it often seemed as if the entire population would show up to root for a Yellowjacket victory. Seated in the school gym are, from left to right, (first row) Jimmy Lofland, Harold Crawford, and Jerry Anderson; (second row) Lem Nichols, Don Cornelius, and Max Raney. At right, Mike Reinhardt is about to take the snap for the Rockwall Yellowjackets.

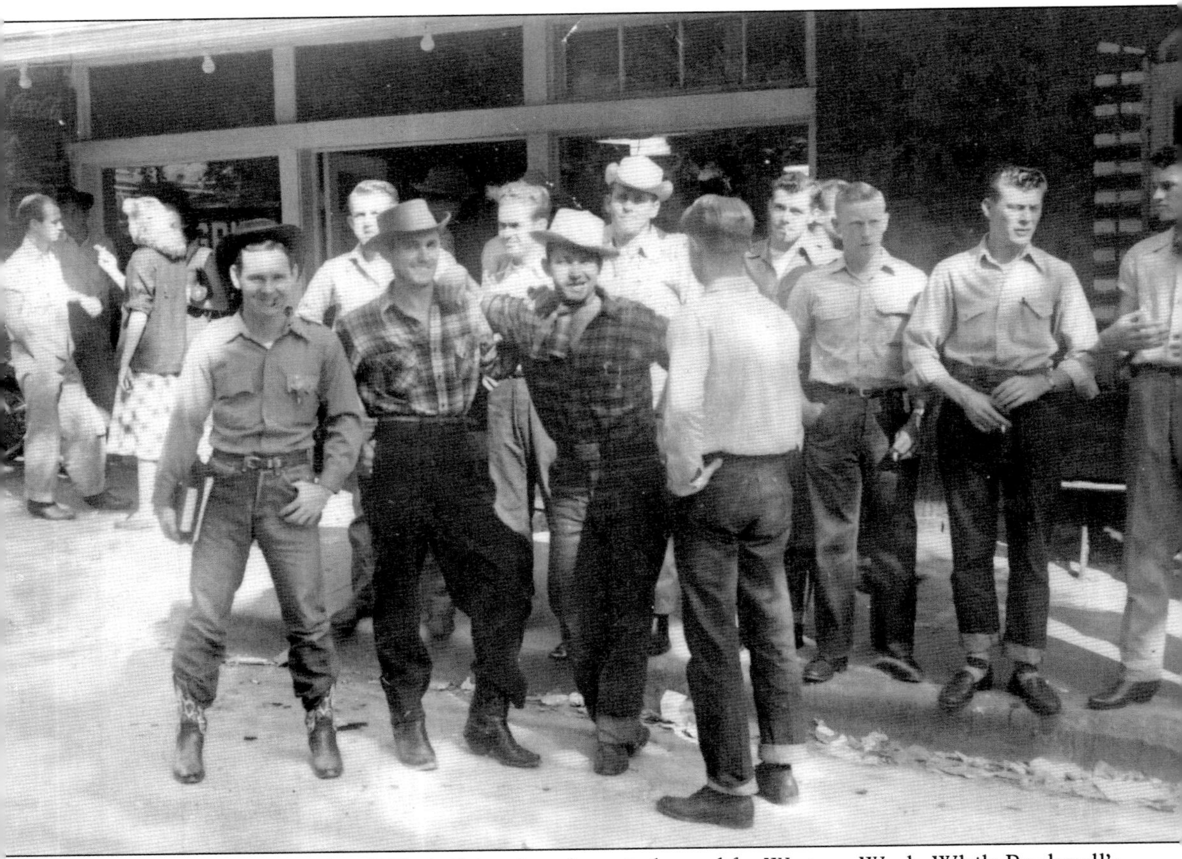

A group of 1950s Rockwall High School students is dressed for Western Week. While Rockwall's Wild West days were long gone, the 1950s revived a fascination with Western culture that permeated the entire nation and made a lasting impact on the youth of the day. During this decade, both the big and small screens were filled with cowboys. By this time, television was a household product, and all ages were watching shows featuring family-friendly stars such as Roy Rogers and Hopalong Cassidy. By the end of the decade, shows such as *Wagon Train* and *Have Gun Will Travel* had made their debuts. John Wayne, Audie Murphy, and Randolph Scott rode roughshod across the big screen. The cowboy image fit perfectly into a 1950s culture based on the heroism of the postwar male. In small towns like Rockwall, the cowboy was celebrated and revered. (Courtesy of James and Pat Flores.)

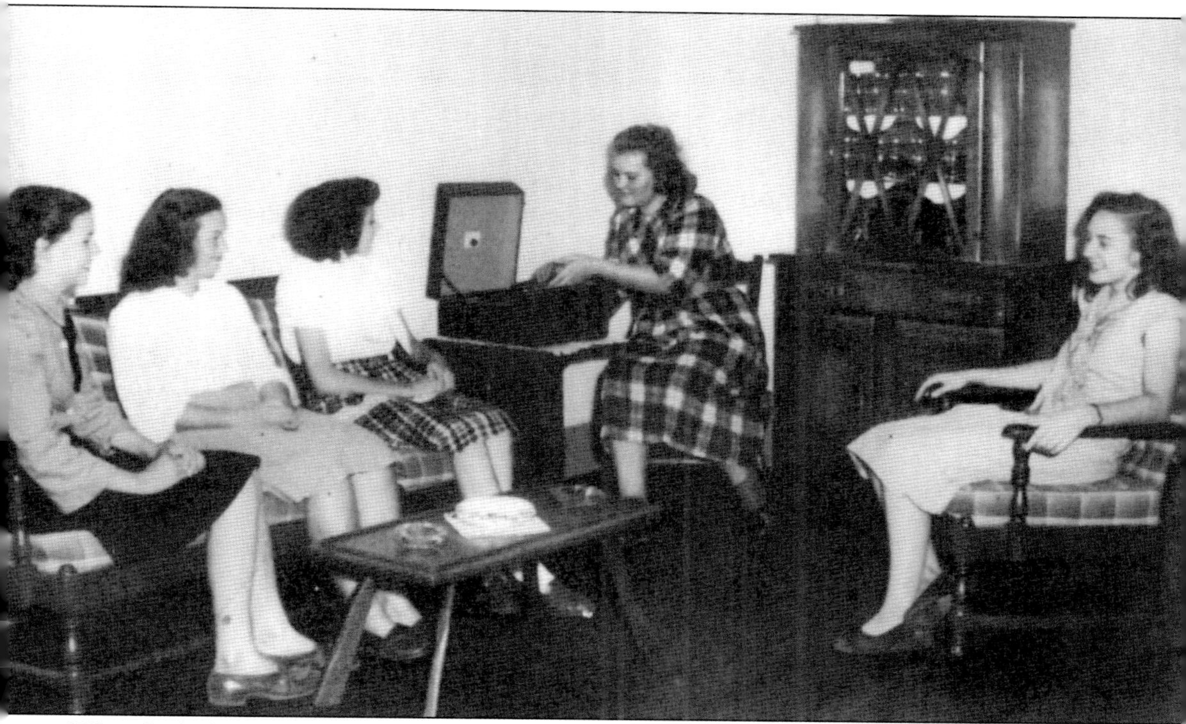

When looked at through a historical lens, the origins of home economics courses actually have their roots in a progressive academic effort in the late 19th and early 20th centuries aimed at bringing science to the farm and home through the areas of nutrition and child development. As the decades progressed, home economics contributed to the development of such fields as fiber science and consumer economics. While the local course offerings certainly adhered to the larger, global goal of improved rural and urban living, the average home economics student at Rockwall High School in the 1940s and 1950s most likely saw his or her class curriculum as simply covering the basics of managing a household—cooking, sewing, entertaining, and etiquette. Above, students in the living room of the home economics lab at Rockwall High School have a lesson on entertaining and etiquette. This photograph was published in the 1948 yearbook.

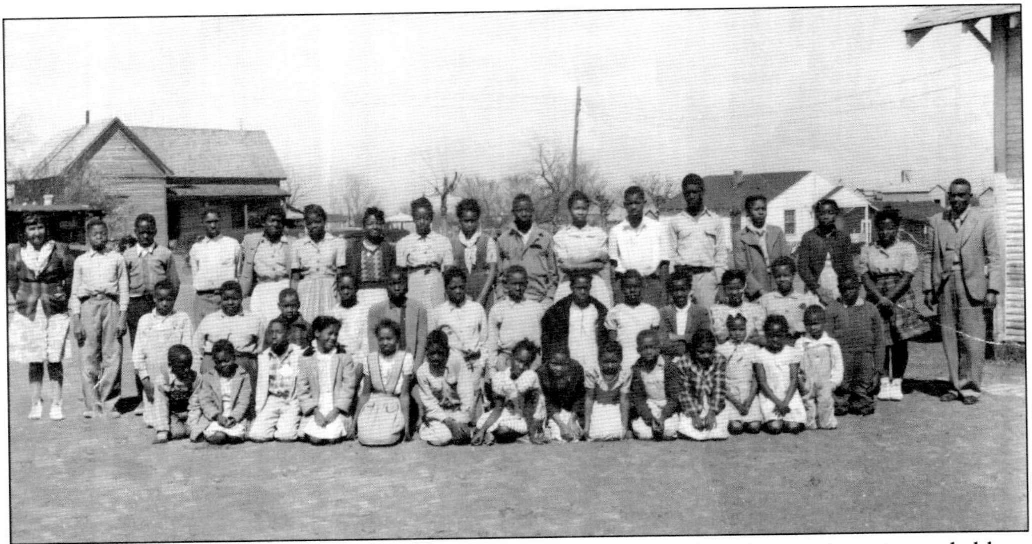

As early as 1880, Rockwall offered educational opportunities for African American children in segregated settings, but often the school terms were shorter than those available for white students and the grades offered were not as advanced. Prior to 1951, Rockwall's African American students had no opportunity for a high school diploma without leaving the county. But in 1951, the Rockwall High School for Negroes graduated its first class with three members. In 1956, the Bourn Avenue School was completed, a new nine-classroom school building built especially for Rockwall's African American student population. Above, Rockwall's African American students were segregated in the 1940s. Below is the 1958 eighth-grade class of the Bourn Avenue School, with principal Dorris Jones seated at far left in the first row.

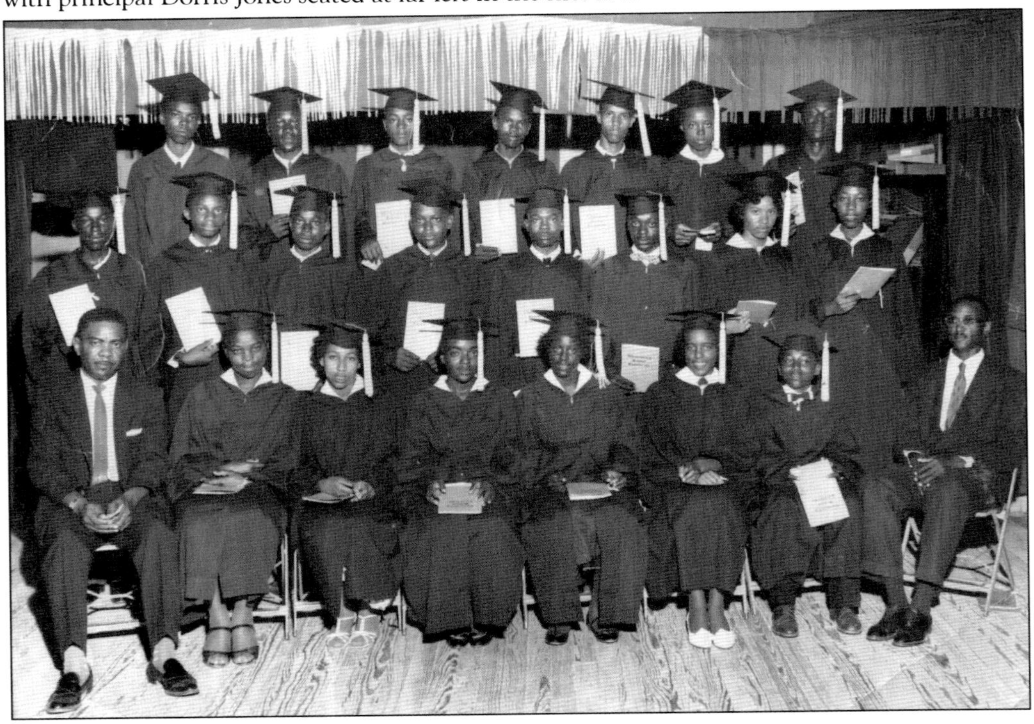

The week of June 8–13, 1954, was Rockwall's Centennial Celebration, which included a parade, a pageant, numerous contests, and the crowning of a queen. Mary Sue Reinhardt was named Centennial Queen, and a parade was supposed to officially kick off the celebration. However, the parade was slightly delayed when the chairman of the festivities, local physician Dr. Sherman Sparks, was called to the house of Mrs. Vernon Stanley, who was in the midst of delivering a baby girl, Lisa Kay. Dr. Sparks made it back, and the parade continued as planned. At right, Annie Anderson Lofland gets ready to ride sidesaddle in the parade.

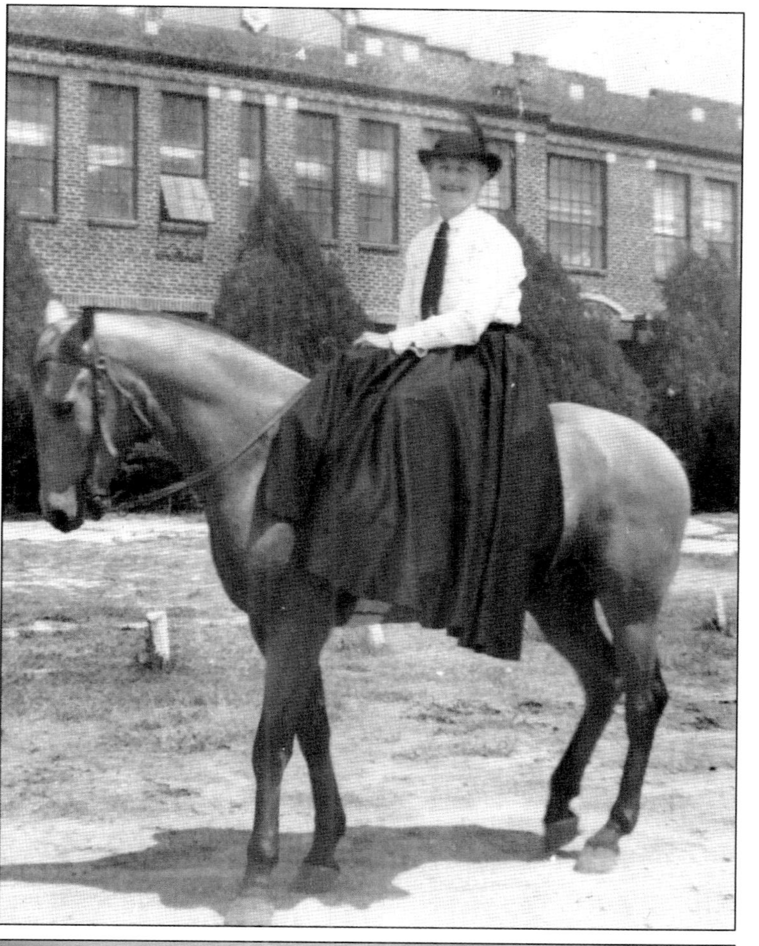

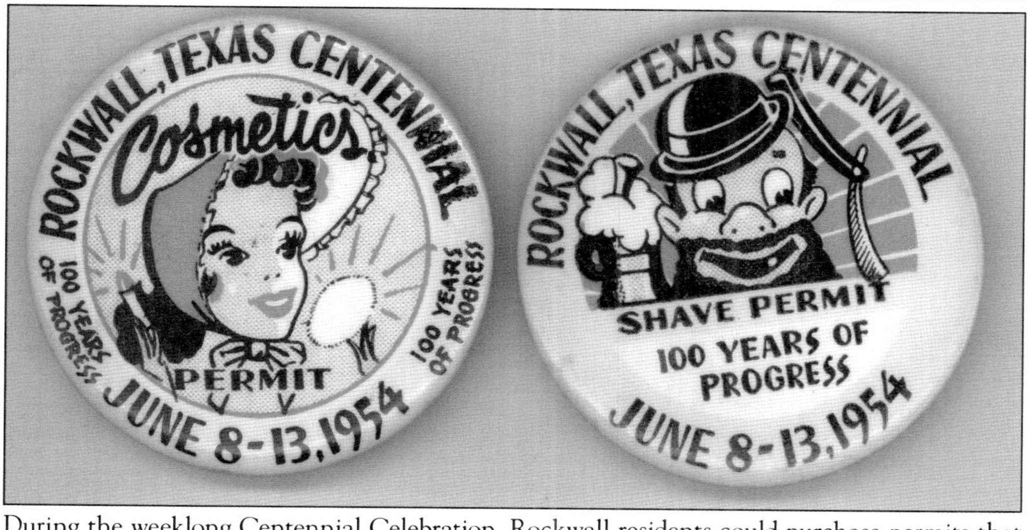

During the weeklong Centennial Celebration, Rockwall residents could purchase permits that allowed them to shave and wear makeup. (Courtesy of James and Pat Flores.)

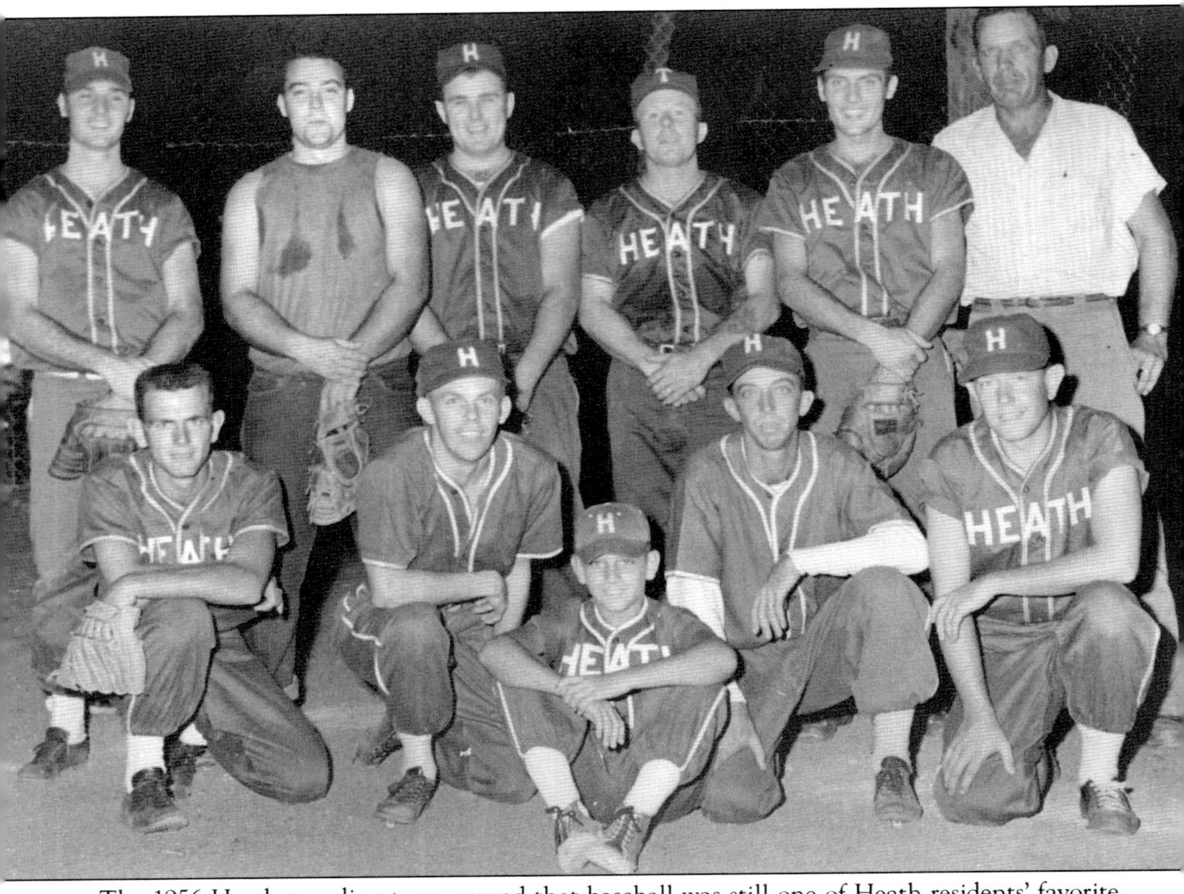

The 1956 Heath traveling team proved that baseball was still one of Heath residents' favorite pastimes. The team, made up of local men, included, from left to right, (first row) A. R. Seabolt, Joe Frank Isbell, mascot and batboy Kenny Terry, Roy Gene Mitchell, and Harold Evans; (second row) Charles Terry, Lloyd Oakley, James Terry, Grady Isbell Jr., Huey Smirl, and coach Jake Hall. The baseball field, which was right in the middle of "downtown Heath," had been a local gathering place for decades as dedicated fans came out to watch the hometown boys play nearby rivals Forney, Rockwall, and Fate. In those days, the traveling teams were often family affairs, and it was not unusual for brothers, cousins, and in-laws to all play together. The current coach, Jake Hall, had taken his own turn on the field a number of years earlier when he played third base for Heath. His brother Curtis played catcher, and brother Clifford pitched.

In the 1940s, the Soil Conservation Service was brought in to consult with Rockwall's civic leaders. By the 1950s, flood detention dams had been put in place on Camp, Squabble, Long Branch, and Buffalo Creeks, resulting in small man-made lakes. Chamber of commerce records indicate that, prior to the construction of Lake Ray Hubbard, there were 10 of these lakes along tributaries of the East Fork of the Trinity River—all providing excellent fishing. This is the catch of the day.

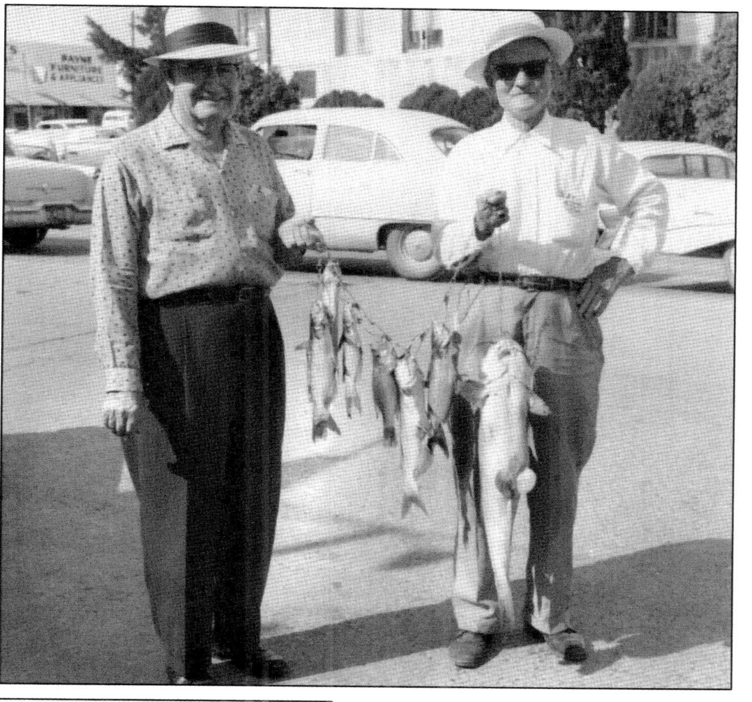

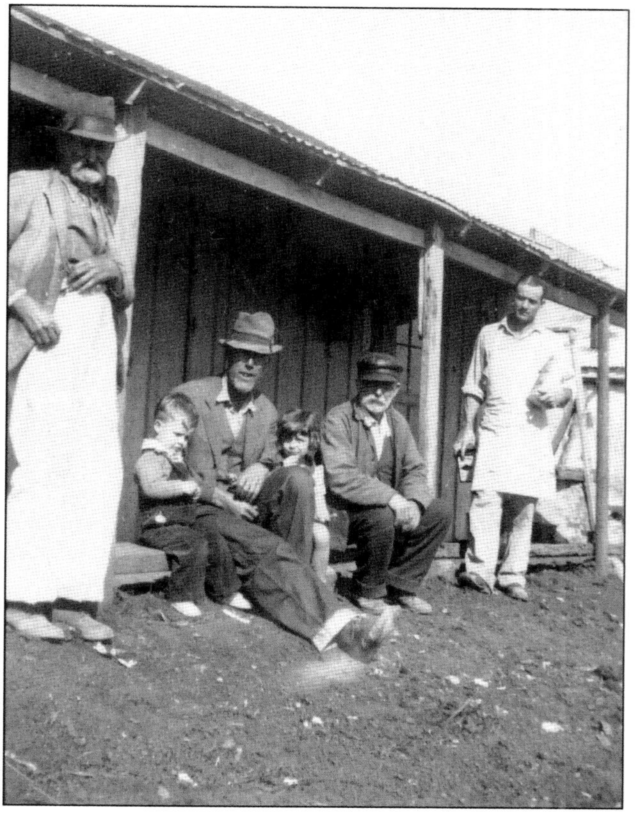

The Zollner Ranch was established in Rockwall County in 1876 and soon became a safe haven for transient men looking for an opportunity to work. Through the years, hundreds of homeless men rode the rails to Rockwall looking for the "Hobo Ranch" that offered an honest day's labor, a hot meal, and a warm bed. During its heyday, the Zollner Ranch had many buildings, including a sleeping dorm, a dining room that would seat 200, a chapel, and a domino hall. Pictured in front of the domino hall are, from left to right, Dad Reeves, Dickie Fowlkes, John Neville, Maxine Zollner, Brocky Bennett, and Edd Parsons. Transient men provided farm labor into the 1970s.

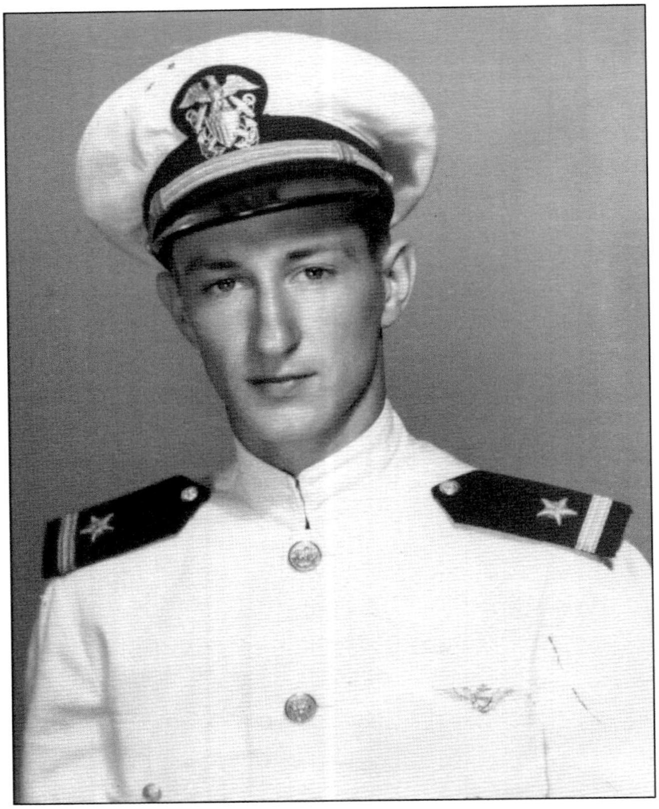

Ralph M. Hall, a native of Fate, has represented Rockwall County at the local, state, and national levels of government. He has served as county judge for Rockwall County and as a representative in the Texas Senate. He was first elected to the U.S. House of Representatives in 1980 and has been reelected to each succeeding Congress. Prior to his political service, Hall served in the U.S. Navy as a lieutenant (senior grade) aircraft carrier pilot from 1942 to 1945 (left). He is also shown below during his service to the Texas Senate with then-governor John Connally and local Rockwall residents, from left to right, Dianne Myers, Sue Davis, Pamela Hargrove, and Louise Hargrove.

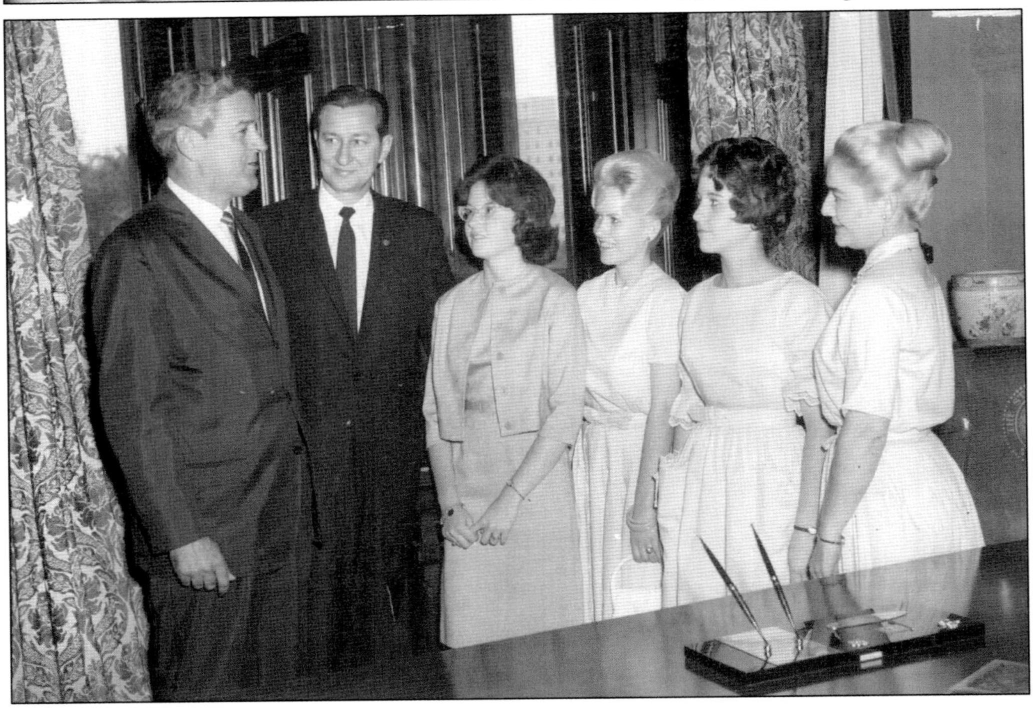

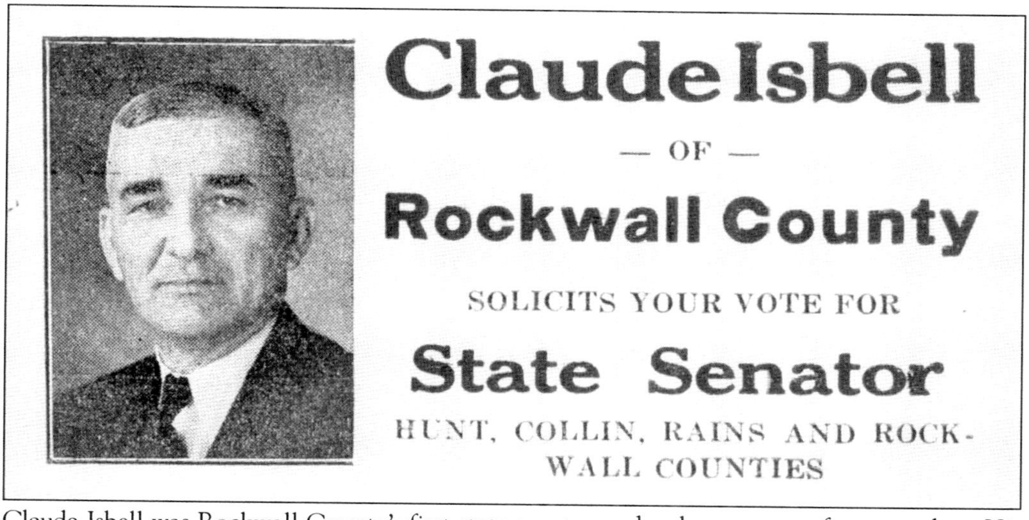

Claude Isbell was Rockwall County's first state senator and only secretary of state to date. His mother died when he was young, and he was raised by his grandmother, Mary Emma Isbell, who lived in Heath. He served as Rockwall County judge from 1927 to 1935. In 1935, he was elected to the Texas Senate. In early 1944, Gov. Coke R. Stevenson appointed him secretary of state, an office he held until 1947.

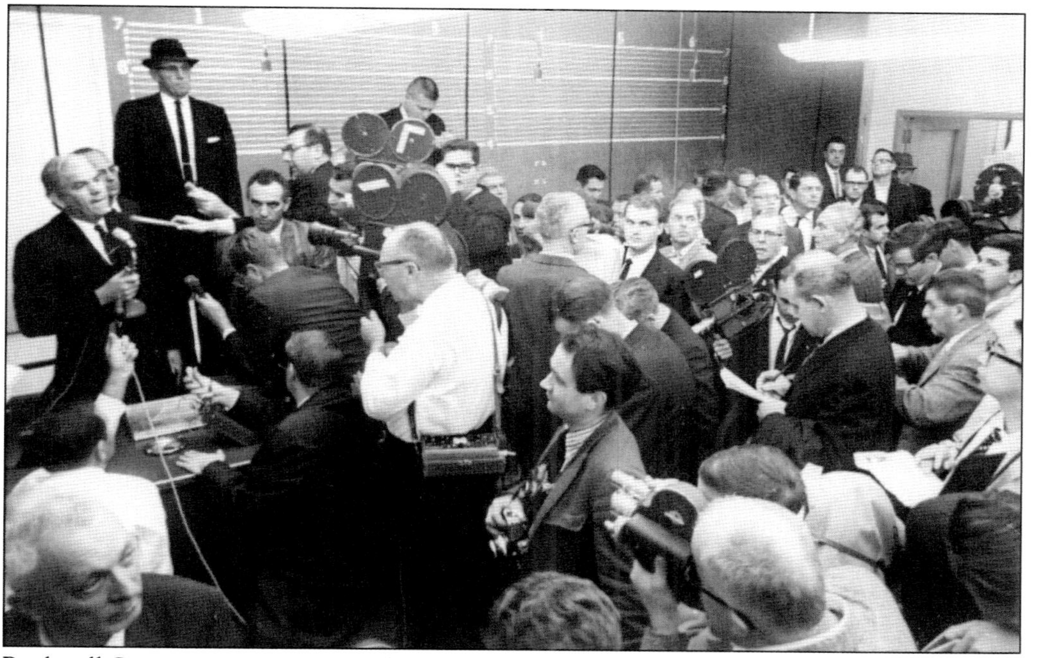

Rockwall County native Henry Wade was one of 11 children born to Henry M. and Lula Michie Wade. He was valedictorian of his senior class at Rockwall High School in 1933. He attended the University of Texas and UT Law School, and served as Rockwall County attorney before being accepted as a special agent by the FBI in 1939. After serving in World War II, he joined the Dallas County District Attorney's Office, and in 1950, he was elected criminal district attorney of Dallas County, a post he held for more than 36 years. Above, Dallas district attorney Henry Wade conducts a press conference in 1963 following the Kennedy assassination.

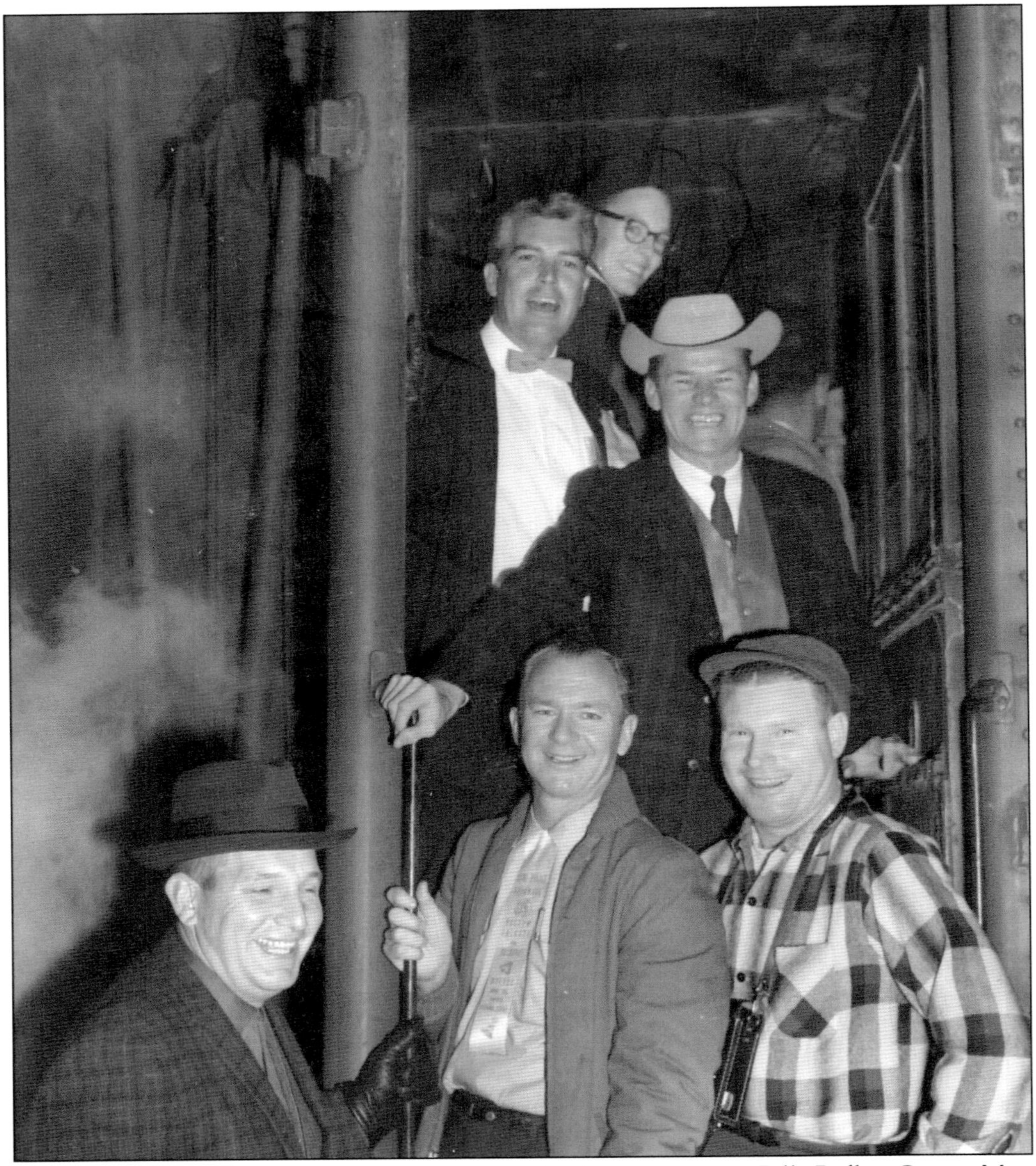

Rockwall residents (from bottom to top) Harry Knight, James Mayo, Billy Ridley, George May, Billy Peoples, and unidentified board the train to Vernon on Saturday, December 14, 1963, to watch the Rockwall Yellowjackets play the semifinal game against Dalhart on the road to the AA State Football Championship. The Jackets won 35-7 and earned a spot in the championship game against John Foster Dulles. Just four days before Christmas, in freezing rain, the Jackets took to a wet and soggy field at Baylor Stadium. The game remained scoreless until late in the third quarter, when Dulles scored but missed the extra point. Late in the fourth quarter, the score was 6-0 and many Rockwall fans had already left. With a fourth and five situation, and Rockwall in its own territory, there was less than a minute to play. Quarterback Kenny Terry threw down the field to Marc Noel, who miraculously caught the ball, avoided numerous tackles, and got in the end zone to secure a tie for Rockwall. Jackie Anderson kicked the extra point. With the final score Rockwall 7 to Dulles 6, the Yellowjackets became the 1963 AA State Champions.

Four

Construction of Lake Ray Hubbard and the Economic Shift to Suburbia

1965 to Present

By the mid-1960s, agriculture had decreased significantly as an occupation in Rockwall County. In fact, there were less than 300 farms in operation. Yet a chamber of commerce publication stated, "Industry and agriculture are mutually supporting in this community with a number of people making homes here and commuting to the industrial area west of the county. The population of the city has doubled within the past ten years and new residents are steadily making homes here."

This carefully worded verbiage shows that community leaders were walking a fine line between a rich agrarian heritage and an economic future that would be dependent on residential commuters. In fact, it was even more complex than that—one of the things that made Rockwall so appealing to those looking to move away from the density of the larger "industrial area west of the county" (Dallas and Garland) was the rural, small-town atmosphere Rockwall offered. The open farmland and grazing cattle offered a bucolic existence that appealed to the city dwellers and called them eastward. The construction of Lake Ray Hubbard in the late 1960s figuratively opened the floodgates, and city and county officials were faced with a dilemma that continues decades later: How do you effectively manage growth and still maintain the small-town atmosphere that drew people to your community in the first place?

As Rockwall County completes the shift from an agrarian-based economy to a bedroom community, issues of historic preservation, open space and parkland development, traffic control, and old versus new are all in the forefront. As people drive through present-day Rockwall County, they will still see a few cattle and horses, old red barns, and a number of historic structures that help maintain Rockwall's small-town feel. But with issues of annexation, road expansion, massive commercial development, and eminent domain, how can city and county official ensure they can preserve the history of the community for future generations? It is a daunting task.

The mid-1960s chamber publication stated, "The leadership of the community is in the hands of a progressive group of citizens constantly striving to improve the city and planning for the future." It is a statement that each succeeding group of officials hopes can be written about them.

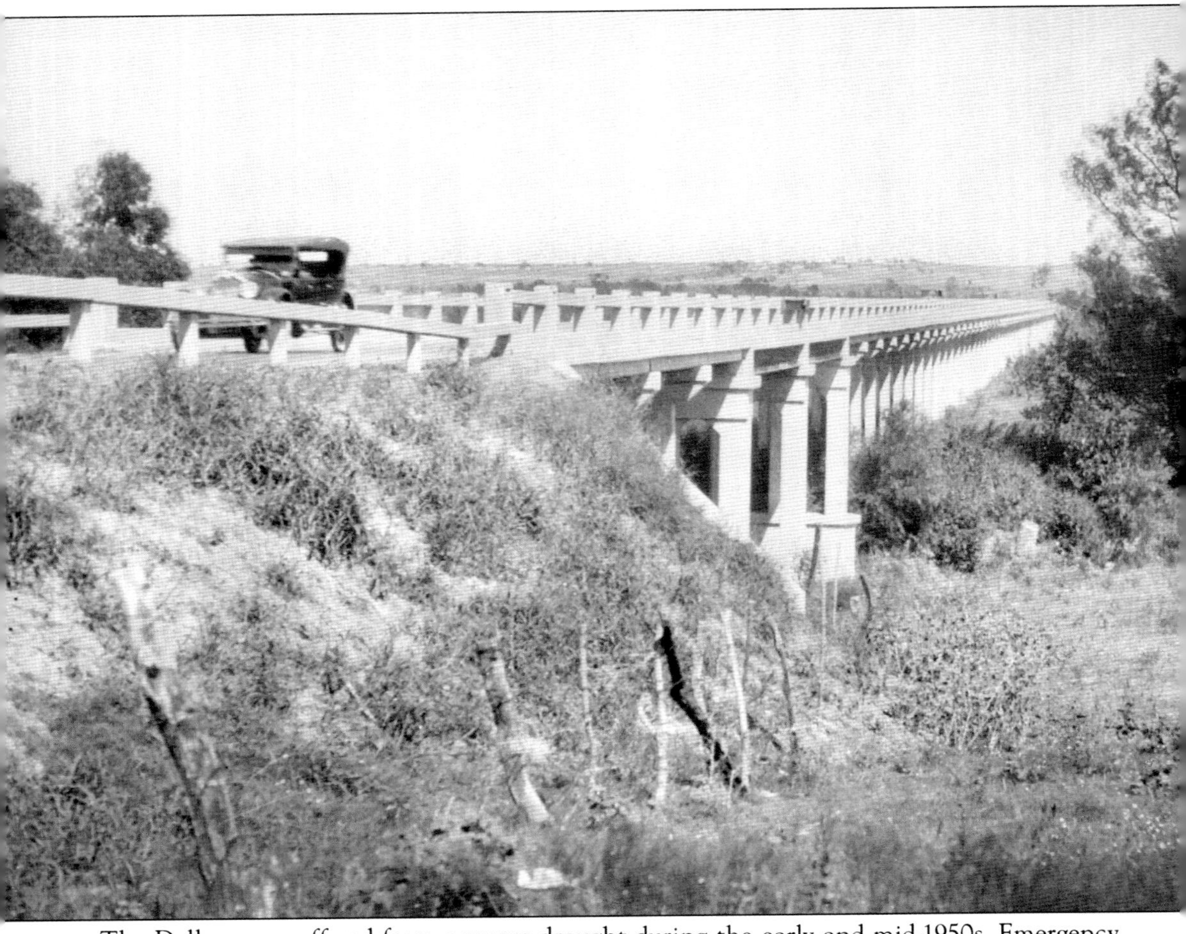

The Dallas area suffered from a severe drought during the early and mid-1950s. Emergency pipelines were installed, bringing water to Dallas from the Red River. When the drought ended, Dallas mayor Bob Thornton led efforts to build a reservoir using the lands of the East Fork of the Trinity River so Dallas residents would never run out of water again. Some of Rockwall's richest farmland was in this bottomland, and many area residents were vehemently opposed to the "Big City" taking their property. Dallas's acquisition of the land resulted in messy legal proceedings. Entire farms had to be displaced, roads were relocated, and even one discovered outcropping of the rock wall is now forever underwater. This photograph shows the bottomland of the East Fork of the Trinity River prior to the building of Lake Ray Hubbard. Pictured is the bridge looking east toward Rockwall. Originally built by Rockwall County in 1920–1921, this bridge was the first paved concrete road in the county. It was part of the famous Bankhead Highway (U.S. 67).

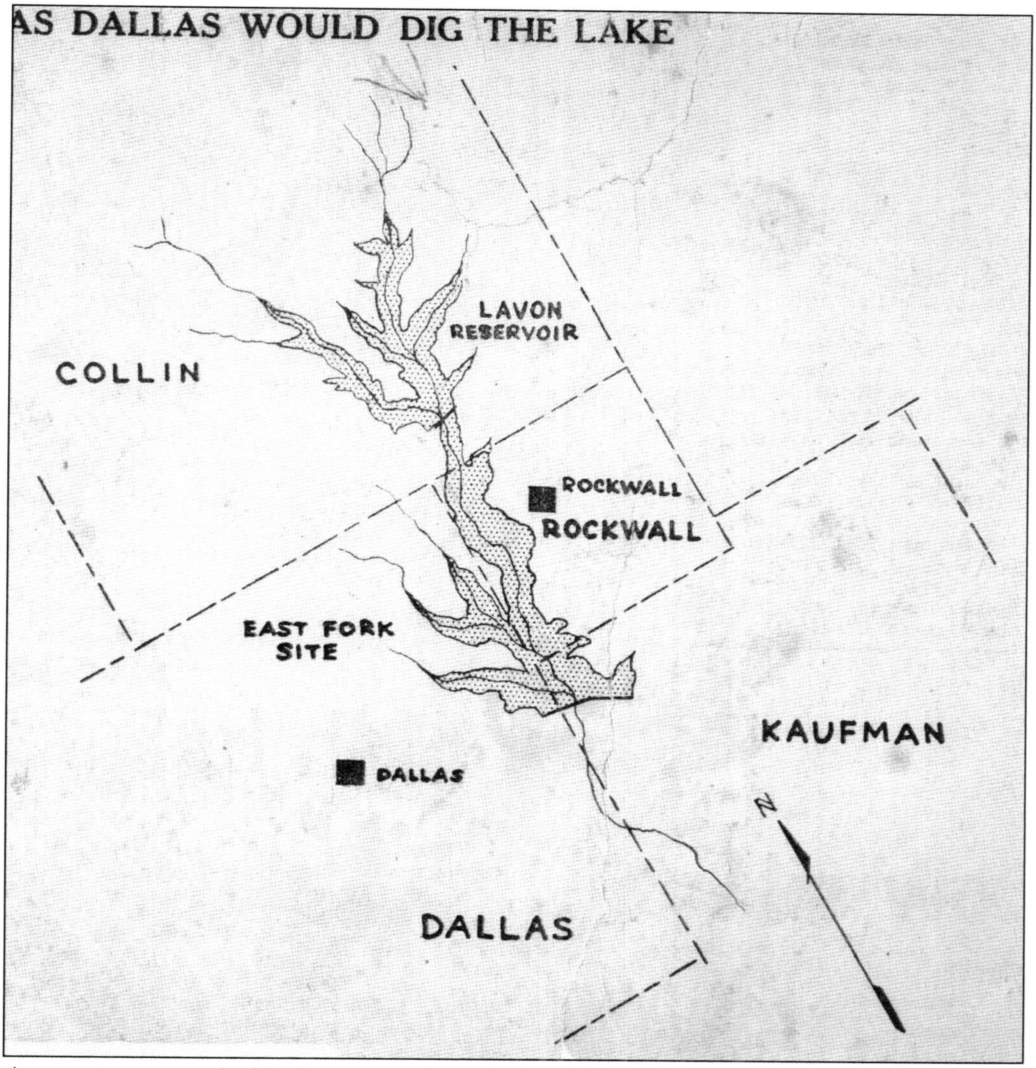

Attempting to ease bad feelings over taking the land for the lake, Mayor Thornton held public meetings in the Rockwall County Courthouse and initially offered to name the lake after Rockwall. Mayor Thornton was not pleased with the treatment he and his wife received from a number of local citizens, so he withdrew his offer, and the lake was called Forney Reservoir. Later it was named Lake Ray Hubbard after the man who served as president of the Dallas Parks and Recreation Board from 1943 until 1972. The project took 29,000 acres of land in Dallas, Collin, Kaufman, and Rockwall Counties. The lake measures 22,745 surface acres and has a maximum depth of 40 feet. The lake was impounded in 1968, but the gates were not closed until 1970 in order to allow for road relocations and some tree removal. Above, a clipping from the *Rockwall Success* newspaper shows local residents the proposed location of the lake.

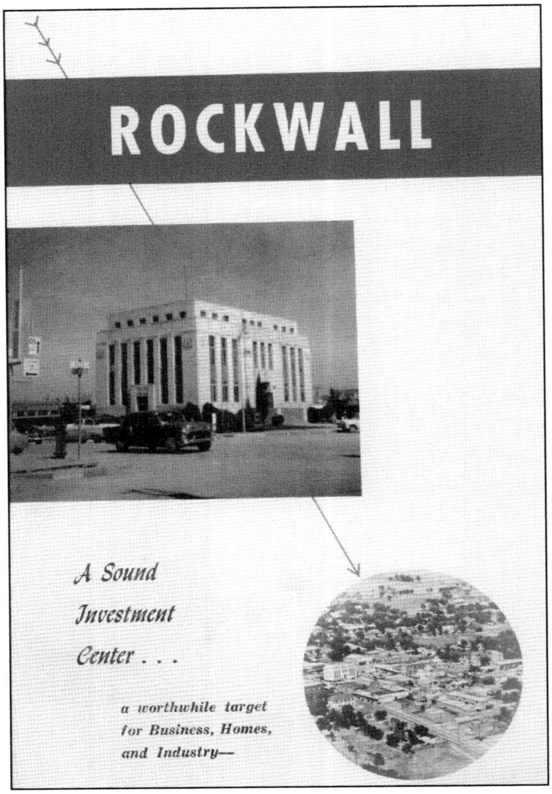

Although new residents were finding their way to Rockwall, the community was still considered small in the 1960s. To encourage growth, the chamber of commerce began to market Rockwall as "A Sound Investment Center." The marketing materials touted the area's new modern swimming pool, the expanding building program of the Rockwall Independent School District, a growing industrial business, and new homes and amenities such as a "water and sewer system . . . that will adequately serve five times [the city's] population." At left, this chamber publication advertised Rockwall's ability to provide "modern roads and living conveniences" while still maintaining a small-town rural atmosphere for families. Below is a map (before Lake Ray Hubbard) from the chamber of commerce marketing booklet.

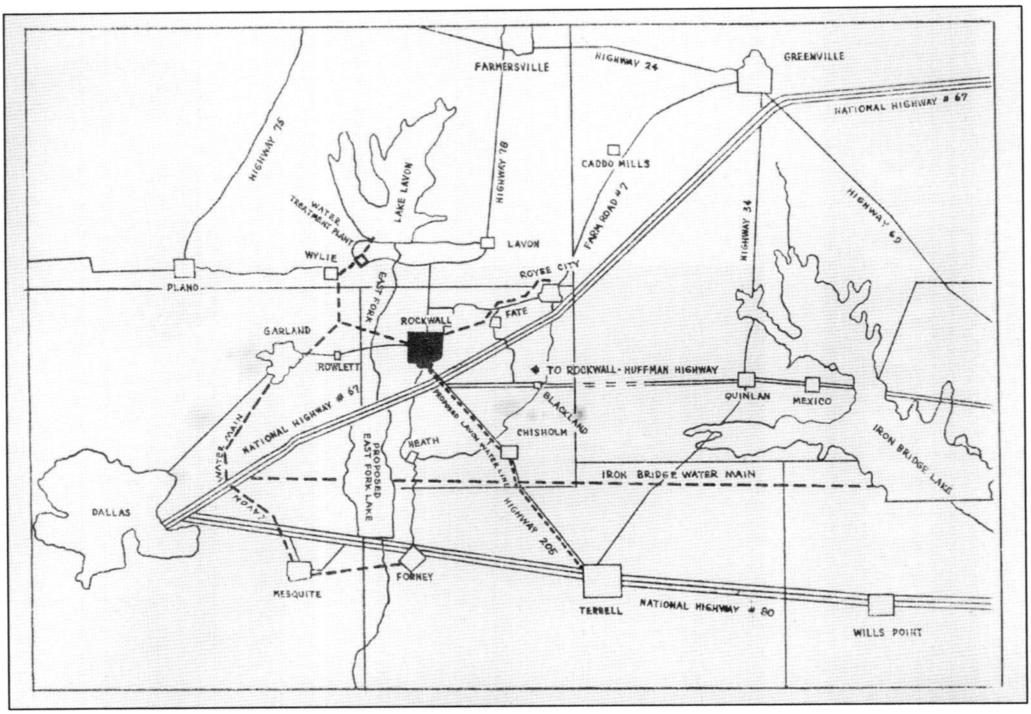

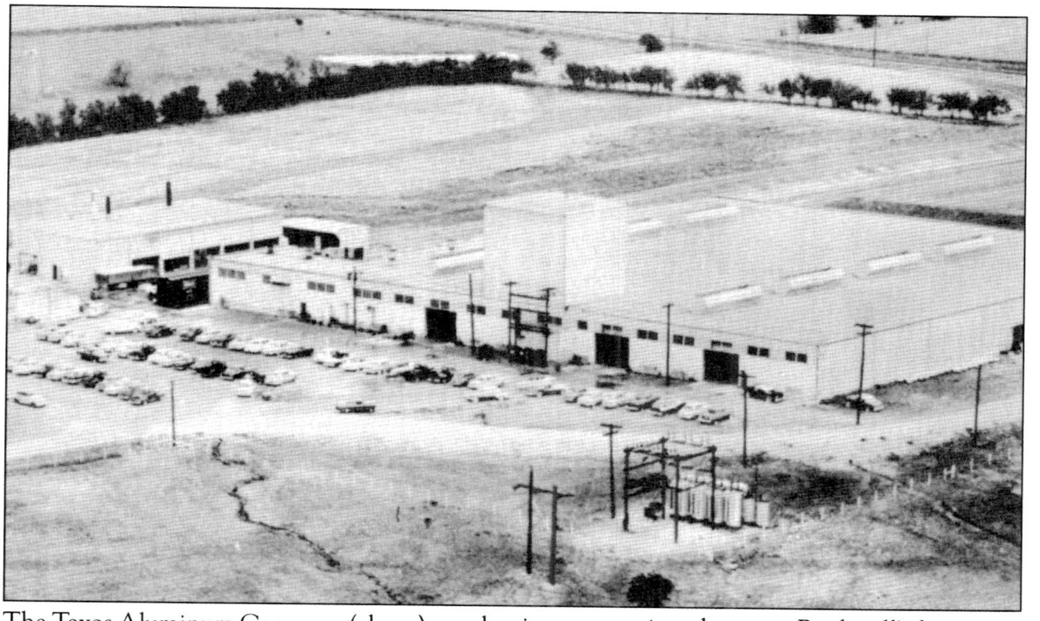

The Texas Aluminum Company (above), an aluminum extrusion plant, was Rockwall's first major manufacturing company. Although Rockwall had been home to several small-scale manufacturing businesses, Texas Aluminum was by far the largest at that time, employing several hundred workers. Richard ("Dick") Pickens had worked for both Alcoa and Reynolds metals before moving his family to Rockwall in 1953. With two partners, he founded the Texas Aluminum Company and operated the facility until 1973.

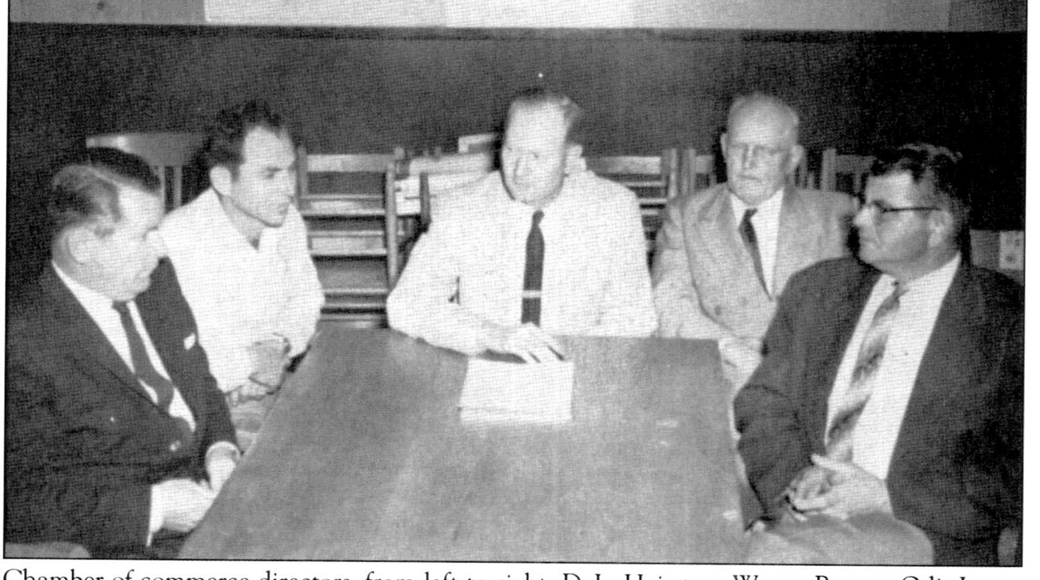

Chamber of commerce directors, from left to right, D. L. Hairston, Wayne Rogers, Odis Lowe, Dr. James L. Glenn, and Raymond Cameron touted Rockwall's finest qualities. Promotional material about the area stated, "Rockwall is well organized with a progressive City Council planning and working toward the future of the city. The Chamber of Commerce provides a coordinated program for the area in all phases of community development."

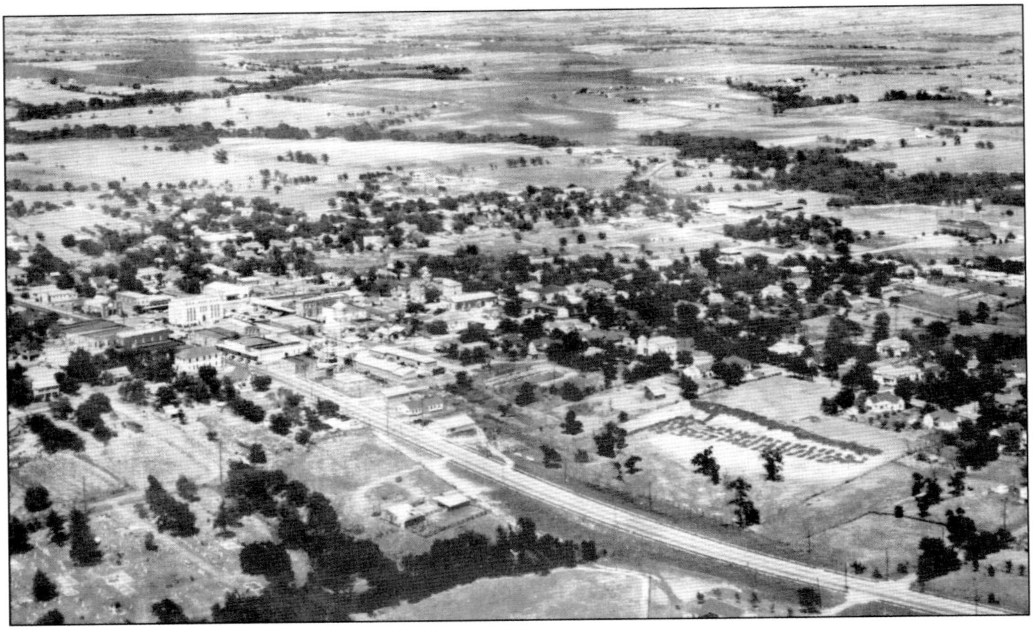

Here are two aerial views of downtown Rockwall. Above, surrounding the courthouse square, old-time Rockwall residents will be able to identify the First Presbyterian Church, the Stephenson Hotel, the old water tower, and other structures no longer present. Note the vast amount of open farmland surrounding the city, particularly leading into the town square on what is now Goliad Street (Sate Highway 205). Today a number of businesses as well as Rockwall's city hall occupy these parcels of land. Below, approximately 25 years later, even though some of the surrounding buildings had changed, the courthouse still served as the centerpiece of the town square.

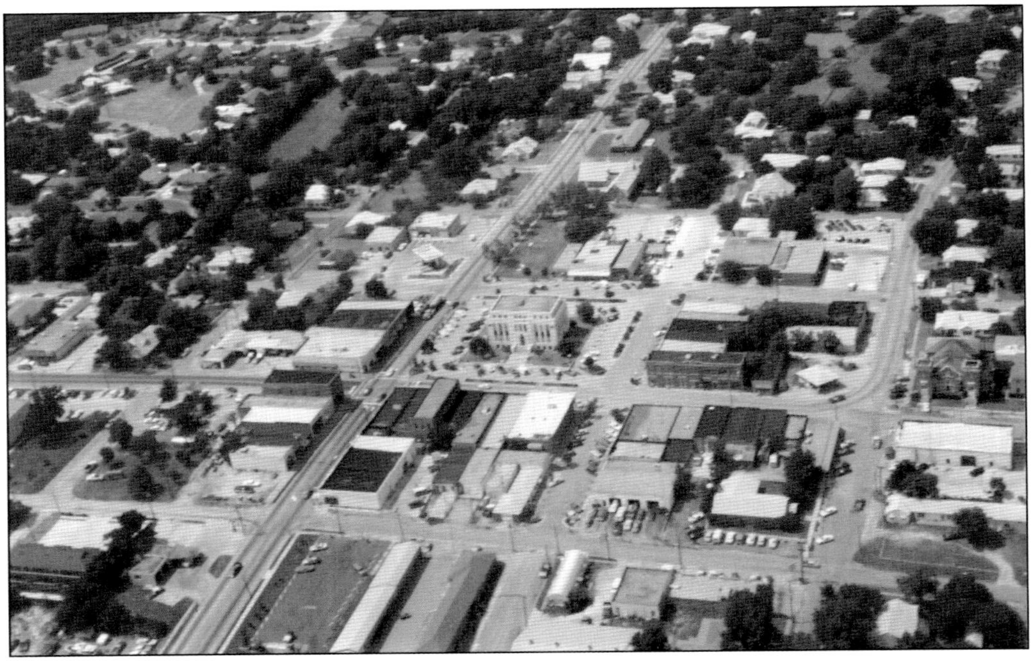

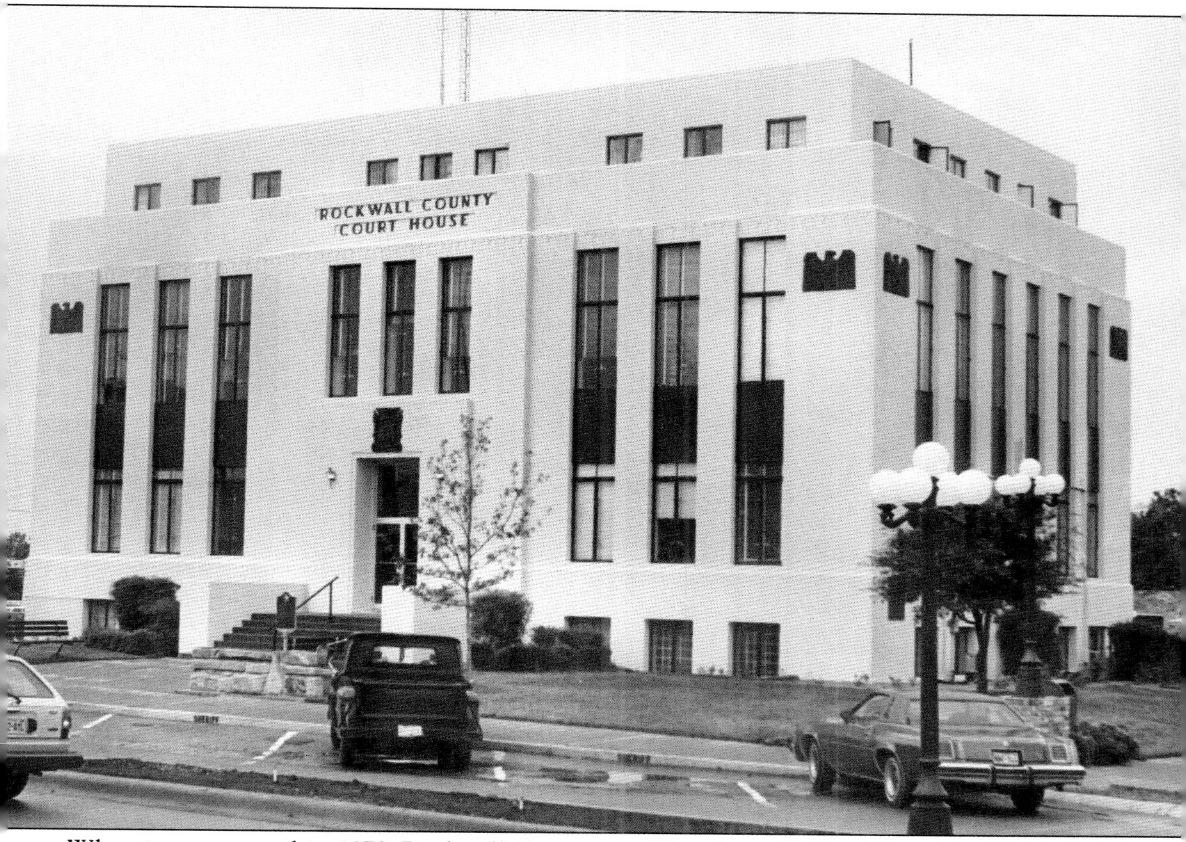

When it was created in 1873, Rockwall County was Texas's smallest county, measuring just 149 square miles. Today's statistics for the county include 129 square miles of land and 20 square miles of water. Records from the U.S. Census show that in 1900 the county population was 8,531. A decline in farming as an occupation and an increase in industrial jobs in Dallas and Garland caused the population to decrease to 6,156 by 1950. The somewhat difficult birth of Lake Ray Hubbard resulted in the creation of a picturesque lakeside community and started a resurgence in population that has yet to wane. Between 1970 and 1980, the population of Rockwall County increased from 7,046 to 14,528, a 106.2-percent increase. By the year 2000, the population registered 43,080 and was still growing. Although land-wise still small, Rockwall County has been consistently ranked as one of the fastest growing counties in the United States.

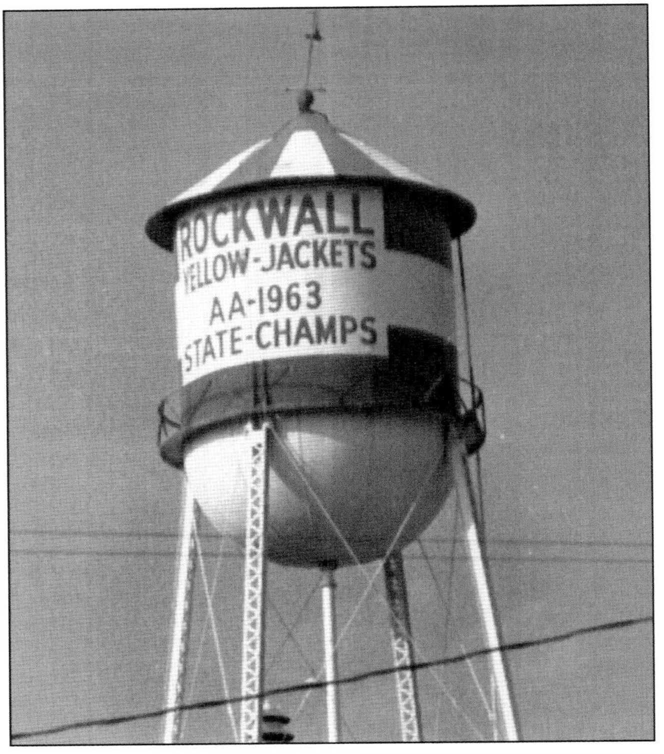

With orange and white paint and commemorative wording, Rockwall's long-standing water tower paid homage to the 1963 AA State Championship football team. The 1963 Yellowjacket team beat John Foster Dulles in a miraculous last-minute come-from-behind finish to secure the state title. (See page 106 for more information on the Yellowjackets' historic football game.)

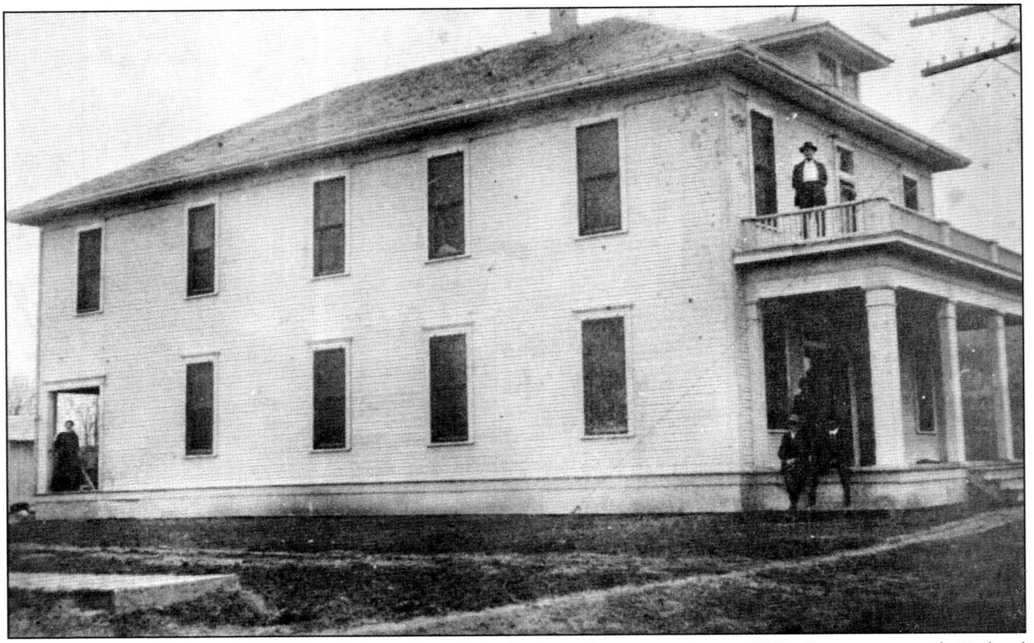

In 1908, the Stephenson Hotel was built on the northwest corner of Washington and Goliad Streets, the same spot the Bailey Hotel had occupied just a few years earlier. The Stephenson Hotel would remain in operation until 1966, operating as both a hotel with short-term room rental and a boardinghouse that rented rooms on a long-term basis.

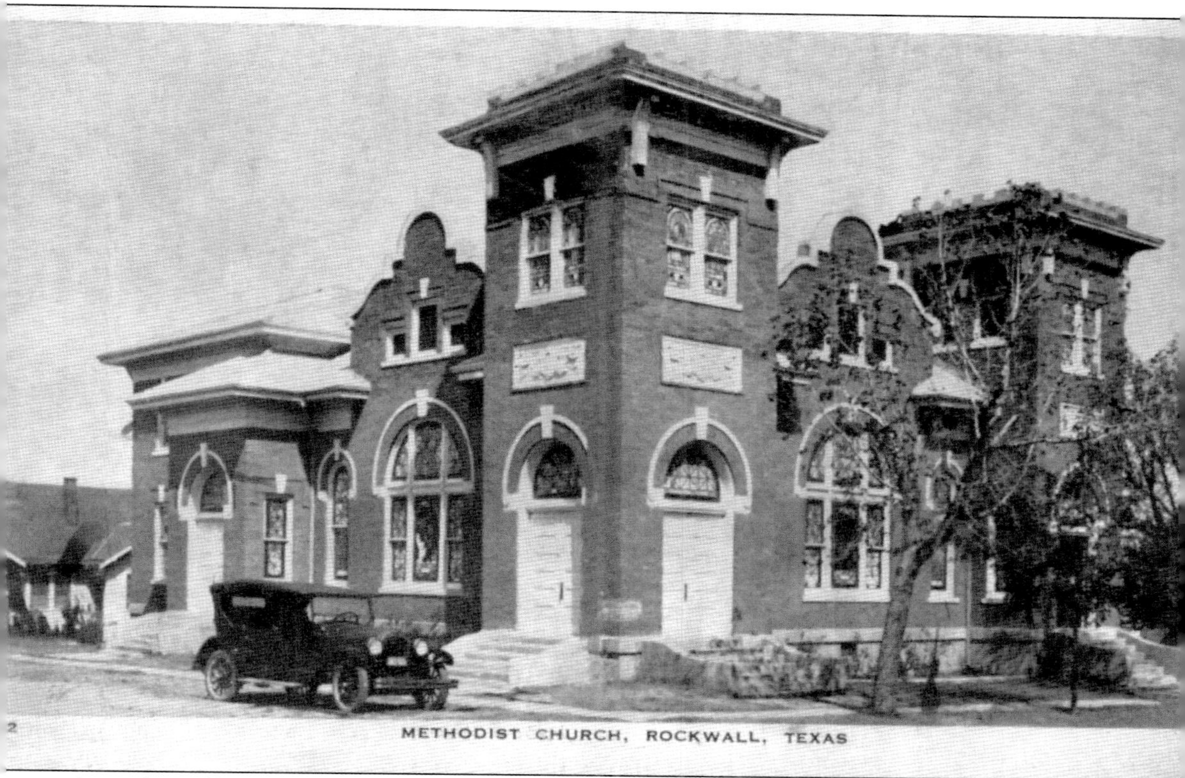

A number of historical structures built early in the 20th century still stood in Rockwall at the beginning of the 21st century. The building that once served as Rockwall's First United Methodist Church is located on the corner of Rusk and Fannin Streets just east of the downtown square. It was constructed around 1913. Rockwall's Methodist congregation had been founded around 1856, possibly earlier, and first used a schoolhouse as their place of worship. Around 1875, the congregation constructed a one-room wooden church building. In the early 1900s, the congregation began discussing their need for a new building. George Lindsey of Greenville served as architect for the new church; the contractors were Harris and Shuman of Nevada, Texas. Newspaper records from 1913 stated, "The building when finished and furnished will cost more than $15,000 and will, with grounds and all, be estimated as an $18,000 plant." Above is a picture postcard of the 1913 Methodist church structure. The congregation moved to a new building in 1981, but the old structure still stands near downtown.

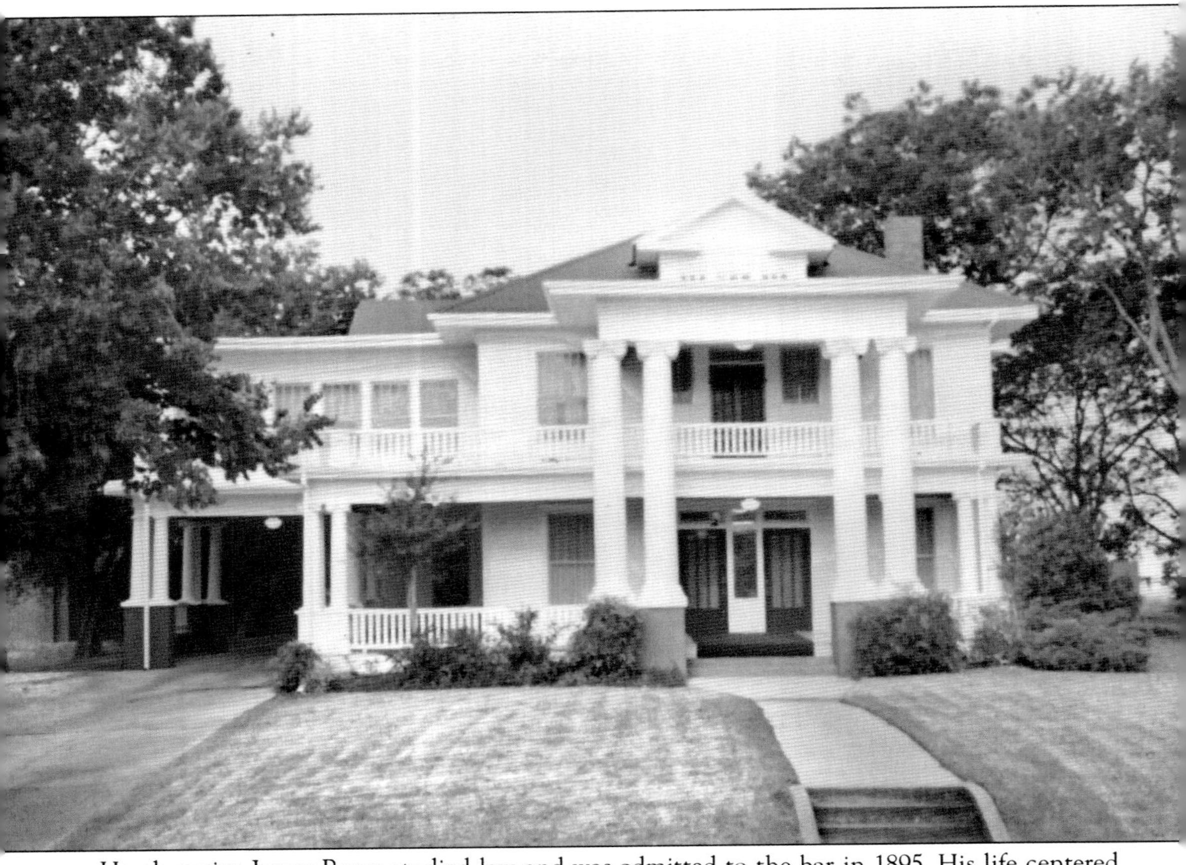

Heath native James Reese studied law and was admitted to the bar in 1895. His life centered around the law and public service, so it was a logical choice when, in 1911, he built this Greek Revival home on South Goliad. The Greek Revival style of architecture represented a spirit of democracy. It had reached its height of popularity in the mid-1800s and was considered the first truly national style of architecture in the United States, as examples could be found in all regions of the country. While it was appropriate for Judge Reese to choose this style, it was highly unusual for Rockwall at that time. Most of the homes of that period leaned toward Victorian architectural influences with gingerbread trim and gabled rooflines. The house was slated for demolition in 2004 to make room for a parking lot, but local residents Ken and Glenda Jones—at considerable personal expense—moved the structure to a lot on North Goliad Street and preserved the city's only original Greek Revival structure.

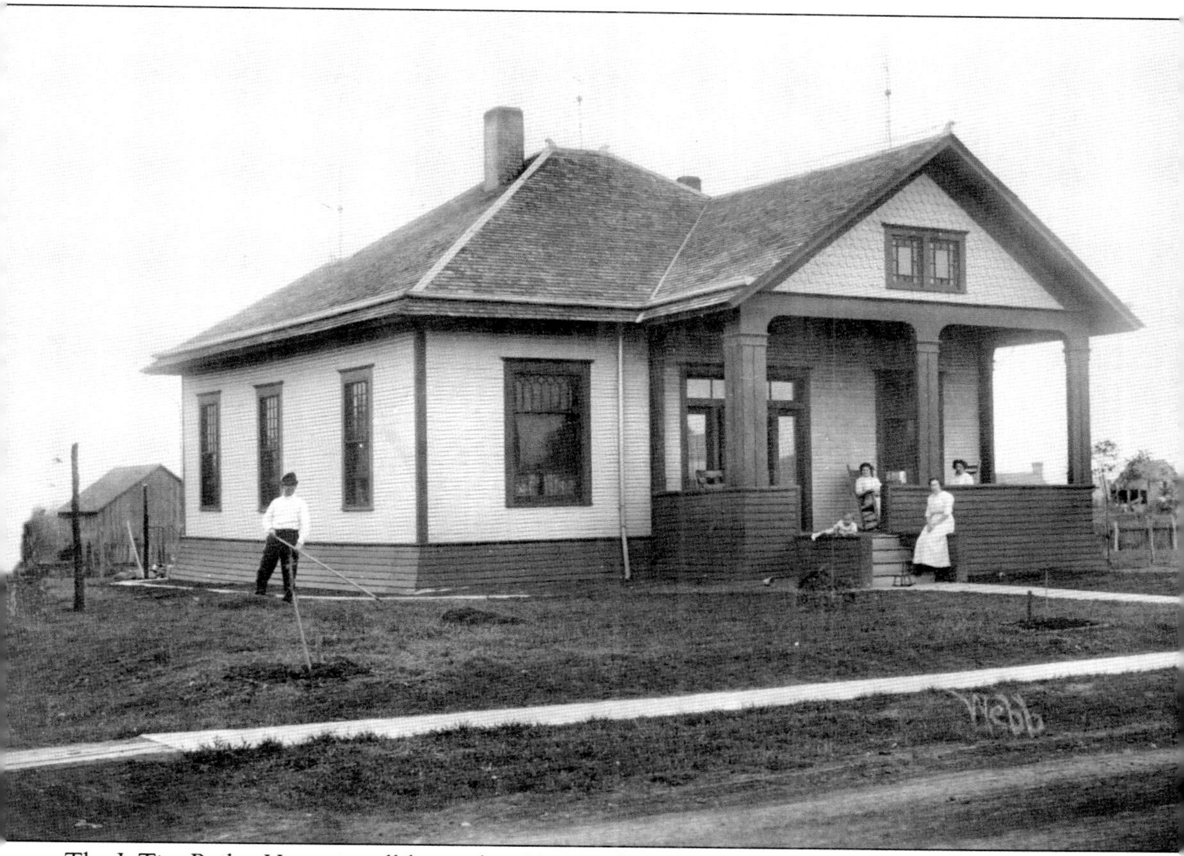

The J. Tite Bailey Home is still located at 301 North Goliad Street, just north of the Rockwall town square. It was built in 1909. John T. "Tite" Bailey was the son of local merchant and civic leader T. W. Bailey and his wife, Hittie. Tite was born in 1875 in Kentucky and came with his family to Texas, finally settling in Rockwall in 1890. He married Lucy Estelle Curry in 1906. Tite was cashier of a local bank. Prior to her marriage, Lucy had been a telephone operator. Later she was Rockwall's first female county clerk, holding office from 1927 to 1935. Tite passed away in 1919; Lucy passed away in 1982 at the age of 102. Through the years, the Bailey home has housed numerous businesses, but it has retained many of its original architectural elements.

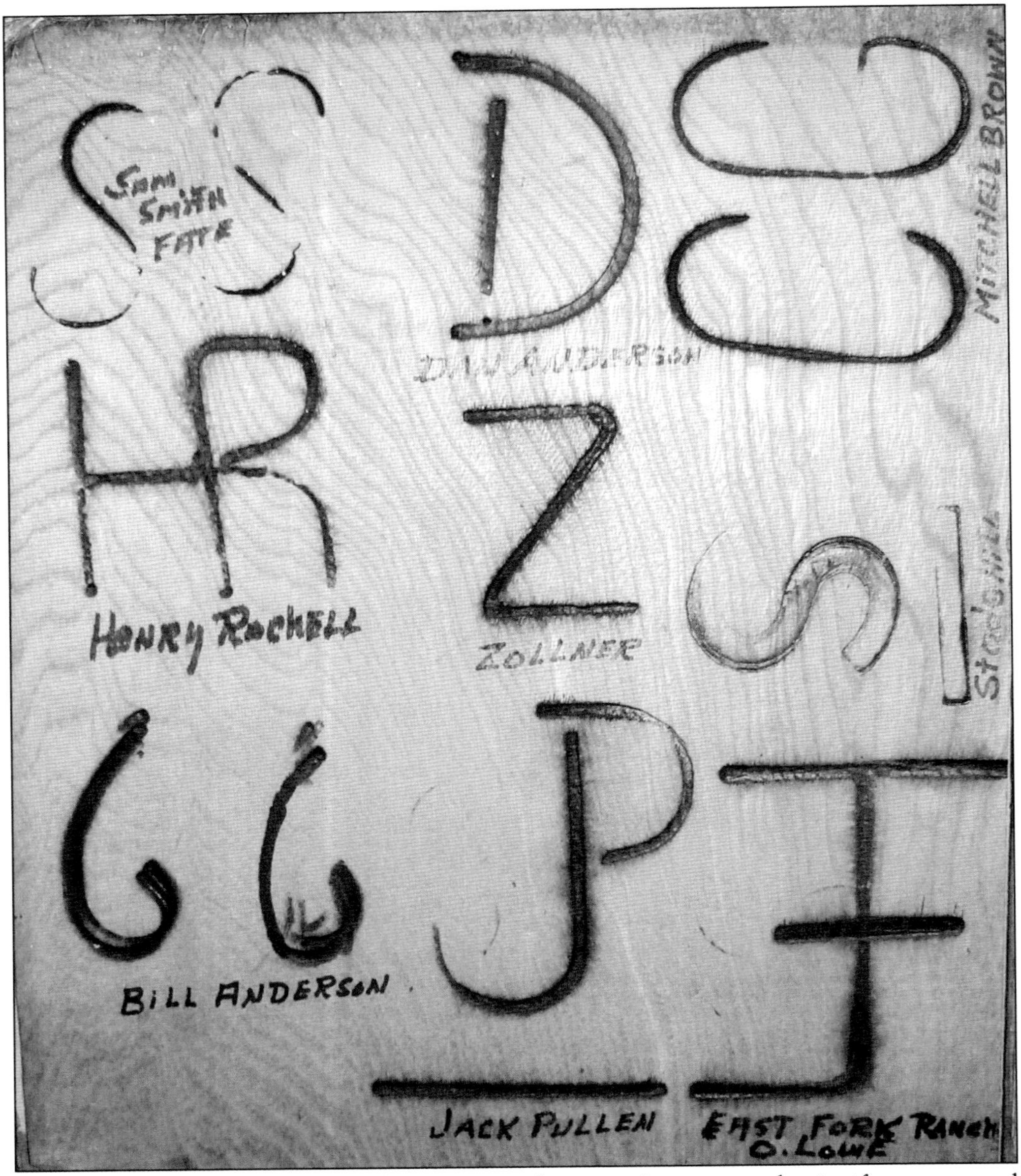

Although cattle have always played some part in the county's economy, the significance seemed to increase with the passing decades. In the 1920s, there were approximately 1,850 cattle reported in the county. By the late 1960s, that number had increased to 6,000 head of cattle. By the early 1980s, only 191 farms were reported in the entire county, but they reported 16,000 head of cattle. A few of these were still farmer-ranchers whose Rockwall roots ran deep. In fact, when the county extension agent was asked to bring local cattle brands to the new Robert J. Kleberg Animal and Food Sciences Center at Texas A&M University in order to record them for posterity, he took some of Rockwall's most recognizable—Zollner, Rochell, Anderson (Bill and Dan), Brown, Smith, Pullen, and Stodghill. This is a copy in wood of the brands used for that project.

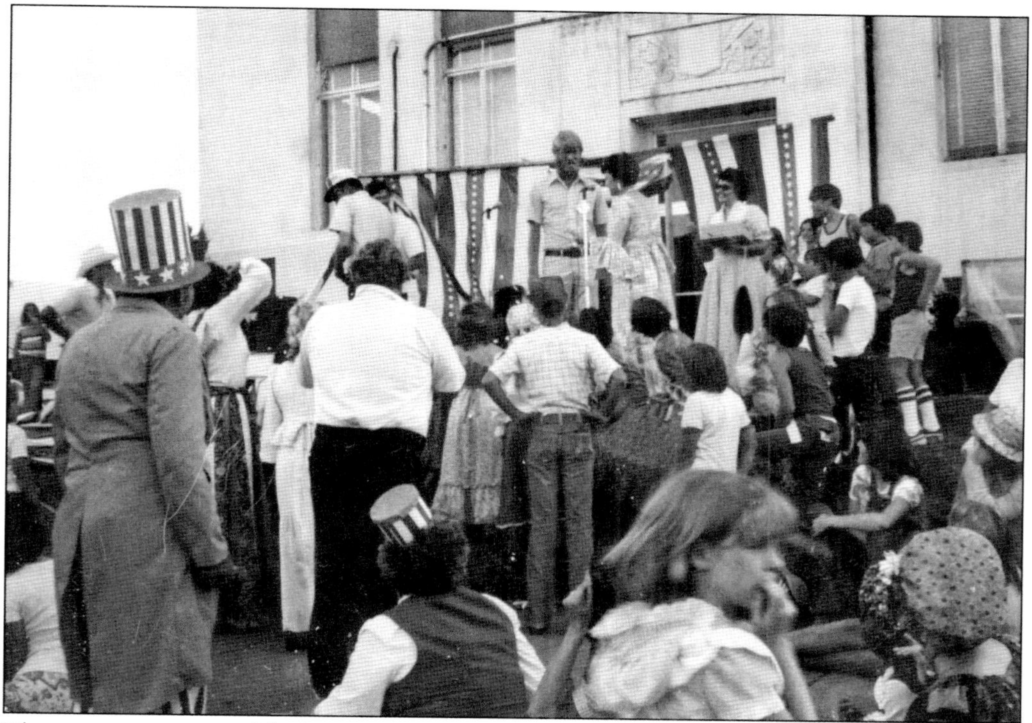

The commemoration of the bicentennial of the United States went on for an entire year and was considered a major cultural event. Communities across the nation were asked to prepare major celebrations and events in honor of the nation's 200th birthday. Rockwall County, in conjunction with the Rockwall Chamber of Commerce, organized a number of events to help the area celebrate the historic occasion. Above, chamber president Marge Gambill and chamber manager Jackie Ferguson participate in the bicentennial festivities on the courthouse lawn. Below, a long shot looking south shows a musical group performing and a 1976 view of the downtown square.

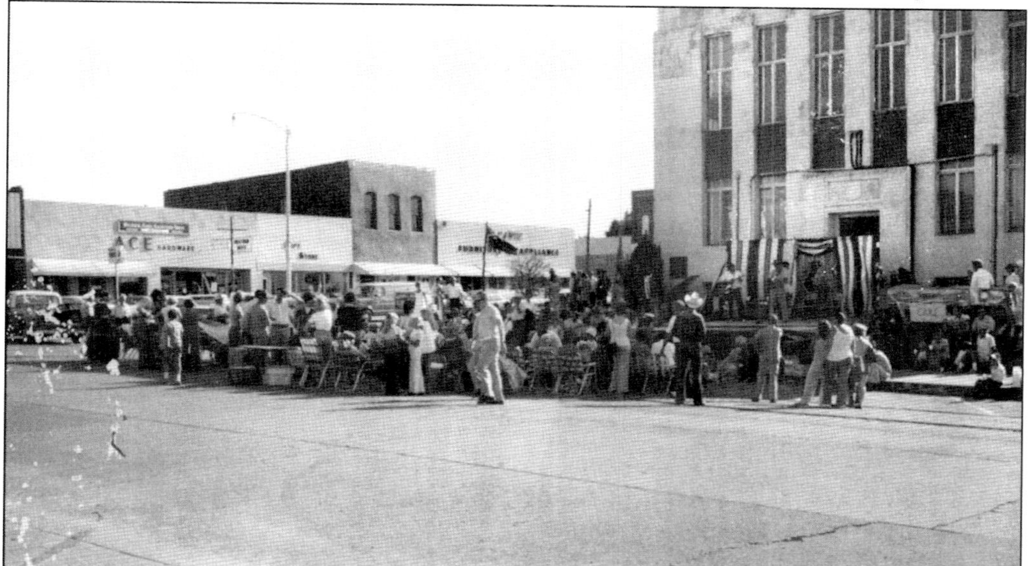

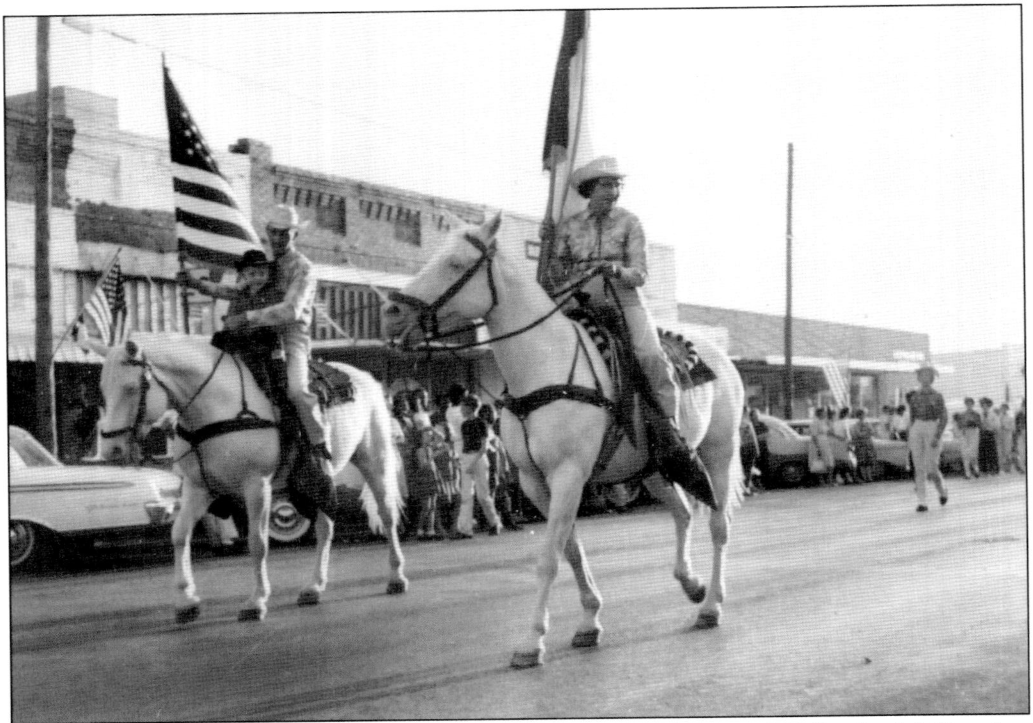

Woodrow Stodghill—with grandson Steven—on his horse Whitey and Willie Stodghill on her horse Snowball lead a parade through downtown Royse City in 1963. During the 1960s and 1970s, the Stodghills led parades throughout Rockwall County. Hometown parades continue to be part of an effort by city and county leaders to help preserve Rockwall's small-town charm despite a rapidly growing population.

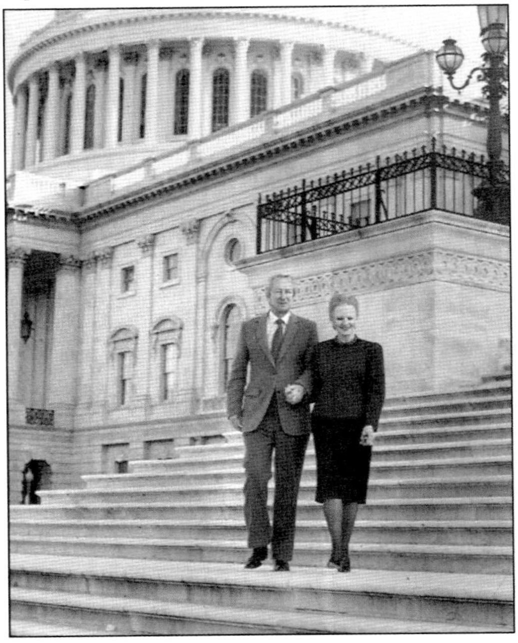

Fate native Ralph M. Hall is only the fourth person to represent the U.S. House of Representatives 4th District since it was created in 1903. The district's second congressman, Sam Rayburn, represented the district for 48 years. The district's third representative, Ray Roberts, represented the district for 19 years. Congressman Hall (here with his wife, Mary Ellen) was first elected in 1980 and is still holding office in 2009.

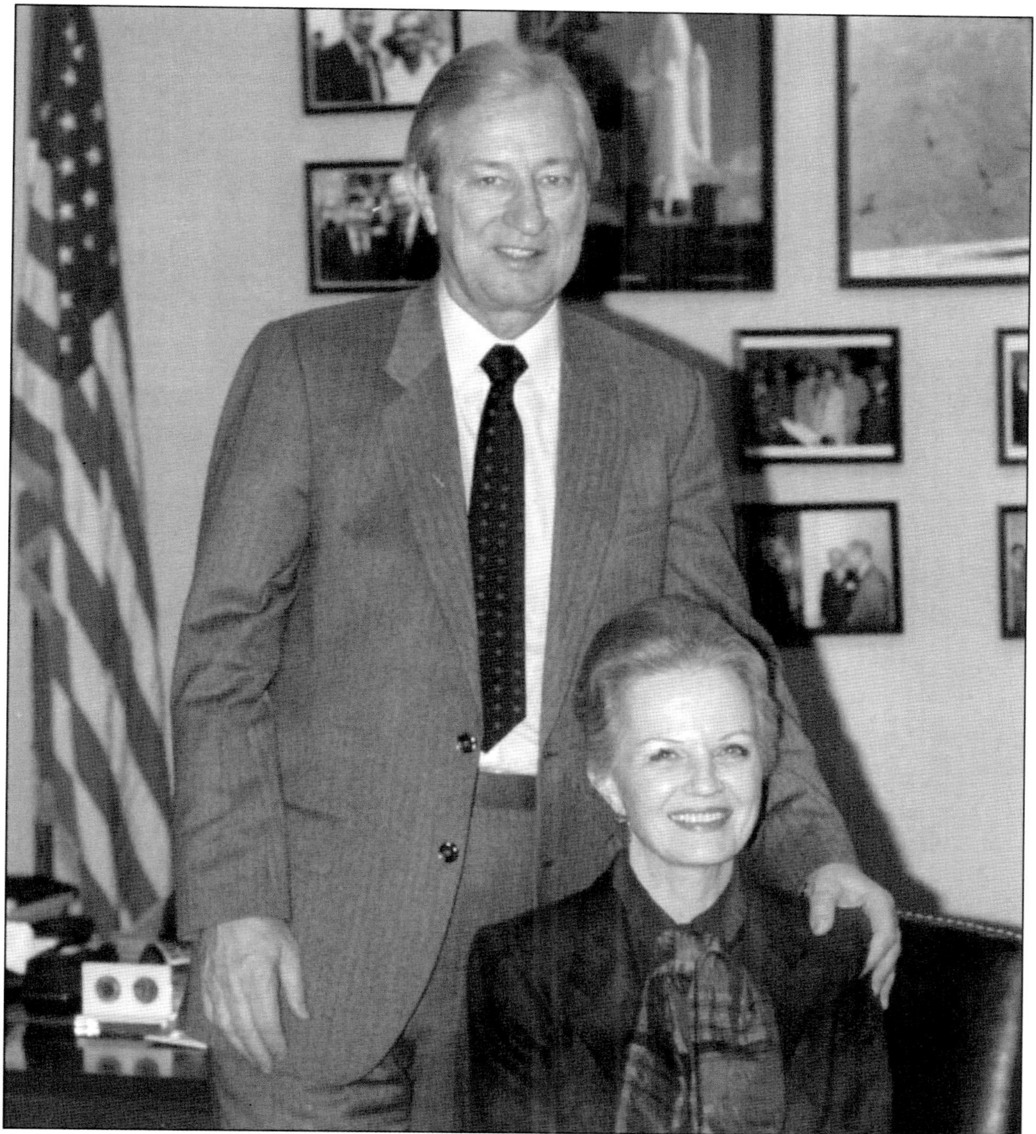

Although Mary Ellen Murphy was not a Rockwall County native, once she moved to the community, she became so beloved that it was hard to imagine Rockwall was ever without her. She was born on January 15, 1925, to Argo Murphy Henry and Jahalon Murphy in Kemp, Texas. She married Ralph Hall on November 14, 1944, when he was a navy lieutenant stationed in Pensacola, Florida. Ralph and Mary Ellen primarily lived in Rockwall, where they raised their three sons: Ralph Hampton Hall, Brett Allen Hall, and J. Blakeley Hall. They briefly lived in Austin while Ralph represented Rockwall in the state senate. Mary Ellen served the Rockwall community in many capacities, including as a member of the Rockwall Independent School District Board of Trustees from 1973 to 1978. They were a consummate political couple: Ralph could spin a tale and never miss a punch line, and Mary Ellen would fill a room with grace and elegance. Mary Ellen passed away on August 27, 2008.

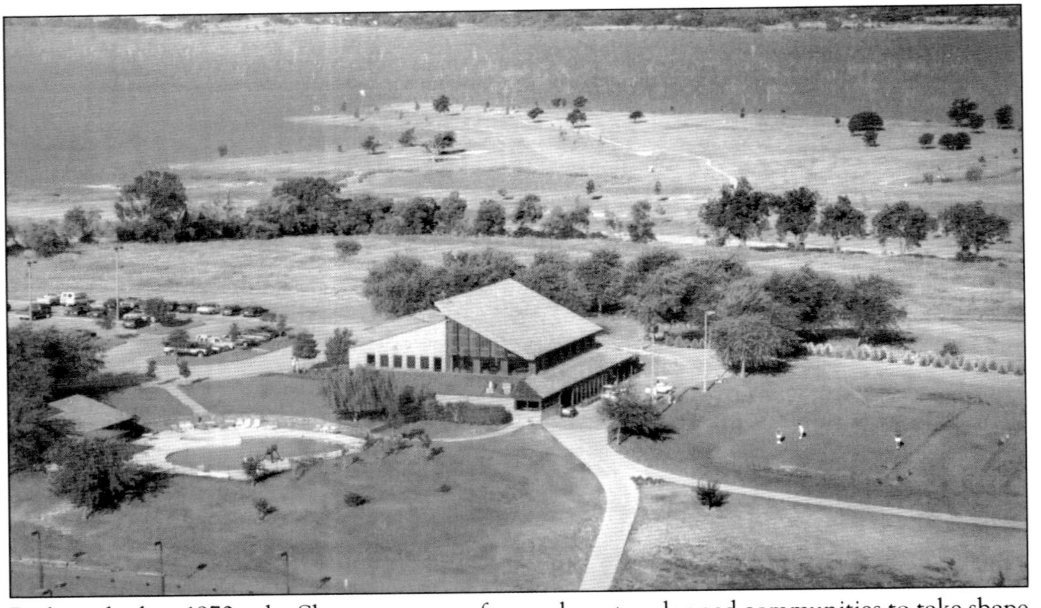

Built in the late 1970s, the Shores was one of several master-planned communities to take shape in the Rockwall area. Featuring an 18-hole golf course with a beautiful view of Lake Ray Hubbard, the Shores marketed homes to families looking for weekend recreational opportunities at their back doors. This c. 1979 picture postcard shows the Shores original country club and pool area.

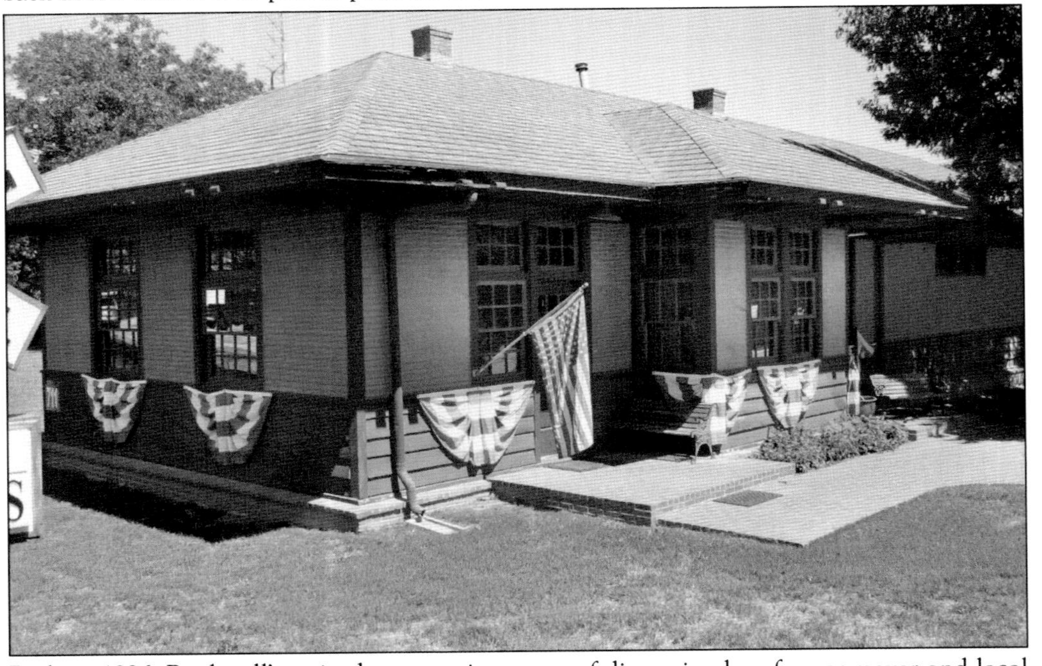

Built in 1926, Rockwall's train depot was in a state of disrepair when former mayor and local orthodontist Frank Miller decided to save the irreplaceable piece of Rockwall history and use it as his office. Dr. Miller moved the depot from its original location by the railroad tracks to a prominent piece of property on South Goliad Street, where he and his son, Dr. Bart Miller, serve patients daily in the restored train station.

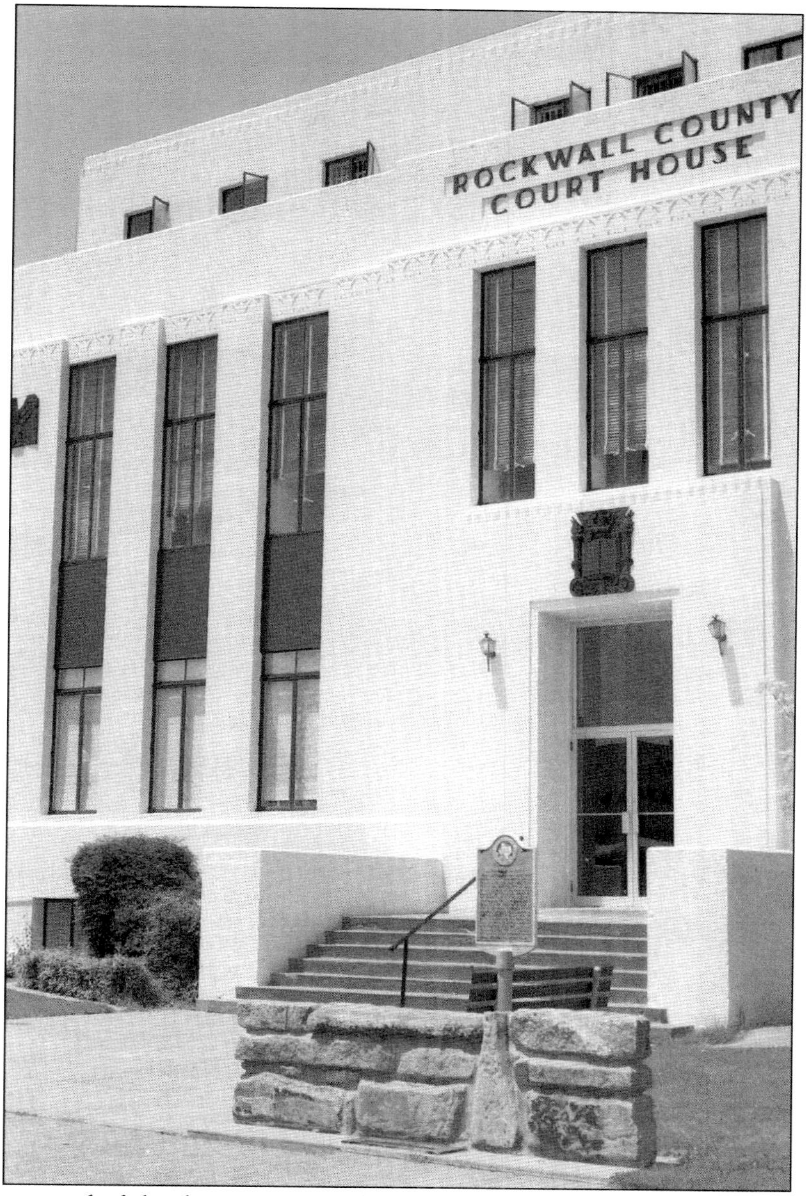

A picture postcard of the downtown courthouse shows the new rock wall display erected in conjunction with the 1976 bicentennial celebration. Along with the national celebration, Rockwall County had coordinated an excavation of the rock wall for public viewing on private property east of town. The property owners had agreed to allow the extraction of a number of rocks for permanent display on the courthouse lawn. Unfortunately, when the rocks were re-assembled, one was inadvertently placed in a straight vertical position. In all recorded excavations and known outcroppings of the rock wall, there are no recordings or photographs of vertical placements as shown on the courthouse lawn; in all the excavations of straight wall sections, the rock wall rocks appear in horizontal patterns. The historical marker that accompanies the rock wall display commemorates the formation of Rockwall County and discusses the underground formation for which the county is named.

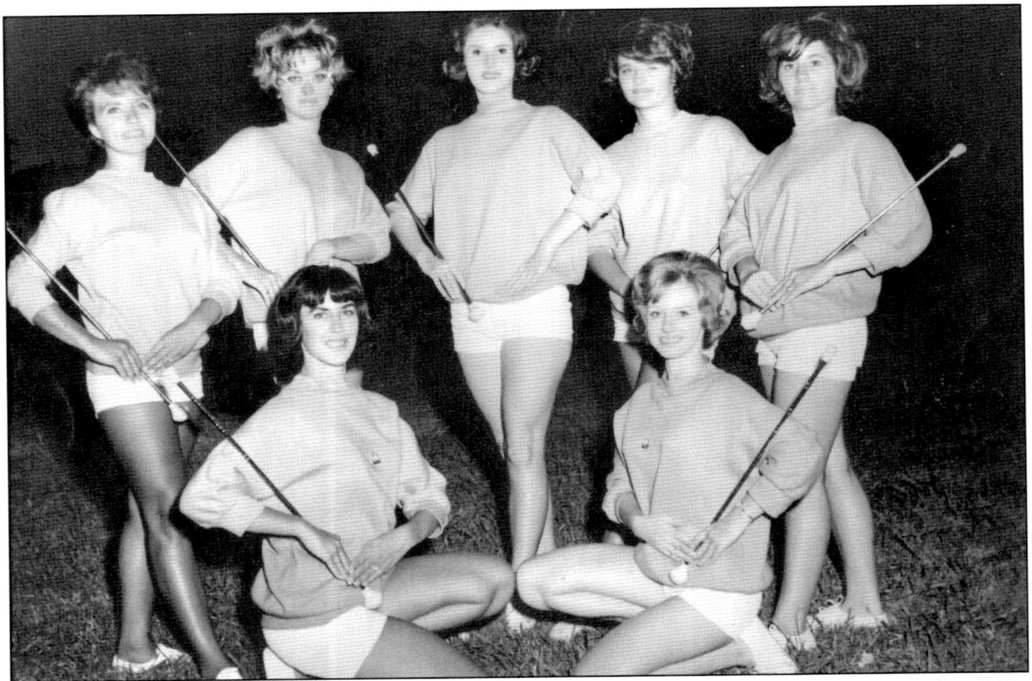

Above, Rockwall twirlers strike a pristine pose. Below, from left to right, Mary Nell Butler, Eddy Heath, and Linda McGuffy take a sneak peak at the class record book in a posed picture. Extra- and cocurricular activities have always played a role in the offerings at Rockwall High School. In the 1920s, students could participate in the literary society, the drama club, or a number of interscholastic competitions. In 2009, Rockwall ISD offers more than 150 student activity options.

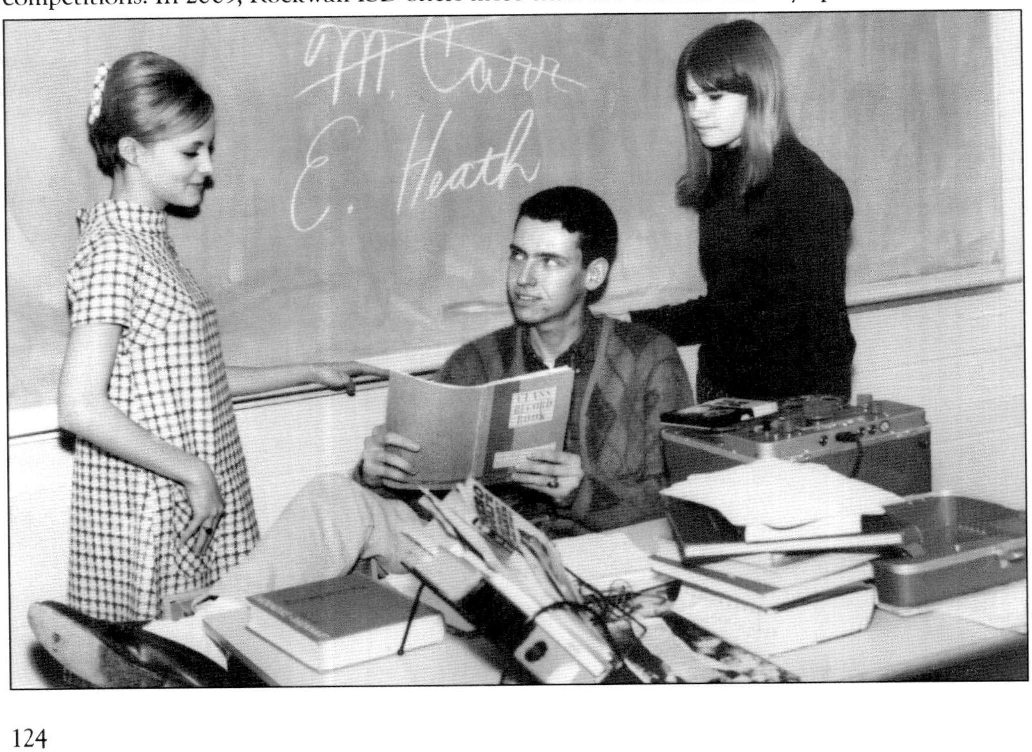

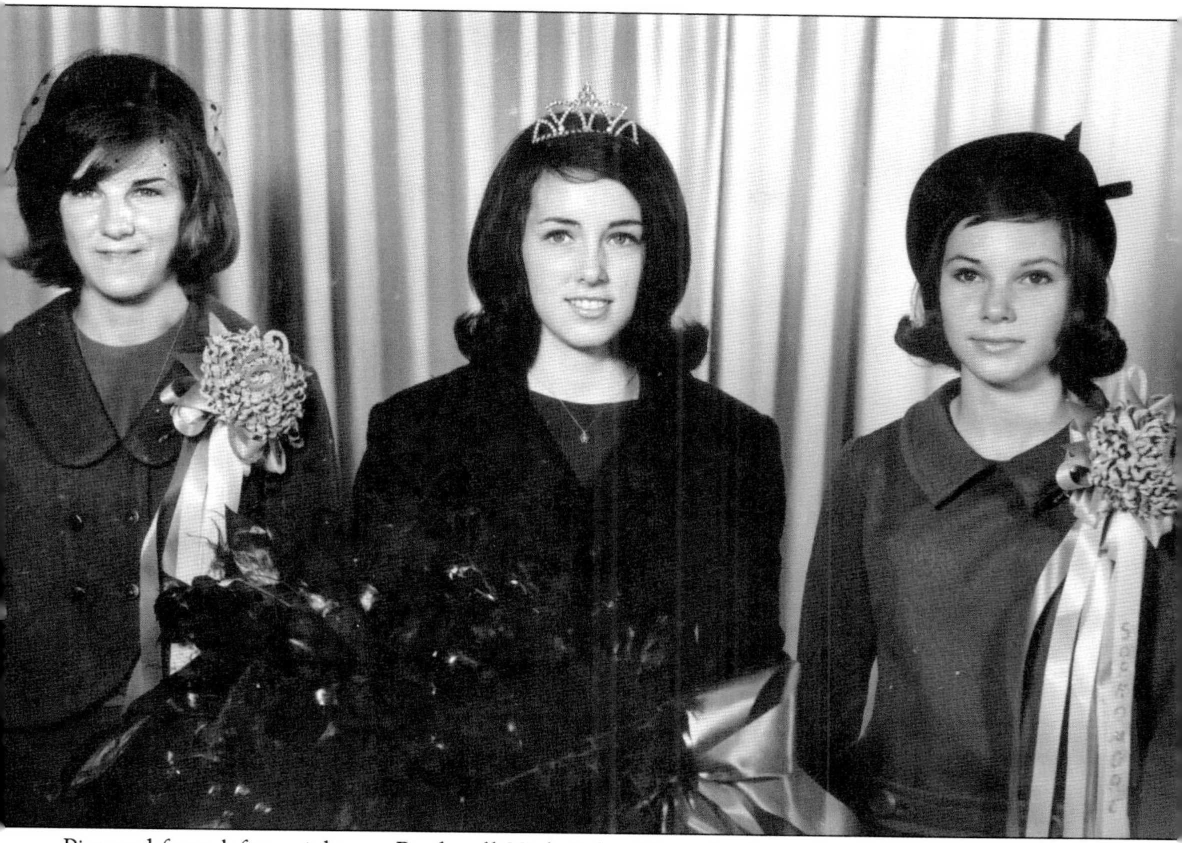

Pictured from left to right are Rockwall High School beauties from the 1960s Sue Jones, Sue Florence, and Susan Herring. From their origins in the one-room country schoolhouses, the school systems in Rockwall County have experienced times of growth and times of consolidation. In 1970, the county's population was approximately 7,000 and climbing. At that time, Rockwall ISD had one elementary campus, one intermediate school, and one high school. Forty years later, Rockwall ISD operates more than 20 campuses and facilities. Demographic projections indicate that, at the time when the city reaches its growth capacity, Rockwall ISD will consist of 44 schools—32 elementary campuses, 7 middle schools, and 5 high schools—that will accommodate approximately 43,600 students. In 1983, the graduating class of Rockwall High School had approximately 80 students. Twenty-five years later, the Rockwall Independent School District's two mainstream high schools will graduate approximately 850 students.

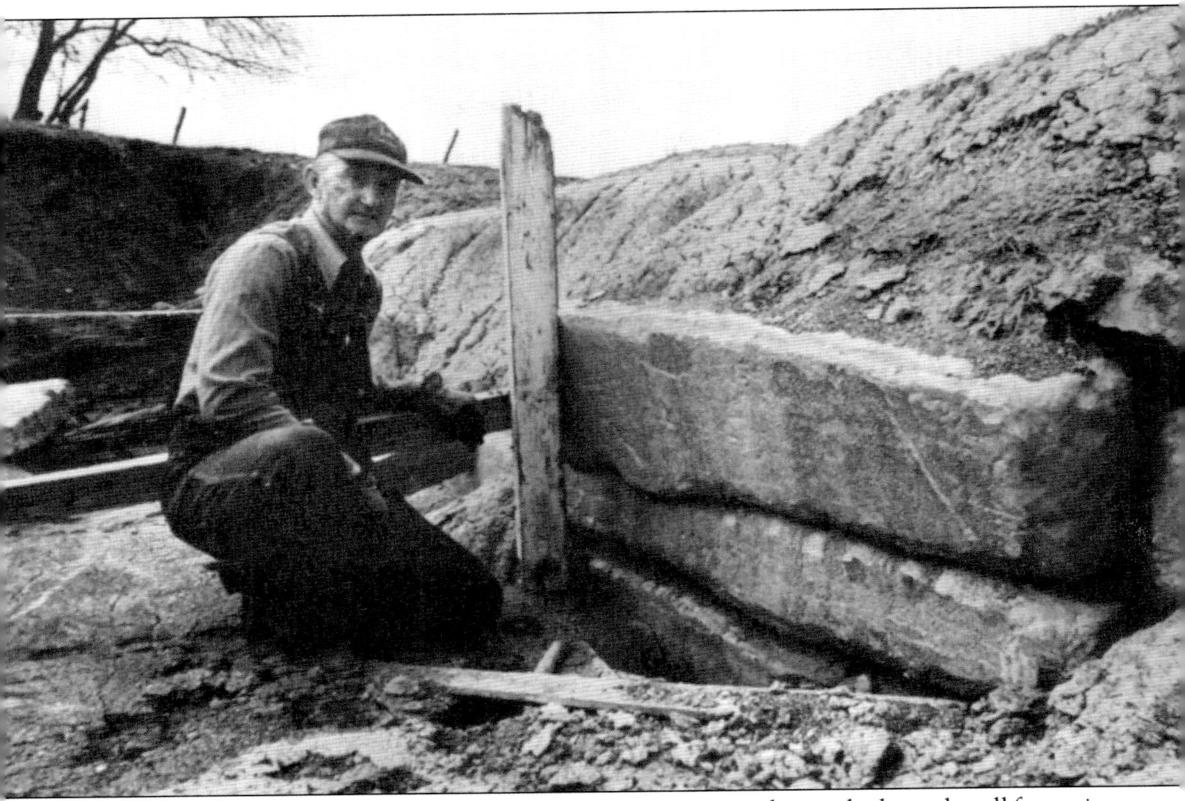

During the second half of the 20th century, scientists continued to study the rock wall formation and debate its origins. In 1979, Dr. Kenneth Scharr of the University of Texas at Arlington examined two sections of the wall and concluded that both were natural formations, but he did not rule out the possibility that another portion could be man-made. In 1988, geologist Brooks Ellwood concluded that the wall was a natural formation. In 1996, architect John Lindsey examined excavations and past records, and concluded that "evidence of a prehistoric structure built by man is mounting." One of the most rewarding excavations was in 1976 when, under the direction of the county, a portion of the rock wall was excavated on land near Farm-to-Market Road 549 and Cornelius Road owned by Woodrow and Willie Stodghill. The excavation coincided with the nation's bicentennial. It was open to the public, and hundreds of schoolchildren came and saw the wall for which the city and county were named. Above, Woodrow Stodghill shows some of the largest examples of rock wall rocks exposed during the 1976 excavation.

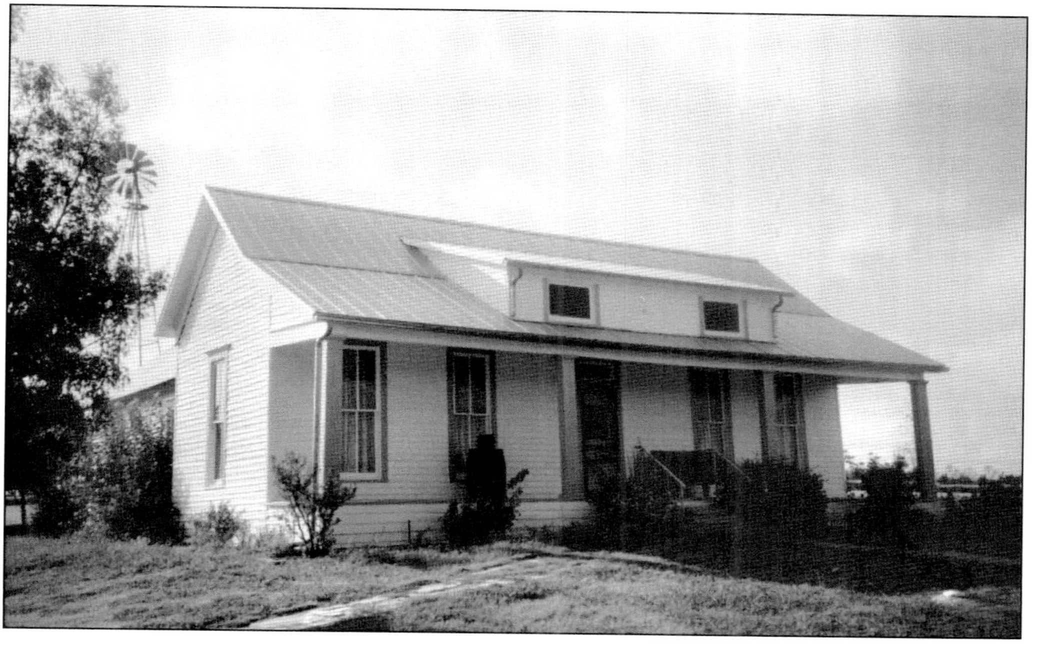

About the Rockwall County Historical Foundation

Records of the Rockwall County Historical Foundation state, "Rockwall County Historical Foundation was organized January 16, 1978, with 21 people attending the first meeting at the Chamber of Commerce building. The desire to preserve the heritage of Rockwall County was the main focus of these people as they adopted by laws and elected officers and directors. Charter members numbered sixty-two."

The RCHF maintains a museum housed in the Manson-LaMoreaux-Hartman House (pictured above), which is considered to be the oldest home in Rockwall County, with its original structure dating to the mid-1850s. The museum is located in Harry Myers Park at 901 East Washington Street in Rockwall. For museum hours or more information about the Rockwall County Historical Foundation, please call 972-722-1507.

In addition to maintaining historical artifacts and written and oral histories, the RCHF is in the process of developing an extensive photograph archive. Numerous families have contributed to this project, and many of the images and stories they have chosen to share are contained within the pages of this book. Individuals and families that have participated in the RCHF photograph archiving project include Theola Barnes, Lucille Bell, Susan Bernal, Jane Bounds, Mary Spelce Byrd, Dewayne Cain, Andrea Heath Chandler, Diana Chapman, Doris Cullins, the city of Fate and the Fate Girls, Carolyn Francisco, Terry Garrett, Joy Bounds Greenwalt, Blakeley Hall, Ralph M. Hall, Amy Isbell Hanschen, Carol Hawkins, Ray Holt, Linda Hopkins, Jeanne Crawford Isbell, Ollie Marian Jacob, Jennie Johnson, Joanne Loftis, Gary Lovell, Jeff Lowe, Martha Myers, Sherry Pittman, Billy and Autumn Quinton, Susan Reinhardt, Virginia Lawhorn Rice, Rosemary Hall Scott, Mary Sue Smith, Bill and Billie Marion Stevenson, Katherine Ann Strain, Patsy and Don Stodghill, Garvin Tate, Virginia Vaughn, Emma Wendt, Frank Williams, Gloria Williams, Jerry Wimpee, Mary and Hobart Wisdom, James and Pat Flores, and the many others who have allowed their personal photographs to be used to preserve Rockwall's history.

—Rockwall, Texas
Sheri Stodghill Fowler

Discover Thousands of Local History Books Featuring Millions of Vintage Images

Arcadia Publishing, the leading local history publisher in the United States, is committed to making history accessible and meaningful through publishing books that celebrate and preserve the heritage of America's people and places.

Find more books like this at
www.arcadiapublishing.com

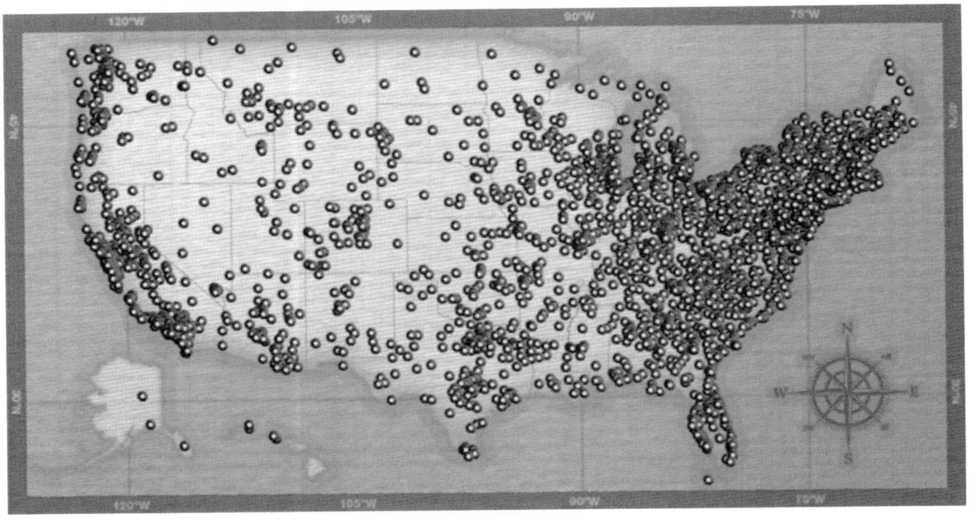

Search for your hometown history, your old stomping grounds, and even your favorite sports team.

Consistent with our mission to preserve history on a local level, this book was printed in South Carolina on American-made paper and manufactured entirely in the United States. Products carrying the accredited Forest Stewardship Council (FSC) label are printed on 100 percent FSC-certified paper.

MADE IN THE USA